*Representative Government
and the Revolution*

THE MARYLAND CONSTITUTIONAL CRISIS OF 1787

Maryland Bicentennial Studies

SPONSORED BY THE MARYLAND BICENTENNIAL COMMISSION

The Honorable Louise Gore, CHAIRMAN

EDITORIAL BOARD

Jack P. Greene, The Johns Hopkins University, CHAIRMAN

Rhoda M. Dorsey, Goucher College

Benjamin Quarles, Morgan State College

MONOGRAPHS

A *Spirit of Dissension: Economics, Politics, and the Revolution in Maryland,* by Ronald Hoffman

In Pursuit of Profit: The Annapolis Merchants in the Era of the American Revolution, 1763-1805, by Edward C. Papenfuse

DOCUMENTARY EDITIONS

Maryland and the Empire, 1773: The Antilon-First Citizen Letters, by Peter S. Onuf

Representative Government and the Revolution: The Maryland Constitutional Crisis of 1787, by Melvin Yazawa

REPRESENTATIVE GOVERNMENT and the REVOLUTION

The Maryland Constitutional Crisis of 1787 + EDITED WITH AN INTRODUCTION BY *Melvin Yazawa*

THE JOHNS HOPKINS UNIVERSITY PRESS
Baltimore and London

Publication of this volume was assisted
by the Maryland Bicentennial Commission.

The Johns Hopkins University Press, Baltimore, Maryland 21218
The Johns Hopkins University Press Ltd., London

Library of Congress Catalog Card Number 75-6546
ISBN 0–8018–1664–5

*Library of Congress Cataloging in Publication data will be found on the last printed
page of this book.*

TO MY MOTHER AND FATHER

Contents

PREFACE   ix

INTRODUCTION   1

DOCUMENTARY SELECTIONS

The Appeal of the House of Delegates, January 16, 1787   35

The Reply of the Senate, January 20, 1787   47

A Proposal from Anne Arundel County, February 8, 1787   53

Samuel Chase to His Constituents, February 9, 1787   55

William Paca to the Citizens, February 15, 1787   61

"A Constituent" to the Printers, March 8, 1787   69

Thomas Stone to the Printers, March 28, 1787   80

Alexander Contee Hanson to the People, April 1, 1787   87

"A Constituent" to the House of Delegates, May 3, 1787   97

William Paca to Alexander Contee Hanson, May 10, 1787   107

Alexander Contee Hanson to the People, May 11, 1787   117

Alexander Contee Hanson to the People, June 9, 1787   118

William Paca to Alexander Contee Hanson, June 22, 1787   129

Alexander Contee Hanson to William Paca, July 12, 1787   137

Alexander Contee Hanson to William Paca, August 2, 1787   150

William Paca to Alexander Contee Hanson, August 6, 1787   159

From *Considerations on the Proposed Removal of the Seat
of Government, by Aristides*, March 17, 1786   169

From *Remarks on the Proposed Plan of an Emission of Paper,
by Aristides*, February 26, 1787   172

INDEX   185

Preface

THE DYNAMICS of politics in the decade after 1776 made conceptual clarification of the idea of representation increasingly imperative. The right of the people to instruct their representatives was not a novel claim by the time of the Revolution. The political rhetoric of separation, however, left unclear the precise application of this doctrine to the upper houses of the Confederation assemblies. That senators represented the interests of the people, as did delegates in the lower houses, seemed to follow the logic of the developments of the Revolutionary era. But to admit that they were therefore bound by constituent instructions threatened to remove what many thought were the remaining foundations of order and authority in the new republic and render the traditional notion of representation obsolete by making the representative a mere tool of the people.

In this volume I have attempted to portray the intellectual struggle that occurred in Maryland as men perceived the implications of, then attempted to come to terms with, a situation in which concepts that had seemed familiar took on new meanings. The defenders of the Senate—perhaps the most tradition-oriented of the senates in the new nation—faced the fundamental task of providing a new justification for the conventional understanding of society and politics. Although objectionable to men rooted in the deferential order, constituent interference in the administration of the ordinary business of government stemmed from the idea that the people were sovereign. Hence, unless that sovereignty was qualified, and until a refined constitutional argument supported that qualification, the opponents of instruction were unable to challenge the right of popular interference without appearing to deny the very principles of the Revolution.

The documentary selections explicitly address the immediate issues of representation and instruction during the 1787 paper money emission controversy. In order to maintain a developmental perspective they also logically follow the outlines of the larger constitutional debate. Earlier pieces have been omitted primarily because the striking thing about them was an emphasis on the content of the proposed measures and a relative absence of constitutional objections. In addition, the concentration of selections presented here reveals the emerging parameters of a refined opposition to popular participation in the administration of government. The first selection, the January address of the House of Delegates, thus serves as an effective introduction: it reflected prior arguments in its assumptions concerning the constitutional privileges of a sovereign people, and at the same time, became the basis of the succeeding essays.

The contributions of Samuel Chase and Thomas Stone describe the essentials being contested. It is revealing also to note that the major premises of Chase varied little from those of William Paca; whereas those of Stone were transformed by Alexander Hanson. It was with Hanson, then, that the constitutional qualification of popular sovereignty was most clearly evidenced. The additional excerpts from two of Hanson's pamphlets are offered to further explicate the nature of this evolution.

The great majority of the Hanson-Paca exchanges appeared in both of the state's major newspapers—the *Maryland Journal* (Baltimore) and the *Maryland Gazette* (Annapolis). Paca's arguments remained essentially unchanged throughout the controversy. The Paca selections illustrate this theme: the people, as sovereign, have the right to judge the actions of their trustees; this right they possessed perpetually and could exercise at any time; and finally, the right to judge and instruct had to be differentiated from the right of dissolving the government—the former was continuous, the latter should be reserved for those instances when redress through prescribed means was ineffectual. Hanson's defense of the Senate was a rejection of the "representation as attorney-ship" notion which, as Bernard Bailyn has said, had prevailed by the time of the Revolution. What the final Hanson essays embodied, in short, was a clarification of the Lockean view of representation and consent. The logic of Paca notwithstanding, Hanson reasserted the idea that consent was not continuous; that indeed constituent interference was restricted to those climactic occasions when the people resumed their original power and thus dissolved the government.

I am indebted to Jack P. Greene for his perceptive criticism of the introduction. His scholarly enthusiasm is an unfailing source of inspiration, and his uncommon patience has made this edition possible. Alan Tully provided an incisive commentary on an earlier version of the introduction, and I have benefited from his suggestions. I am grateful for the assistance rendered by the staffs of the Maryland Historical Society and the Milton S. Eisenhower Library, The Johns Hopkins University. My wife Jennifer helped in every stage of the editorial task.

Baltimore, Maryland   M.Y.
November, 1974

*Representative Government
and the Revolution*

INTRODUCTION

Representation and Constituent Instruction in the Maryland Assembly, 1776-1787: A Study in the Evolution of American Political Thought

THE MARYLAND paper money emission crisis of 1787 generated a lengthy series of articles on the nature of constitutional government. These essays, perhaps among the most significant political tracts of the Confederation, were overshadowed by the affairs of the Federal Convention and the appearance of *The Federalist*. Yet the writings of Publius and those of the emission disputants were complementary. Alexander Hamilton, James Madison, and John Jay confronted questions concerning the propriety of a federal government and the particular requisites and ramifications of such a system. The Maryland writers, on the other hand, especially William Paca and Alexander Hanson, debated the more abstract issues of representative government: the relationship of government and society, the quality of representation, and the implications of political trust. Moreover, the Maryland essays were the culmination of a process of accommodation that made the revolutionary idea of the people as constituent power acting through special conventions so commonly acknowledged that, in R. R. Palmer's words, the revolution in America had "become domesticated."

Gordon S. Wood, in *The Creation of the American Republic, 1776–1787*, examined the Maryland exchanges at some length. Wood attempted to bring the intellectual perspective of the Confederation into focus, and the Maryland experience exemplified what he considered a revolution in political theory. What was this metamorphosis, this creation of the American system of government? In 1776, Wood contended, the American people thought of government largely in terms of the traditional orders of mixed government. They believed that legislative power in particular resided in a lower house that represented the people and an upper chamber that incorporated the aristocratic elements of society. Closely identified with property, the upper house neither represented nor reported to the people. During the decade after 1776, however, an aura of "suspicion and uneasiness" eventually destroyed the mutuality of interest that united the people and the lower houses of assembly. This bond broken, the people realized that they "could never be fully embodied in their houses of representatives." The distinction between representatives and senators was blurred, and the representatives of the people in the lower houses, like the "traditional rulers and upper houses," came to be distrusted.

These developments undermined the idea that the people stood in a one-to-one association with a single branch of government. Rather than sharing a part of the government—embodied in the lower houses—the people remained outside the entire structure and maintained authority over all branches. The traditional conception of representation, according to Wood, broke down. Representatives were no longer independent agents but became tools for their constituents. Election became the sole criterion of representation. The transformation, then, involved a "transferal of sovereignty" from a branch of government to the people at large. The logic of this transfer sanctioned the American development of a double representation of the public. Both the upper and the lower houses of legislature represented the people.

The Maryland debate of 1787 most clearly exposed the constitutional issue because, Wood argued, the Maryland Senate most nearly resembled the traditional aristocratic body: it represented a separate interest and was not directly responsible to the people. The advocates of the paper money emission challenged the conservative notion of representation, the privileged position of the upper house. Senate defenders then discovered that they could no longer justify the Senate as the exponent of an interest apart from that of the people. They admitted that senators, like the members of the lower house, were indeed representatives of the people. Thus, Wood concluded, the novel action of the House of Delegates—the appeal for constituent instructions—procured an unprecedented admission from the Senate.[1]

If Wood is correct, the constitutional response during the emission controversy was the culmination of the gradual movement, throughout the decade, toward the idea of popular sovereignty. If the people were sovereign, then dual representation—by a senate and a lower house—and concurrent jurisdiction of two legislatures—federal and state—could be ideologically justified. The Maryland writers in 1787 struggled with the fundamental questions of the location of authority and the position of the people in government. But did their arguments exemplify this pattern of transformation? Was this the culmination of the American theory of representation?

II

The language and ideas of the Commonwealthmen abounded in Revolutionary Maryland. The members of the Maryland Convention in 1775 subscribed to the Association of Freemen and anxiously viewed "the long premeditated, and now avowed Design of the British Government," the "arbitrary and vindictive statutes passed," the "unlimited power assumed by Parliament," and the threat to alter "the constitution of all the colonies, thereby destroying the essential securities of the Lives, Liberties and Properties of the Colonists." The imperatives of the situation more than justified resistance. The call to arms was "no longer dictated by prudence merely, but by necessity." The alternatives, the association declared, were "base submission or manly opposition to uncontroulable Tyranny."

With their options thus defined, the leading men in Maryland were decisive. "By the God of Heaven," Samuel Chase fumed, "I owe no allegiance to the King of Great Britain. What American can hesitate in the choice between independence and slavery?" We should not trouble ourselves "about becoming independent," Chase advised, but we should "act as if we were." Men less volatile than Chase were no less determined. Matthew Tilghman pondered "whether freedom or slavery is most likely to be our portion." He could only "revere the spirit of the northern people," for he believed that "their warm and unrelaxing opposition" was right, and indeed he was "ashamed to think that the southern colonies" did not "keep pace with them." Thomas Johnson "wished for reconciliation . . . but if the terms are so hard as slavery to America," he favored "employing every means of self defense." The almost universal goal in America, Johnson said, was "in the first place to establish our liberty." Thomas Stone declared, "war, anything, is preferable to a surrender of our rights." John Adams best summed up the Maryland situation before 1776. "That is so excentric a colony—sometimes so hot, sometimes so cold, now so high, then so low—that I know not what to say about or to expect from it." But, Adams prophesied, "when they get agoing, I expect some wild extravagant flight or other from it."[2]

Having made up their minds, Marylanders pursued their calling with kindled emotions and awakened optimism. The people of Baltimore greeted the Declaration of Independence "with a Discharge of Cannon, &c. and universal Acclamations for the Prosperity of the FREE UNITED STATES," while an effigy of George III burned "to the no small Mirth of the numerous Spectators." A writer who styled himself "America" exclaimed, "The whole world has beheld the Congress of America, struggling amidst the storms of unwarranted power, and patiently

pleading with their apostate brethren a cause that Heaven delights in!"
He continued, "Happy people! happy even in your distress. . . . Go on
you brave asserters of never dying freedom! Persevere in your glorious
undertaking."[3] Their cause was just, their faith was in the "favours of
Providence," said another, and it was "unmanly, unchristian and
unworthy of any free mind to discover the least degree of timidity."[4]

The sense of the "glorious undertaking" permeated the air. The
people, "happy even in distress," turned to the task of reconstituting
government by reformulating their constitution. It would be credulous
to assume that the men who met in the state convention shed all but
their self-interest, and that external exultation failed to penetrate the
sanctuaries of thought. "The people," explained a writer in the *Maryland Journal*, "ought to form a new constitution of government." The
men in convention would derive all authority "from the people whom
they are to govern."[5] Those men, added another, "should always, with
pleasure, receive their constituents' instructions . . . and the constituents ought from time to time, to instruct them in those things they
conceive would be to their advantage."[6] These assertions presaged
future frustrations.

The leading political personalities in Maryland under the Confederation were part of the pre-Revolution antiproprietary "country party,"
but it does not follow that the new state government was consciously a
conservative and aristocratic one. The Declaration of Rights and the
state constitution of 1776 manifested the ambivilence of the Maryland
leaders. Drawn up by the prominent men of the state, both documents
nevertheless subscribe to the notion of popular sovereignty. Those who
have focused their attention on the "aristocratic" features of the constitution—especially the provision for senatorial electors—have not
given due weight to the repeated stress on government through compact
and to the declaration that all executive and legislative officials were
"trustees" of the people, "and, as such, accountable for their conduct."[7]
The high property qualifications and the indirect election of senators
did not void the popular basis of sovereignty. They were the progeny
of the inertia of tradition. Maryland had a highly deferential political
operation.[8] The object of the power of the people in such a system
was to keep the interest of the rulers dependent on the interest of the
ruled. This responsibility the "provincial leadership was willing to
bestow on a populace which they nonetheless considered incompetent
to participate directly in the esoteric decisions of government."[9] Whig
thought reinforced deferential government. Jackson Turner Main has
stated that a vital element of Whiggism was the "conviction that most
men were incompetent to rule, and that the elite should govern for
them."[10]

How were the people to exercise their allotted power? The Declaration of Rights recognized "That the right in the people to participate in the Legislature, is the best security of liberty, and the foundation of all free government." Participation would be realized through "elections . . . free and frequent, and every man, having property in, a common interest with, and an attachment to the community, ought to have a right of suffrage."[11]

But it was more than a yearning for a deferential system that accounted for the juxtaposition of elitism and popular sovereignty. The men of the Revolution understood, Hannah Arendt has argued, that government consisted of both power and authority. Power had to be balanced "with the additional weight of authority." The colonial charters and the "loyal attachment of the colonies to king and Parliament in England" had maintained that balance. Hence the "chief problem of the American Revolution, once this source of authority had been severed," according to Arendt, was the "establishment and foundation not of power but of authority."[12]

The search for the location and the distinction of authority coincided, and eventually fused, with the quest for the separation of legislative power—the dual representation of the people. In *Thoughts on Government*, a pamphlet widely circulated in Maryland, John Adams argued that the depravity of human nature necessitated a separation. The representative assembly "should be in miniature, an exact portrait of the people at large." To avoid misunderstanding, Adams clarified: "It should think, feel, reason, and act like them." But the people must not lodge legislative power in one assembly, for such a body was "liable to all the vices, follies, and frailties of an individual." They needed some "controuling power." A "distinct Assembly" serving as "a mediator" also ensured a proper balance between legislative and executive functions. This distinct assembly, Adams emphasized, should have a "free and independent exercise of its judgment, and consequently a negative voice in the legislature."[13]

Proposals for a unicameral legislature in Maryland did arise. The author of "The Common Rights of mankind" recognized that "many distinct bodys . . . tend to Create opposite interests as well as to retard business." He favored "one house of Representatives of the People in whom alone the Legislative Power shall be Lodged." Rather than divide the legislature, a "Council of Seven or some other convenient number" could be "chosen annually by the house of Representatives."[14] Daniel of St. Thomas Jenifer warned in 1777 that "the Senate does not appear to me to be the Child of the people at Large, and therefore will not be supported by them longer than there subsists the most perfect union between the different Legislative branches."[15]

Jenifer's solution to this malady paralleled that suggested in the "Common Rights." "There is but one remedy," said Jenifer, a bill must be passed "incorporating the Two houses into one for twelve months, and out of this conjunction to create an Executive Council."[16]

Men versed in the tradition of Whiggish suspicion, however, reflected the thoughts of Adams. Power must be checked. "Bodies of men," they believed, "have the same selfish attachments as individuals, and they will be claiming powers and prerogatives inconsistent with the liberties of the people." The end would inevitably be a disruption of free government. "All men, by nature fond of power, are unwilling to part with the possession of it." Unless the people curbed this "natural" tendency, the "desire to command" would grow consistently. The exercise of power "creates affection, and what was granted as a trust is soon claimed as a right." The legislature must be "so constituted as never to be able to form an interest of its own separate from the interest of the community at large." Two independent branches were necessary to "balance each other, and all dependent on the people."[17]

The search for distinguishing characteristics for the members of the "controuling" assembly eventually led to an emphasis on the readily available property qualification. The "senatorial part" of society must consist of the wise and the virtuous. The Maryland constitution called for "men of the most wisdom, experience and virtue." But these were intangibles and, unlike property, were difficult to measure.[18]

Whig tradition contributed to the elevation of the importance of property. J. R. Pole has observed that the bedrock of Whig philosophy of government was the compact formed to insure the natural right of property ownership. For Locke the "property" which the union into commonwealths would preserve included the "Lives, Liberty and Estates" of men. However, the subtlety of his definition escaped Locke's successors. The Maryland essayists constricted the scope of the argument. "Governments have been instituted," a Marylander declared, "not to provide the governed with the necessaries of life, but to secure them to those who have earned them." The problems "that so generally prevail," he continued, resulted from laws that often failed to "give the necessary protection to property."[19]

The criterion became rigid. It perverted, as Wood put it, the "classic meaning of mixed government, which had placed honor and wisdom, not wealth and property, in the middle branch of the legislature."[20] But the criterion satisfied the urgently felt need for a negative authority within the legislature, for a balanced separation of power. It must be remembered, too, that an essential premise of political thought was, as Theophilus Parsons asserted, that the desired intangibles "will most probably be found amongst men of education and fortune." The immediate distinction hinged on property, but the end in mind was the identification of quality. Daniel of St. Thomas Jenifer clearly sounded this in his criticism of the Maryland constitution. "In attempting to excell," Jenifer complained, "there have been so many gradations, and exclusions that there will not be men enough found of sufficient abilities to turn the Machine with that velocity which the present exigencys of our Affairs require."[21]

The convention of August 14, 1776, adopted the Declaration of Rights and the constitution. The delegates, having gone through both documents "paragraph by paragraph," altered none of the essentials. Attempts to reduce franchise qualifications from £30 currency to £5 currency "or paying taxes for the support of government" were unsuccessful. Yet it is significant that the delegates attempted such reductions, and that the latter criterion failed by a margin of only five votes. The convention maintained the practice of *viva voce* elections, but it also defended annual election of the lower house against proposals for two or three year terms. The convention set personal property required of a candidate for sheriff at £1000 current money, but it also vigorously asserted that the position be filled through election, not appointment. The convention allowed the indirect election of senators and enabled the Senate to fill its own vacancies, but it stipulated that the upper house would set priority according to the order in which senators stood in the electoral returns, and further, that "senators elected by the senate" would be "junior to the senators elected by the electors." And if, in the "paragraph by paragraph" examination of the documents, the convention did not question the requisites of senators and delegates, the bastion of popular sovereignty was also unassaulted.[22]

The men in convention accepted the necessity of an assembly divided into two houses and the property distinctions without feeling they were betraying republican doctrine. The Declaration of Rights decreed "That all government of right originates from the people, is founded in compact only, and instituted solely for the good of the whole." But few, if any, perceived the "compact" and the "good of the whole" as incompatible with deferential government, property qualifications, or the creation of an upper house of "mediate" representatives whose primary function would be to moderate power and thus procure stability. On the contrary, these qualifications seemed to secure the common good. It would be presumptuous to contend that a select minority in Confederation Maryland operated as a coordinated demagogue, manipulated ideas and manufactured situations, and thus advanced their economic interests. Rather, in the disordered state of society, traditional paradigms existed alongside new, hastily perceived ideas. That sovereignty resided in the people at large, and that they were the source of all power was common coin. Evidence indicates that, as Bailyn has said of the inflammatory rhetoric of the Revolutionaries, the words and ideas "meant something very real to both the writers and their readers."[23] The disharmony that characterized the politics of Maryland in the decade after 1776 resulted largely from a realization of the revolutionary consequences of the new ideas. The disparity between deferential expectations and popular sovereignty, between traditional forms and new formulations, became distinct through repeated confrontations. With reckoning came adjustment. Defenders of the conventional order hammered into shape a refined constitutional argument and used it to reconcile the traditional political structure with the notions nurtured by the Revolution.

The evolution of political thought in Maryland is best studied through the crises and the consequences surrounding three critical issues: loyalty oaths, 1777; confiscation of British property, 1779–1780; and paper money emission and debtor relief, 1786–1787.

III

Because providence was aligned with the "glorious undertaking," it was well to castigate timidity as "unchristian and unworthy." But a people who must "assert independence and freedom with an open and manly boldness" in order to preserve their "happy state," must insure that timidity was at least benevolent.[24] If it were not, then mortal and material effort would augment divine "favours."

It is scarcely surprising, in view of these sentiments, that oaths and affirmations of loyalty served as the first sparks of controversy. The state constitution proclaimed "That every person who shall offer to vote . . . shall (if required by any three persons qualified to vote), before he be admitted to poll, take such oath or affirmation" as the legislature prescribed. Persons appointed to offices of "profit or trust" were to declare not only faith and allegiance to the state, but also "belief in the christian religion."[25] But these were far from sufficient. "To our internal foes are we indebted," cried an irate observer, "for the present war, the immense expense incurred, and the devastation, ravage and ruin suffered by us, in consequence of it." The necessity for more stringent loyalty measures was obvious. "Scotch treachery might have been expected, and British enmity may be forgiven," for they had affections for their "native country." But our "internal *secret* enemies," he charged, arouses my greatest "detestation." "A native traitor is a villain of the blackest hue: His parricide ought never to be pardoned." When "friends of liberty" contend with "wicked designs," no man should remain "neuter."[26]

Suspicions seemed grounded in fact when disruptions forced the

General Assembly to deal with the "dangerous insurrection in Somerset and Worcester counties." The House of Delegates thought it "necessary to send one thousand men from the western, and the same number from the eastern" shores to quell the disturbance.[27] The resolution of a joint committee of the House and the Senate provided a force "upwards of seventeen hundred men" for the "suppression of insurgents" whose actions "have not only maintained the authority of the cruel and unrelenting tyrant of Great-Britain, and his venal and corrupt parliament . . . but maliciously and advisedly have endeavoured to raise tumults and disorders."[28]

The appearance of an article in the *Maryland Journal* signed "Tom Tell-Truth" aggravated the already fevered state of patriotism. The contributor spoke of the "terms of peace offered, by General Howe, to America," and praised the "magnanimity, generousity, humanity, and virtue of the British nation."[29] Immediately the "Whig Club" called upon the *Journal's* editor, William Goddard, and ordered him to reveal the author of the article. When Goddard refused, the club gave him twenty-four hours to leave Baltimore and three days to leave the country. The harassed editor fled to Annapolis and appealed to the Committee of Aggrievances of the House of Delegates. The committee concluded that the proceedings of the Whig Club were "a manifest violation of the constitution . . . and tend in their consequences . . . to the overthrow of all regular government."[30] Reason prevailed in the House, but tension remained. The people would not tolerate "internal secret enemies."

During the February Session of the General Assembly, Samuel Chase introduced in the lower house a bill entitled "An Act to punish certain crimes and misdemeanors, and to prevent the growth of toryism." The House approved the measure and sent it to the Senate. On April 9, 1777, the bill, with amendments attached, returned to the lower chamber. Contention centered on the proposal for an "oath of fidelity and support to this government." The Senate had rejected the entire test clause. This action by the Senate incited the delegates. "This house are at a loss," they replied, "to conceive the reasons which influenced your honours judgement." The question was "whether the oath proposed was improper, whether your honours conceive that no test is necessary to distinguish whigs from tories, friends from foes." The bill contained no more than was "*implied* in the oath prescribed in the form of government." In their opinion, the delegates declared, it was "high time that some test should be established to discover, if possible, our internal and secret foes."[31]

The Senate modified its opposition. The senators withdrew their objections to oaths for men in offices of "trust or profit," but they would not concur with the House on oaths directed at all male persons above eighteen. A general test, the Senate maintained, was improper and "contrary to the spirit of our declaration of rights." The senators made a bold defense of individual rights. "No government," they said, "has a right to dive into the secret thoughts of subjects." The state must not sanction the sifting of "political principles" from the bosoms of the people "by an appeal to their consciences, in order to lay the foundation of a persecution, or for purpose of inflicting pains and penalities." It was true, the senators conceded, that general tests were "imposed by our ancestors." But we must "imitate their wise, not impolitic institutions." Tests of this nature "will not prevent the dangerous practices of wicked and designing men," the upper house warned, but they "have been and may be abused" to the detriment of the public. The constitution and Declaration of Rights intended only the application of particular oaths to enumerated positions, and "we may fairly presume, no other persons" were required to subscribe to tests.[32]

The House of Delegates acquiesced. "With great reluctance" the members of the lower house consented to "strike out of the bill the test to the disaffected." The message continued forebodingly, "We are not to learn your honours power over our bills, and flatter ourselves that it will never be exerted to prevent any useful and necessary regulation, and that your honours will ever afford every effectual security to our new government." The arguments of the Senate, the delegates added, did not convince them that tests to expose "internal enemies" were contrary to the "spirit of the declaration of rights." The matter would be "subject to future consideration."[33]

The "future" alluded to came two months later. In June the House passed "An Act for the better security of the government" with elaborate procedures and punishments for the enemy within. The preamble decreed that in every free state "allegiance and protection are reciprocal, and no man is entitled to have the benefit of the one, who refuses to yield to the other." If a person enjoyed "the protection and benefit of the government," then surely he should willingly "give testimony of his attachment" to the state. The act stipulated that any person refusing to take the oath would be "considered as an outlaw" and deprived of all rights due him in courts of justice. Such persons were not to pursue "the science of physic or surgery," not to participate in trade, and not to exercise "any office, civil or military, within this state."[34]

When the Senate rejected the proposal, the House, by a vote of 49 to 5, ordered the immediate printing of the bill in the *Maryland Gazette*, with "fifteen copies thereof sent to each county in this state."[35] Two weeks later "Rationalis" addressed the "People of Maryland." "Whenever a diversity of sentiment takes place between your two branches of legislature," he advised, "it remains *solely* with you to determine in favour of the one or the other." Both houses of the assembly "originate from you, and from you alone derive all their authority. You are their constituents." The separation of legislative power meant that the "senate are the *mediate*, and the house of delegates the *immediate* representatives of the people." Both branches, though "free and independent of each other," he continued, were "equally bound" by the will of the people. The controversy in the assembly over loyalty tests must be decided. "Your delegates have published the bill for your consideration, and made their appeal to you." It was the duty of the people, "Rationalis" proclaimed, "to approve the one, and condemn the other." Both houses would "cheerfully acquiesce in your determination."[36]

The June Session of the General Assembly adjourned at the end of July. Adjournment delayed action on the loyalty proposal. But only temporarily, for in the October Session of 1777, the bill "for the better security of the government" again appeared. The House of Delegates approved the general test "to be offered to the people of this state." The sponsors of the measure defeated all attempts to qualify it. They rejected modifications which would have required only "disaffected persons" to take the oath, excused "quakers, menonists, and dunkers," and allowed those who refused subscription to retain their rights in courts of law.[37]

The Senate postponed consideration of the measure for over three weeks, then succumbed. The senators, like the members of the lower house, repulsed efforts at curbing the harshness of the bill; instead they augmented its strictest clauses. They upheld the treble tax against nondeclarers, maintained the court restrictions, and preserved the ban on professional and mercantile practice.[38] Reasons for the Senate's retreat are unclear. The senators, many leaders of the Revolutionary movement in Maryland, were almost surely caught in the fervors of independence. They were in the midst of and vulnerable to the crossfire of conspiratorial fears. Yet why was there no defense of the Senate when the patrons of constituent instruction called for popular interference in the proceedings of the legislature? The senators and their allies were jealously aware of the benefits of an upper chamber, of the separation of legislative power, and would not have allowed a usurpation of its privileges. These partisans, it seems, were victims of their ambivalent inclinations. Realizing the intense popular demand for tests of loyalty, they were morally, if not legally, bound to follow the popular will.

The immediate crisis was over. But the combatants left unanswered a question of far greater constitutional consequence—constituent instruction. And even before these first sparks had settled, fresh breezes of discontent swept through the assembly and through Maryland.

The debate over confiscation of British property intensified inter-cameral tensions. The Continental Congress recommended in 1777 that loyalist property in all states be seized and sold, yet the Maryland upper house was reluctant to encroach upon property rights. When the confiscation measure, approved by the House in December 1779, appeared before the Senate, the members of that august chamber declined to consider the proposal. The "extreme severity of the weather" and the "danger to the eastern shore gentlemen" of being caught in such hazardous winter conditions, necessitated that "the whole business of the session . . . remain unfinished."

The delegates were unimpressed by this evasive response and returned the bill to the Senate. Congressional requisition and the Maryland quota of over 14 million dollars must be met, the House declared. The difficulties involved in levying still another tax, and especially the "very great and rapid depreciation of our continental currency," placed the required sum "beyond the abilities of our constituents." Indeed the obstacles were insurmountable "without a seizure, confiscation and application, of the British property within the state." If the senators were "still inflexibly determined" to reject the measure, the delegates concluded, "we shall return to our constituents with the consolation" that the consequences of legislative inaction, disastrous though they may be, "will not be justly imputable to us."[39]

The senators attacked the ambiguity of the confiscation plan. "We are not convinced," they said in a tart rejoinder, "of the justice of the bill, less of its policy, and least of all its necessity." The distinctions "set up by the bill are in some instances arbitrary, and without sanction of law." They found it difficult "to ascertain who shall be deemed British subjects, without wounding the constitution"; therefore, the senators asserted, "we would rather err on the side of indulgence . . . than violate the constitution."[40]

If the lower house had hinted before of returning "to our constituents," it was now explicit. After restating their position, the delegates went on to declare, "Our appeal is now made to our constituents. We are both bound by what they shall determine." Should popular opinion oppose confiscation, "this house will comply" with the decision of the people. But, "if they should coincide with us . . . we flatter ourselves your honours will not oppose the voice of your country." The house then adjourned until the first of March in order to allow time for constituent expression and instruction.[41]

The Senate chose not to reply. The November Session of the General Assembly ended. The House resolution materialized in the state's newspapers. The delegates "earnestly requested" voters to "express their sentiments on the present difference between the two branches of the legislature."[42] In response, Charles Carroll, Sr., under the pseudonym "Senator," defended the decision of the upper chamber. It is significant to note that Carroll, staunch old-line advocate, did not question the procedure of the House of Delegates. Rather, Carroll recognized that "the delegates having appealed to their constituents for their instructions" made necessary further investigation "to attempt to throw such lights upon the subject as may enable" the public "to form a right judgement of the controversy." Carroll went on to outline the argument that the Senate had used. The bill did not provide an accurate "description of British subjects" and was "contrary to the law of nations, our common law, and the principles of our constitution." The plan of confiscation, he said, was *bad policy.* Only "engrossers and speculators" stood to gain at the expense of public welfare. "Whether there is force in the foregoing observations and reasoning," Carroll concluded, "the public, to whom the appeal is made, must determine."[43]

The controversy in the assembly provoked a wave of replies of all persuasions. The bulk of the exchanges followed the example of Carroll. The polemicists approved or condemned the confiscation proposal on the quality of its content. No one questioned the constitutionality of the delegates' appeal or the right of constituent instruction.[44] Those who dealt tangentially with constitutional concerns did so from premises of dual representation. "A Plebean" lamented the resolves of the delegates which "so severely censured the senate." The upper house of the assembly, he reminded all, "is elected by the people." It was a creature of the constitution and served as "a check and controul to the house of delegates, to correct their errors." Senators, he emphasized, had no "distinct and separate interest from the people." The asset of the second branch of the legislature was its limited membership, for it could "prevent those popular passions, prejudices, and predilections, to which every numerous body are liable."[45] Under the old constitution, explained another writer more explicitly, "a perpetual jealousy subsisted between the two houses of assembly." The members of the legislature served different interests. The delegates represented the people, but the upper house was devoted to the lord proprietor. Under the new constitution, he argued, "notwithstanding some ancient names are preserved," the basis of the assembly had changed. "The senate are as truly the representatives of the people, as the house of delegates." Another contributor urged "Counter-Instructions" to neutralize the petitions which were in "Agitation, in some Counties." Inactivity was "unpardonable."[46]

The House of Delegates reintroduced the confiscation scheme in the March Session of the General Assembly of 1780. The bill, identical to the previous one, again faltered in the Senate.[47] The stalemate might well have continued had not the lower house acquired an added advantage through external circumstances. The old proprietary government of Maryland had at one time invested in the Bank of England funds belonging to the province. The proprietary government had also appointed London merchants Osgood Hanbury, Sylvanus Grove, and James Russell as trustees. In 1779 the new state government, pressured for paper money, attempted to draw on the invested funds. The trustees refused to honor the bills of exchange.[48] Consequently, the June Session of 1780 authorized the treasurer of the Western Shore to issue bills of credit for £30,000 sterling. If the London trustees failed to honor these bills, property belonging to them or to the heir of the late proprietor would be liable for confiscation. The compounded assault forced the Senate to submit. The October Session of 1780 extended the provisions of the act; it allowed the state to confiscate all property, "debts only excepted, belonging to British subjects."[49]

Intercameral disputes thus characterized the Maryland legislature from its inception. The House of Delegates and the Senate divided on the question of loyalty tests and on the issue of confiscation. Both were fevered and volatile concerns; both involved popular commitment. Yet all the while, the Senate and its defenders maintained the strained alliance between the inertia and expectations of old and the energies of new patterns. The delegates called for the exercise of popular sovereignty in legislative affairs; the defenders of the Senate vied for popular approbation. The lower house declared its opinions and asked for instructions; the advocates of the upper chamber challenged the content of the proposals, not the manner of the proceedings.

Such was the motif of the legislative debates. During the confiscation crisis, however, cells of a new growth began to take shape. Its evolution would shift the center of contention. The idea that senators were "truly the representatives of the people" did not diminish the belief in the necessity of a separation and "controul" of legislative power, for men adhered to the notion that such a separation "affords stability."[50] Here the advantage belonged to the Senate. The upper house incorporated this argument into its defense of May 1780. The senators rejected a bill entitled "An Act for bringing into the treasury the sum of twenty million five hundred and forty thousand dollars," on the grounds that though it was a money bill it also dealt with valuation of the bills and therefore violated the constitution. The proposal of the delegates, they said, contradicted Article XI, which specified that the House should not attach matters of general legislative concern to money bills. Article XI further stipulated "That the Senate . . . may not be compelled by the House of Delegates, either to reject a money bill . . . or to assent to some other act of legislation, in their conscience and judgment injurious to the public welfare." This consideration, the senators explained, prompted their rejection of the plan of the lower house. The constitution and the privileges of both houses must be maintained. If the assembly sacrificed Article XI, the Senate would become a "useless and miserable appendage of legislature."[51] The argument soon matured to dominate the reasoning of the Senate's defenders.

IV

Speculation and postwar deflation in Maryland made inevitable the eight months of agitation for paper money and debtor relief in 1786–1787. Total monetary investment in confiscated property for the years 1781–1785, a large portion of which had been on credit, was over £650,000. The two currency emissions of 1780 were pledged for redemption on or before May 1, 1786, and the state had already begun to call them out of circulation. When British creditors resumed the collection of prewar debts, the situation worsened.[52] In addition to these circumstances, the November Session of 1784 sanctioned a "consolidating act," which scheduled the liquidation of the public debt, especially in confiscated property, by January 1, 1790. The act, as Philip Crowl has said, "destroyed the happy uncertainty which had hitherto prevailed."[53]

The House of Delegates in the November Session of 1785 resolved that "an emission of credit is necessary and proper at this time of so great scarcity of specie and heavy and necessary taxes, and that the greater part of the emission be lent out on loan on interest." The bill reached the Senate on December 22, failed ratification two days later, and returned to the House.[54] The deadlocked session ended, but currency emission was a heatedly debated issue during the state elections of 1786. Opponents of the proposal warned that the "scheme for issuing paper money *on loan* . . . was calculated only to enable speculators" to pay debts in depreciated currency. In addition they pointed out that the paper money question was not the "only subject of concern." They advised that the people carefully preserve the two independent branches of the legislature.[55]

The House of Delegates, during the November Session of 1786, again approved an emission of bills of credit. And again the Senate rejected it. The "general and perfect confidence" needed to "establish the credit of a paper money," the senators declared, was missing. The House, upon receiving the Senate's rejection, moved to adjourn until the twentieth of March, and appointed Robert Wright, Samuel Chase, and William Paca to prepare a message to the constituents.[56]

The address of the delegates dealt preponderantly with the necessity and the practicality of the measure. There was no need to dwell upon the validity of instructions or the propriety of appeals. "Both branches of your legislature" the lower house informed the people of Maryland "are bound by your instructions" and on disagreements between the houses of assembly "you alone are to decide, and to you only can there be any appeal." That the delegates devoted only one paragraph to this assertion in their twenty-four page message indicated that the practice was not new, and needed no justification. Paca implied as much by reacting with mock dismay to the Senate's protest. "And what is this address which the senate call an appeal?" Judging from the "severe comments," exclaimed Paca, one would suppose "there was something in it of a very dangerous tendency indeed!" Yet the message of the delegates merely gave "information of the federal debt . . . requisitions of congress for the current year, the expences and charges of our own government, the circumstances of our trade and commerce, the amount of our private debts and arrearages of taxes, the quantity of gold and silver in circulation . . . the necessity of some systems to relieve the people in payment of their taxes and private debts, the measures adopted by the house of delegates, the reasons by which they were influenced, and the senate's dissent to these measures."[57]

Samuel Chase explained the reasoning behind the delegates' address. The power of the people, he said, "is like the light of the sun, native, original, inherent, and unlimited," whereas the power of "rulers or governors . . . is like the reflected light of the moon, and is only borrowed, delegated and limited by the grant of the people." Thus the "*mode* of choice by the people" made no "difference in the *political relation* between the people and the house of delegates, and the people and the senate." Both branches possessed "only a *derivative* and *delegated* power." Unless the people of Maryland were willing to surrender their fundamental right as freemen, Chase advised, they must reject the notion of noninterference in legislative proceedings. Paraphrasing Article V of the Declaration he concluded, "The right of the people to participate in the legislature is the foundation of all free government." Only from this right "proceeds a government . . . by representation."[58]

The Declaration of Rights, however, specified the manner of participation. In concert with the assumptions of a deferential system, participation would consist of "free and frequent" elections. Defenders of the Senate echoed these sentiments. Instructions, they warned, would not secure "freedom and liberty." Instead they might subvert "every equitable principle of legislation." "Liberty stands on a much firmer basis . . . the best possible security for it." Liberty depended upon "the perpetual right of Election."[59]

Advocates of the lower house scoffed at such notions. It was folly, said Chase, to argue that the people could not constitutionally interfere with the deliberations of the legislative houses during the terms for which they were chosen. If representatives of the people were not bound, the "very idea of *election*, and of delegated power" ceased to exist. William Paca dismissed the thought that the people should apply for redress "by *petition* and *remonstrance*" so as to leave "both branches *at liberty* to exercise their judgment." Suppose the legislature rejected the application? "What then?" The people, Paca insisted, must retain "*supreme authority*" and may resume the powers of government whenever they found the public trust violated. These were the very "principles of the *American Revolution*." To say that the people should judge the actions of government only through elections, Paca later asserted more emphatically, was absurd. If they were otherwise incapable of intervention, when "the time is come for a new election, then the people may—I beseech you what?" During the interim between elections the people may well have lost their "liberties and become slaves."[60]

Others endorsed the opinions of Chase and Paca. "We choose" the members of the upper house as well as those of the lower, a contributor argued, "and they ought not to be above us who make them, for if they do, they will be our masters, and we their servants." We have more reason to interfere in the proceedings of the Senate than in those of the House, he added, for the latter body was turned "out every fall, and the other lasts for five years." The assertion that senators were free of popular control, observed another, was "new and dangerous to liberty," and should the senators ever claim as much "they would from that moment cease to be the constitutional representatives of the people."[61]

The more substantial defense of the Senate had as its theme the necessity of a separation of legislative power. The message of the upper house, prepared by Thomas Stone, Charles Carroll of Carrollton, John Henry, George Gale, and Richard Ridgely, emphasized this constitutional safeguard. The senators condemned the delegates' plan as "utterly incompetent to afford relief," but the core of their message was a careful elaboration of the earlier defense of Article XI. "Appeals to the people," they said, tended "to weaken the powers of government." "If this practice should prevail," it would soon destroy the legislature "consisting of two branches, equally free and independent." The

House, because of its numerical superiority, "will have greater opportunities of influencing the people." Hence if the procedure of appeals, as outlined by the House of Delegates, were allowed, "it is probable that . . . the majority of the people will be induced to adopt the sentiments of the delegates." Consequently, "the powers of the senate would be annihilated, and though its name and semblance might remain, its real utility would cease." The system of checks and balances rendered inoperative, "force instead of reason will govern, and liberty must finally yield to despotism."[62]

The tone and the temper of the subsequent exchanges became crystallized. "An appeal is made by the house of delegates" on the subject of a paper-money emission, cried a Senate defender, but "the question which gave rise to the appeal . . . is far less important than the appeal itself." The measure, said another, was ill-conceived, but the "means of effecting it, should they succeed, appeared far worse than the measure itself."[63] Constitutionalism indeed became the central concern of these men. The crucial corollary, soon apparent, involved the authority of constituent instruction. If the appeal of the delegates destroyed the independence of the legislature, then to what extent were citizens to participate in government? If constituent instruction contradicted the intentions of the constitution, how could popular sovereignty be realized? The search for answers clarified the divergence between the inertia of traditional expectations and the momentum of new formulations. These vectors eventually converged through a relocation of power and a reconsideration of the governmental compact.

Arguments for the preservation of a bicameral legislature were powerful. Even the most impassioned partisans of constituent instruction recognized the propriety of the institution. Chase declared that "*both* bodies must be subject to the instructions of the people," but he also admitted that "the *legislative* power" resided in "*two* distinct bodies of men, to operate as *checks* upon each other." He recognized "that *each* body should be entirely and absolutely free and independent *of the other*."[64] It was a tenuous position to maintain, as writers asserted again and again the provisions in Article XI of the constitution: that the Senate "may not be compelled" to accept or to reject legislation. If the procedure of appeals prevailed, they insisted, "the distinction required by the constitution will be at an end. There will, in fact, be only one branch in our legislature."[65] Confronted with these charges, the advocates of instruction could only retort, "It will be *insinuated* that some design is formed to abolish the Senate." "Such a fear," they assured, was unfounded. That the legislature consisted of two branches operating "*as checks upon each other*," and that "the system would be destroyed if *either* depended on the *other*" need not be said for "who denies the truth of the position?"[66]

The partisans of the lower house found, too, that in stressing the similarities of the two branches they wielded a curiously doubled-edged blade. Popular approbation was theirs when they declared that both houses "derive *all* their authority from the people, and *equally* hold their *commission* to legislate," and that "there is no difference between them but *only* in the *duration of their commission*." But if both chambers were "co-equal and co-extensive," then the necessity of instructions could be questioned. "In legislatures composed *partly* of the representatives of the people, and *partly* of those . . . independent of them," the "Constituent" argued, the need for popular interference might arise. "But in our constitution, there is no such body." A common interest bound the legislature and the citizens. The former, "framed *entirely* of the representatives of the people," undistinguished from their constituents, elected regularly, and subjected to the same laws, would not oppose the welfare of the whole.[67]

The senators and a majority of their allies, however, had not yet challenged the right of constituent instruction. They still objected primarily to the mode of the proceedings of the House of Delegates. Their contentions climaxed in the reasoning of Thomas Stone. The delegates, said Stone, "did not want instructions to regulate *their* conduct," for having already approved the measure "the only sensible end to be answered, by obtaining instructions in favour of the measure, was to *oblige* the Senate to agree to a bill which they had unanimously dissented to." Such coercion would disrupt the independence specified in the constitution. Although he recognized the right of the people to instruct their legislature, the exercise of that right, Stone insisted, had to be "of their own accord." If the procedure of appeals and instructions "were to become a part of ordinary legislation, it would be more wise . . . to take the sense of the people before any formal determination," and in this way avoid subjecting "either branch to the odium of having acted contrary to the sense of the people." The populace, Stone continued, "left to form their opinions freely and without bias or prejudice, are said never to err." But such freedom was impossible "after a decision upon the question has been given."[68]

Stone's carefully structured complaint nevertheless was an uncomfortable one. Even if constituents forwarded instructions "of their own accord"—and not as a consequence, as Stone said, of "an appeal to the people by one branch of the legislature against the other"—and thus preserved the integrity of the houses of assembly, the entire operation remained unsatisfactory. The people had initiated representative government for reasons other than mere convenience. In matters of ordinary legislation, the "Constituent" explained, "the people at large cannot be supposed to be competent judges." Only in situations of extraordinary legislation, "cases that forcibly strike the senses, and operate upon the feelings," were they qualified to decide. The Maryland constitution decreed that "men of the most wisdom, experience and virtue" be entrusted with the powers of government. The "refined mode of electing a senate" aimed at achieving quality for the benefit of the whole. Stone therefore tempered his remarks with the qualification that "the *existence of a right*, and the forbearance to *exercise that right in particular cases*, are perfectly consistent ideas." "Forbearance," he reassured, did "not in any degree affect the existence of the right." A contributor to the *Maryland Journal* mirrored the minds of many when he wrote: "Planters, Farmers, Parsons, Overseers, Lawyers, Constables, Petifoggers, Physicians, Mechanicks, Shopkeepers, Merchants, Apprentices, Watchmen, Barbers, Beaux, Draymen, Porters, Labourers, Coblers, and Cooks, all are to order the honourable, the legislature of Maryland what they *must* do upon the most *intricate* questions in government . . . it appears queer to me."[69]

The dilemma was obvious. How could men like Stone resolve the incompatibility of representation and instruction? How might they bridge the chasm between deferential orientation and the application of popular sovereignty? The problem involved more than the mode of conduct of the House of Delegates, it challenged the validity of constituent instruction. The issue implied more than the maintenance of a bicameral legislature, it questioned the basis of government itself. The quest shifted toward a definition of the relationship between governors and governed. The call led to an elucidation of the compact.

This need for an elaboration of the meaning of the compact stemmed from what Hannah Arendt has observed to be the "unique but theoretically inarticulate background of the American experiment." According to Arendt, American contractual conceptions evolved through need and practice, and were the results more of events than of theory. The colonial experience resembled some of the circumstances postulated by Enlightenment theorists. As a result, the colonists, and later the men of the Revolution, did not perceive the abstract distinction between the implicit contract of community and the more explicit contract of government.

Thad W. Tate has reinforced the observations of Arendt. Tate concluded that American statements concerning the contract were brief and uninquiring. The recurrent premise of the Revolutionaries equated the suspension of the old royal government with the termination of society and the return to a state of nature. The remainder of their argument, however, said Tate, made it clear that they meant no such thing. The months immediately after Independence saw a fuller development of the contract theory than at any other time during the Revolution. But men were then preoccupied with specific procedures and not with the theory itself. As Tate put it, they were interested in "the constituent convention, some form of constitutional ratification by popular vote, and amendment by a process more rigid than that for ordinary legislation."[70]

The lack of basic theoretical clarity concerning the societal contracts complicated the disparity in Maryland between Revolutionary ideals and Provincial expectations. Contrary to Tate's observations concerning the contract theory during the Confederation, however, the confrontation manifested more than a fascination with specific procedures. The particular disposition of the House of Delegates and the Senate, the debate over representation and instruction, and the attempts to accommodate the deferential paradigm with the popular argument, produced conceptual clarification of the circumstance of community and the implications of government. By 1787 men rooted in the deferential order sensed the cumulative challenge of the preceding decade. The actions of the House of Delegates threatened to erode the basis of deference democracy. If this occurred, the lesser elements of society would no longer fulfill their implicit roles; instead they would breach the realm of the men of merit. The natural political division between rulers and ruled would disappear. But the appeals of the delegates seemed to be true to the principles of American independence. Did not the law of nature and the restrictions of compact dictate that the people were sovereign? If so, then how could the men of the Senate oppose the actions of the House or the instructions of their constituents? One thing was certain, the American situation of late had erased any possible defense of an aristocracy or an imposed hierarchy. The natural rights orientation of the preeminently political argument for separation from England further necessitated that the current crisis deal with the extent of such rights. The opponents of unrestricted popular sovereignty had no other recourse but to refine their contractual concepts.

The political essays of Alexander Contee Hanson manifested the struggle toward theoretical compatibility. Using the pseudonym "Aristides," Hanson championed the cause of the Senate. His opinions exhibited the uneasy coexistence of incongruities. In 1786 Hanson admitted the authority of instructions, provided they were the products of well publicized public meetings where "any matter shall be freely discussed," but he doubted that "people of a county can have a fair comprehensive view of a subject to be discussed in the general assembly."[71]

Early in the emission controversy Hanson made an observation that was identical to Stone's. If the members of the lower house were undecided, "I should have no objection." But, he noted, "these instructions are to govern the senate, and at the same time to be dictated by the delegates." The people "are not volunteers." However there was a critical difference in the arguments of the two men. Stone refused to progress beyond questioning the mode of conduct of the lower house. He consciously confined his objection to demonstrate only that "it would be improper for the people to exercise the power of directing either branch to accede to the measures of the other." Stone proclaimed that he sought to "restrain a practice of the *legislature*" that would otherwise destroy the advantages of the bicameral system, and that he had no desire to "affect the *rights* of the people." Hanson, on the other hand, while emphasizing the ills of "this mode of effecting the plan," ventured beyond Stone and hinted at a qualification which he soon extended to disavow the legitimacy of binding instructions. Addressing the public, Hanson explained that the Senate was "a select body of men of enlarged minds" who had "no interest whatever distinct from yours." Senators bore a "full proportion of burthens, and out of the senate-house at their own homes" composed a part of the people. Having stressed homogeneity, Hanson went on to assert, "the constitution creates two distinct branches only" and neither the constitution nor the Declaration of Rights "anywhere intimates, that the people at large are immediately a part of the legislature."[72]

Charges and countercharges between Senate defender Hanson and House advocate William Paca dominated the final four months of the emission controversy. Paca, as "Publicola," repeated the self-styled syllogism of popular sovereignty whose premises were that the people must act as constitutional judges, and that judgment implied instruction. Paca's argument forced Hanson to confront the confusion caused by ambivalence and to clarify the qualification he had begun to posit—an implicit distinction between society and government.

Paca began with the undisputed postulate, "There is no power, but the people, superior to the *legislature*" because "all legislative power is a grant of the people." The people instituted government for their own welfare and happiness. Therefore, they ought to judge whether those elected to governmental positions acted according to the trust reposed in them. Whenever the people determined that their creation was functioning improperly, that the employment of governmental power was contrary to their welfare, interference "1st. By memorial and remonstrance. 2dly. By instruction and demand," was appropriate. Why? Because interference "resulted as a plain and natural consequence" of the right of judgment. From this right proceeded the intermediate authority of instructing representatives and the supreme power of dissolving government. Moreover, the objection that "representatives of a county" served the whole nation and thus were not bound by the instructions of that particular county, which could only be a *"minority,"* was unfounded. Instructions, Paca insisted, would come "from *every* county, or from the *majority* of the people." These national instructions, the voice of the people, must be conclusive, otherwise "the legislature is despotic."[73]

Hanson, however, did not reject the premise that all power originated with the people, rather he questioned the nature of the trust, hence the obligations of the trustee. "All power indeed flows from the people," he acknowledged, "but the doctrine that the power actually at all times resides in the people, is subversive of all government and law."[74] Hanson agreed that the people must judge legislative actions, but he added a critical qualification. Interference meant dissolution. "Upon every sound principle of government," said Hanson, "the interference of the people is a resumption of all delegated powers; the whole frame is *ipso facto* dissolved; and it becomes their business either to reform its errors and abuses, and to declare it again in force, or to adopt an entire new system." He recognized the significance of this restriction. "The difference between me and my adversaries is whether an interference will not abolish or suspend the constitutional legislature."[75] The basis for his entire doctrine, Hanson explained, could be reduced to a single proposition: "In every free government, founded on a real compact, neither the governing nor the governed, are to be considered on the footing of either master or slave; they both are possessed of certain rights, which ought to be held inviolable."[76]

The divergent interpretations of the potency of instructions evolved, as Hanson remarked, from "the construction of the compact." The conceptions of the creation of government, and the state which preceeded it, determined the course of the debate. This basic disagreement accounted for the argument over the nature of representation and the assumptions of contractual government. The remainder of this introduction examines the implications of these differences.

Paca understood the compact as a set of restrictions drawn up by the people and placed upon those chosen to act as legislators. This contract of government defined the scope of operations of the representatives. Moreover, since the people established the rules and did the selecting, they had "like command over their delegates and representatives, as they had over their *grooms* and *cooks*."[77] There did indeed exist a distinction, regardless of what Hanson had said, if not between master and slave, then certainly between master and servant. It was despotic to argue that the creator might not control his creation. The people could rightfully exercise all powers which they "possessed before the compact, and which are not therein mentioned, parted with, and *transferred*." The right of instruction fell in this category. It antedated the compact "and therefore, if not transferred by compact, might be exercised."[78]

What was this condition before the compact? Paca believed that the establishment of government removed men from the independent, though chaotic, state of nature. But men remained as constitutional judges. And once more, judgment involved instruction. The people, therefore, possessed the right to instruct their trustees because they had never surrendered this privilege through compact. Consequently it remained "a natural right, *paramount* the *compact*." When Locke stated that the powers of legislation could never revert to the people while a government existed, he meant, explained Paca, "those powers which the people possessed *individually*, and exercised *independently* and *exclusively* of each other, in a state of nature, before they established a civil government." Such powers obviously could not be exercised as long as government survived because the two were incompatible. But, "the right of instructing is founded on the national and collected voice of the people," thus it kept men from the state of nature and, in turn, was in harmony with the institution of civil government.[79]

That the inception of community coincided with the establishment of government was Paca's basic assumption. He perceived only one compact. To speak of society and government was tautological. Men lived "in a state of nature before the establishment of civil government." This premise compounded the necessity of instruction and led Paca to reject the logic of Hanson that interference signified dissolution, for was it not, he asked rhetorically, "clearly for the interest and happiness of the state," that the people be allowed to exercise the power of instruction "*before* they proceed to the last extremity of suspending and dissolving government?"[80] Interference through instructions must be allowed and the contract preserved, lest men revert to the precarious state of nature in the wake of the suspension of government.

Hanson repudiated Paca's interpretation of politics and political obligation. Society, not individuals "in a state of nature, (if ever such there was)," had actuated the governmental contract establishing a "government by representation." Furthermore "the whole society has solemnly agreed . . . to be governed agreeably to its provisions."[81]

These terse statements embodied the two central assumptions which become abundantly clear through all of Hanson's essays.

First, although he never elaborated his challenge to the existence of an independent and exclusive state of nature, Hanson consistently argued that the demise of government would not return men to the state of social chaos that Paca envisioned. Rather, men would remain in community. Hence Hanson entertained none of Paca's anxieties over the consequences of governmental dissolution. He implicitly distinguished between the existence of a community and the foundation of its government. "Society and government were instituted solely for the good of the whole."[82] And although there was a homogeneity of interest in the people at large in a community, there existed civil distinctions within that community that resulted from the institution of government. Senators "out of the senate-house" were a part of the people, but the roles of senators and constituents were distinct in the realm of the state. Still, the constitution defined this entire sphere. Differentiation notwithstanding, therefore, "in a genuine republic, there is no such political idea as that of master and servant." Every person "is subject to the constitution." It was "the sovereign and the protector."[83]

The idea of constitutional sovereignty led directly to Hanson's second assumption. The "real compact" of which Hanson spoke represented an agreement that bound the governed as well as their governors. In an essay ascribed to Hanson, "A Constituent" declared that a "constitution established on the principles of freedom and equality" ought not "to be violated on the one hand, by those who were appointed to the execution of it, or to be infringed or rendered useless, by the rest of society."[84] The contract of government thus enumerated rights as well as responsibilities. Representative government, after all, benefitted the whole. That a pure democracy, as Hanson said, with the legislative power lodged in the people suited only a limited domain, "small cities in their beginnings," was beyond argument. That in "a state of equal extent and population to ours," governmental power must reside in a select group of men of talent was likewise the consensus: "men in general cannot . . . so well judge as those who are selected from their fellow citizens, on account of superior talents." The inescapable conclusion, according to Hanson, was that the "people in a government by representation" could not legislate for themselves advantageously "owing to the same reasons, that, in the beginning, recommended the government by representation, in preference to the government of the people at large."[85] Hanson therefore accused Paca, "You most erroneously imagine the constitutional legislature to be nothing more than agents, deputies or trustees." Erroneously because, Hanson clarified, "The compact confers rights as well as duties, on the governing, whilst you would make them mere tools of the governed."[86] Later, Hanson resumed his indictment of Paca, "You remember all which Locke says about deputies and trustees; and yet Locke does not place them on the same footing, as you would place *our* deputies and trustees."[87]

The rejection of the natural right of binding instructions followed the logic of these assumptions. There could be "no rights *'paramount'* the compact," as Paca seemed to think, because the governmental compact was supreme and comprised the entire political world. Thus, if in a system of government "there can be such a department as the people having a constitutional legislative power, as a collective body, the constitution is its creator." In Maryland no such power resided in the people, said Hanson, for "the parties to the compact, *in which each has a right that ought not to be violated,* have agreed that those agents, deputies, or trustees, shall act according to their own judgments, so long as they shall act at all."[88]

Hanson's arguments revealed what R. R. Palmer has termed "The Distinctiveness of American Political Ideas." The case for the supremacy of the constitution was founded on the belief in the constitutional convention which, according to Palmer, actuated the "idea of the people as constituent power" and embodied their sovereignty. Once the convention had drafted a constitution, however, it disbanded, and "constituent power went into abeyance, leaving the work of government to the authorities now constituted." The people "having made law . . . came under law."[89]

The "distinctively American" political theory further substantiated the objections of the defenders of the Maryland Senate. The concept of a constituent convention alluded to the two levels of law: "a higher law or constitution that," as Palmer explained, "only the people could make or amend, through constitutional conventions . . . and a statutory law" that the constitution defined and entrusted to legislators. By 1787 Hanson had perceived the essentials of this theory. The bond of government consisted of "a great original contract" in which undifferentiated participants of society constructed two roles—governors and governed —and although they maintained ultimate power over their construction, the roles thus created could not be altered without ending the agreement and starting anew. If the people relinquished their roles as governed under an existing compact they could then issue binding instructions to the members of the constitutional convention because, Hanson emphasized, we must distinguish between "instructions for forming a compact" and those aimed at "making laws, under a compact already formed."[90]

Hanson's interpretation of American politics sustained the position of the Senate and restricted the scope of popular sovereignty. Hanson had constitutionally determined that the Maryland legislature was "at liberty to examine whether . . . instructions, although signed by a majority really contain the general sense," and even at liberty to decide "whether that general sense be right." He boldly concluded with a comparison that polemicists had shunned and denied throughout the decade. The constitution, stated Hanson, intended the Senate "to be as independent in legislation as the orders of nobility" in other countries. "The idea that senators are representatives of the people of Maryland, is no more just, than is the idea, that the king, and the house of lords, are representatives of the people of England."[91]

The paper money emission controversy soon gave way to the more far reaching question of a federal government. The House of Delegates did not attempt to introduce another emission bill in the assembly. The delegates made no further appeals to the people concerning legislative authority. But men were wary. Although the issue of a new national government was pending, the leading figures in the recent controversy were unwilling to leave the state. John Henry, George Gale, Thomas Johnson, Chase, and Paca refused to be considered in the nominations for delegates to the convention at Philadelphia. Thomas Sim Lee, Thomas Stone, and Charles Carroll of Carrollton resigned after having been elected to represent the state.[92]

The appeal of the House of Delegates for constituent instruction in 1787 and the Senate's early admission that it was a representative body were not novel and unprecedented actions. Rather the confrontation over the currency emission marked the culmination of a movement that began with the Revolutionary ideas formally incorporated into the Declaration of Rights and the state constitution of 1776. Men remained, but the context in which those ideas had been cast had shifted, thus the basis of politics changed. Only the shell of the old order survived—first supported by a nebulous maleability, and later, when men more clearly perceived the consequences of the new formulations, accommodated through refined constitutional reasoning.

In the decade after Independence men struggled with the implications of ideas prescribed during the exultation of constitution-making. The gap in Maryland between the ideal and the actual was pronounced. The political apologists of the deferential order, confronted with inconsistencies, forced reasoning back to the foundations of gov-

ernment in an effort at conceptual clarity and compatibility. Deliberations ranged from the content of loyalty oaths to the constitutionalism
of appeals, and from the constitutionalism of procedure to the nature
of the compacts.

In 1787 these polemicists were no longer preoccupied with the
wisdom of bicameralism. In 1776 they recognized the dual representation of the people and the necessity of legislative checks and balances,
and they certainly accepted the institution in Maryland by 1780. The
actions of the Maryland essayists, especially the defenders of the Senate, during the loyalty oath and confiscation controversies also indicated
that popular sovereignty was an acknowledged premise of government.
The transformation in political thought, therefore, was not in the
transferal of sovereignty to the people. Rather it was in the qualification
of that sovereignty. What was important in the 1787 crisis was that
political writers questioned the nature of popular sovereignty. They
challenged the legitimacy of constituent instruction. The senators and
their allies protested the procedure of the lower house. Even more
basic, they constitutionally defended the traditional notion of representation—representatives were to exercise judgment independent of
their constituents—which earlier had been adequately supported by the
strength of deferential orientation. In making this defense these partisans achieved greater conceptual clarity concerning the societal contracts. The logic of these developments was an evolution in political
theory, a refinement in the separation and distribution of power and
authority. The people remained the ultimate source of all power, but
within the context of politics they were bound by consent. The contract
of government, the sovereign constitution, created specific political—
rather than communal—interests and delegated authority over particular functions to the constituted positions. Although society could
interfere in the formation of government, constituents could not inter-
rupt the deliberations of their delegates unless the constitution specified such a right, or until the people suspended the constitution. Power
in this way was a grant of the people, but, as Hanson explained, the
idea that it at all times resided in them was subversive of all government. The constitution reconstructed the distinction between rulers
and ruled, but theoretically this distinction disrupted neither the contractual rights of the representatives and constituents nor the homogeneity within the community. Thus Hanson reversed the logic of the
entire controversy over binding instructions when he charged that Paca
had reduced "equal liberty" to consist of nothing more than "the peoples not being bound even by the government which they have chosen
themselves."[93]

The immediate issue of constituent interference was beyond resolution for the principal contenders in the 1787 controversy. Each rejected the initial premises of the other. Hanson and Paca contested the fundamentals of politics. Resolution, however, became tangential, for precisely from this disagreement a profound dialogue developed and an extended consideration of political philosophy evolved. The discussions of the nature of government and society, the limits of law and sovereignty, and the scope of constituted authority and political obedience transcended the solitary significance of the emission crisis.

NOTES

1 Gordon S. Wood, *The Creation of the American Republic, 1776–1787* (Chapel Hill, 1969), pp. 249–54, 369–72, 385–87. Also, Wood, *Representation in the American Revolution* (Charlottesville, 1969); and "The Maryland Constitutional Crisis of 1787: A Revolution in Political Theory," Bernard Steiner Lecture presented at the Maryland Historical Society, November 10, 1969. See also R. R. Palmer, *The Age of the Democratic Revolution: A Political History of Europe and America, 1760–1800,* I (Princeton, 1959); quotation from p. 231.

2 *Archives of Maryland, Journal of the Convention, July 26–August 14, 1775,* XI (Baltimore, 1892), pp. 15, 66–67. Herbert E. Klingelhofer, "The Cautious Revolution: Maryland and the Movement Toward Independence, 1774–1776," *Maryland Historical Magazine,* 60 (September 1965), pp. 264, 265, 269, 284–85.

3 *The Maryland Journal and Baltimore Advertiser,* July 31, October 30, 1776. Cited hereafter as *Md. Journal.*

4 *Ibid.,* Dec. 18, 1776. On patriotism and piety, see: Alan Heimert, *Religion and the American Mind from the Great Awakening to the Revolution* (Cambridge, 1966); Perry Miller, "From the Covenant to the Revival," in *Religion in American Life,* edited by J. W. Smith and A. L. Jamison, I (Princeton, 1961), pp. 322–68; Carl Bridenbaugh, *Mitre and Sceptre: Transatlantic Faiths, Ideas, Personalities, and Politics, 1689–1775* (New York, 1962).

5 *Md. Journal,* May 22, 1776.

6 *Ibid.,* July 31, 1776.

7 *A Declaration of Rights, and the Constitution and Form of Government* (Annapolis, 1776) (cited hereafter as Constitution), articles I, IV. The standard account of pre-Revolutionary Maryland is Charles A. Barker, *The Background of the Revolution in Maryland* (New Haven, 1940).

8 On the essentials of a deferential system, see: Richard Buel, Jr., "Democracy and the American Revolution: A Frame of Reference," *William and Mary Quarterly* (cited hereafter as WMQ), 3rd ser., 31 (April 1964), pp. 165–90; and J. R. Pole, "Historians and the Problem of Early American Democracy," *American Historical Review* (cited hereafter as AHR), 67 (April 1962), pp. 626–46. Also see Philip A. Crowl, *Maryland during and after the revolution: A Political and Economic Study* (Baltimore, 1943), pp. 37–39, 84, 136–41.

9 Buel, "Democracy and the American Revolution," p. 185.

10 Jackson Turner Main, "Government by the People: The American Revolution and the Democratization of the Legislatures," WMQ, 3rd ser., 23 (July 1966), pp. 391–407.

11 *Declaration of Rights,* article V.

12 Hannah Arendt, *On Revolution* (New York, 1963), p. 178.

13 John Adams, *Thoughts on Government: Applicable to the Present State of the American Colonies* (Philadelphia, 1776), pp. 9–15.

14 "The Common Rights of mankind and the Evident Principles upon which all Equal and good government is founded," Corner Collection, box I, Maryland Historical Society, Baltimore, Md.

15 Quoted in Crowl, *Maryland during and after the Revolution*, pp. 39–40.

16 *Archives of Maryland, Journal and Correspondence of the Council of Safety*, XVI (Baltimore, 1897), pp. 108–109, Jenifer to Carroll of Carrollton, Jos Nicholson, Jr., Turbitt Wright, Brice T. B. Worthington, and Samuel Wilson.

17 *Md. Journal*, May 22, July 3, 1776.

18 *Constitution*, article XV. Wood, *Creation*, pp. 214–22.

19 Pole, "Historians and the Problem of Early American Democracy," pp. 641–43, and Pole, *Political Representation in England and the Origins of the American Republic* (New York, 1966), pp. 24–26. John Locke, *Two Treatises of Government*, edited by Peter Laslett (Cambridge, 1963), Second Treatise, chapter 9. *Md. Journal*, February 6, 1787.

Wood and Pole have emphasized the dichotomy expounded in the Essex County convention, which met to consider the proposed 1778 Massachusetts constitution. The convention's conclusions, probably authored by Theophilus Parsons, came to be known as the *Essex Result*. "The writers of the *Result*," Pole claimed, "had something important to say about the political rights of special interests, and they adopted the traditional language of Whig thought with which to say it." The basic principle established was that "government operates only on two objects— on the persons and the property of individuals." Wood, *Creation*, pp. 217–18; Pole, *Political Representation*, pp. 17–18, 25–26, 182–89.

20 Wood, *Creation*, pp. 221–22.

21 *Archives of Maryland, Journal and Correspondence of the Council of Safety*, XVI, pp. 108–109. Parsons quoted in Wood, *Creation*, p. 217.

22 *Proceedings of the Convention of the Province of Maryland, August 14, 1776*, October 31, November 1, 2, 3, 4, 5, 1776.

23 Bernard Bailyn, *The Ideological Origins of the American Revolution* (Cambridge, 1967), p. ix.

24 *Md. Journal*, May 1, 1776.

25 *Constitution*, articles XLIII, LV.

26 *The Maryland Gazette* (Annapolis), July 17, 1777; see also February 13, 20, 27, March 6, July 10, 31, 1777. Cited hereafter as *Md. Gazette*.

27 *Votes and Proceedings of the House of Delegates of the State of Maryland*, February 7, 1777. Cited hereafter as *V. and P., House*.

28 *Ibid.*, February 11, 1777; *Votes and Proceedings of the Senate of the State of Maryland*, February 12, 13, 1777. Cited hereafter as *V. and P., Senate*.

29 *Md. Journal*, February 25, 1777.

30 *V. and P., House*, March 10, April 2, 1777; resolution adopted by the House, April 11, 1777.

31 *Ibid.*, April 9, 10, 1777; *V. and P., Senate*, April 11, 1777.

32 *V. and P., Senate*, April 12, 1777.

33 *V. and P., House*, April 17, 1777.

34 *Ibid.*, June 21, 1777; *Md. Gazette*, July 10, 1777; *Md. Journal*, July 15, 1777.

35 *V. and P., House*, June 26, 1777.

36 *Md. Gazette*, July 17, 1777; *Md. Journal*, July 22, 1777.

37 *V. and P., House*, November 13, 14, December 19, 1777.

38 *V. and P. Senate*, November 15, 26, December 8, 16, 1777.

39 *Proceedings of the two Houses of Assembly of the State of Maryland on the Subject of Confiscation of British Property*, December 15, 20, 21, 1779. Cited hereafter as *Proceedings on Confiscation*.

40 *Ibid.*, December 23, 1779.

41 *Ibid.*, December 30, 1779.

42 *Md. Gazette*, January 7, 1780; *Md. Journal*, January 4, 1780; *Messages Between the Two Houses of Assembly on Confiscation*, December 30, 1779.

43 *Md. Gazette*, "A Senator," February 11, 18, 25, 1780.

[44] For example, *Md. Gazette*, March 3, 10, 17, 24, 31, April 14, 1780.

[45] *Ibid.*, "A Plebean," February 18, 1780. A distinction must be made, for in the course of the controversy another "Plebean" appeared. Thereafter, the writers designated themselves "First" and "Second" Plebean, respectively. See March 3, 10, 1780.

[46] *Ibid.*, "A.B.C.," November 26, 1779; "A Republican," March 31, 1780; *Md. Journal*, "Veritas," March 21, 1780.

[47] *Proceedings on Confiscation*, April 4, 12, 14, 1780.

[48] Crowl, *Maryland during and after the Revolution*, pp. 43–45; Kathryn L. Behrens, *Paper Money in Maryland, 1727–1780* (Baltimore, 1923), chapters 7–9; Barker, *Background of the Revolution in Maryland*, pp. 93–94, 122, 292. The proprietary government had purchased stock in the Bank of England in order to establish a redeeming fund for the 1733 currency emission. After the currency had been retired, the province possessed a surplus of £25,000.

[49] William Kilty, *The Laws of Maryland*, I (Annapolis, 1799), June and October Sessions (1780), chapters 24, 45. The confiscation act stipulated that due to the former attachment to England, every property owner in the new state might be considered a "British subject" "unless he hath, by some subsequent act, divested himself of that relation, by adhering to us and our cause, as by entering into the service or employment of the United States, or any of them, joining in the formation of our government, taking the oath of allegiance to it, withdrawing himself from the British dominions for his attachment to the United States, or by doing some similar open act, or by giving his implied assent, by remaining within this or some other of the United States, and receiving the protection and benefit of their government and laws."

[50] *Md. Gazette*, November 26, 1779, February 18, 1780.

[51] *Proceedings on Confiscation*, May 7, 10, 14, 1780; *Constitution*, article XI.

[52] Article IV of the Preliminary Articles of Peace ratified by the United States on April 15, 1783, included the provision that "creditors on either side shall meet with no lawful Impediment to the Recovery of the full value in Sterling Money of all bona fide Debts heretofore contracted." The House of Delegates in 1787 estimated that prewar British debts amounted to £600,000 sterling. Crowl has argued that the Maryland legislators were "comparatively lenient in the treatment of British creditors" and did not prevent the regular collection of these debts. Crowl, *Maryland during and after the Revolution*, pp. 68–81, 86–87.

[53] *Ibid.*, pp. 60–63, 86–89, quotation on p. 62; Behrens, *Paper Money*, chapters 7, 8; Kilty, *Laws of Maryland*, November Session (1784), chapter 55. An act passed in the November Session of 1785 deferred execution on the two 1780 emissions until July 1, 1786 (for "black money"), and January 1, 1787 (for continental state money).

[54] *V. and P., House*, December 1, 22, 1785.

[55] *Md. Gazette*, August 17, 24, 31, 1786.

[56] *V. and P., House*, December 27, 1786; January 5, 6, 11, 1787.

[57] *V. and P., Senate*, January 5, 1787; *Md. Journal*, February 2, 1787; House of Delegates, *The Present State of Maryland* (Baltimore and London, 1787). Paca in *Md. Gazette*, February 15, 1787.

[58] *Md. Journal*, February 13, 1787; *Md. Gazette*, February 22, 1787.

[59] *Md. Journal*, February 16, 20, 23, March 2, 1787.

[60] *Md. Gazette*, Chase, February 22, 1787; "Publicola," February 15, May 10, 1787.

[61] *Md. Journal*, February 13, 16, 1787.

[62] *V. and P., Senate*, January 17, 20, 1787; *Md. Journal*, January 16, February 6, 1787.

[63] *Md. Gazette*, March 8, June 9, 1787.

[64] *Ibid.*, February 22, 1787; *Md. Journal*, February 13, 1787.

[65] *Md. Gazette*, March 8, 1787; *Md. Journal*, "Instructions proposed to the Voters of Anne-Arundel County," February 9, 1787.

[66] *Md. Journal*, February 13, 1787, "Extract of a Letter from Annapolis."

67 *Ibid.*, Chase, February 13, 1787; *Md. Gazette*, "A Constituent," March 8, May 3, 1787.

68 *Md. Gazette*, April 5, 1787; *Md. Journal*, April 6, 1787.

69 *Md. Journal*, February 16, 1787; *Md. Gazette*, Stone, April 5, 1787; "Constituent," March 8, 1787.

70 Arendt, *On Revolution*, pp. 164–78, considered the distinction between the "mutual contract" of people in order to form a community and the "so-called social contract between a given society and its ruler." The former was based on "reciprocity and presupposes equality." The alliance fused the "isolated strength" of the "partners" into a "new power structure." The social contract, on the other hand, she said, was an "aboriginal act on the side of each member by virtue of which he gives up his isolated strength." Instead of gaining power "he resigns" it to a constituted government "whose power consists of the sum total of forces which all individual persons have channeled into it and which are monopolized . . . for the alleged benefit of all subjects." The governed, Arendt observed, "are politically impotent so long as they do not decide to recover their original power in order to change the government and entrust another ruler with their power."

Thad W. Tate, "The Social Contract in America, 1774–1787: Revolutionary Theory as a Conservative Instrument," WMQ, 3rd ser., 22 (July 1965), pp. 375–91. See also J. W. Gough, *The Social Contract: A Critical Study of Its Development* (Oxford, 1963), for a discussion of the historical ambiguity of the contract theories.

71 [Alexander Contee Hanson], *Considerations on the Proposed Removal of the Seat of Government* (Annapolis, 1786), pp. 57–58; *Md. Gazette*, April 19, 1787; *Md. Journal*, April 13, 1787.

72 [Alexander Contee Hanson], *Remarks on the Proposed Plan of an Emission of Paper, and on the Means of Effecting It* (Annapolis, 1787), pp. 5, 10–13.

73 *Md. Gazette*, May 10, 1787.

74 *Ibid.*, June 14, 1787.

75 [Hanson], *Remarks on Emission*, pp. 6–7, 11–12.

76 *Md. Gazette*, June 14, 1787.

77 *Ibid.*, May 10, 1787.

78 *Ibid.*, June 28, August 16, 1787.

79 *Ibid.*, June 28, August 16, 1787.

80 *Ibid.*, June 28, 1787.

81 *Ibid.*, August 2, June 14, 1787.

82 *Ibid.*, August 9, 1787.

83 *Ibid.*, August 2, 1787.

84 *Ibid.*, May 3, 1787; on the association of Hanson with the Constituent, see April 19, 1787.

85 [Hanson], *Remarks on Emission*, p. 6.

86 *Md. Gazette*, August 2, 1787.

87 *Ibid.*, August 9, 1787.

88 *Ibid.*, August 2, 1787.

89 Palmer, *Age of the Democratic Revolution*, pp. 214–15.

90 *Md. Gazette*, August 2, 1787.

91 *Ibid.*, August 9, 1787.

92 Crowl, *Maryland during and after the Revolution*, pp. 109–10.

93 *Md. Gazette*, June 14, 1787.

DOCUMENTARY SELECTIONS

The Maryland Constitutional Crisis of 1787

The Appeal of the House of Delegates
JANUARY 16, 1787

TO THE PEOPLE of MARYLAND

WE, YOUR IMMEDIATE representatives in the general assembly, think ourselves responsible to you for our conduct, and that on all subjects that materially concern your welfare or happiness, you are to be consulted; and your opinions, freely and fairly delivered, ought to govern our deliberations.

We also hold both branches of your legislature bound by your instructions, whenever you please to give them; on a diversity in sentiment between us and the senate, you alone are to decide, and to you only can there be any appeal.

We wish you to be truly informed of the situation of your affairs, and however critical or dangerous, we have a confidence in your virtue, fortitude and perseverance, and that you will never despair of the public safety. Duty and inclination, and a desire to receive your approbation of our conduct, induce us to communicate to you the real state of your government at this time, and the measures proposed by us to afford the best relief, we conceive, in your power to give.

We shall not enter into the detail, but briefly exhibit, in one view, the proportion of this state of the federal expences, *in time of peace*, which stands thus:

	Dollars.
1. The expences of Congress *civil* establishment for 1786	446,876
2. Interest of Congress *foreign* debt for 1786	1,723,626
	2,170,502

Suppose, the proportion of this state one tenth, (though in our opinion above it) is 217,050 dollars, equal to £81,267:12:6 current money. This sum can only be paid in *specie*.

EDITOR'S NOTE: The House Committee—Robert Wright, chairman, Samuel Chase, and William Paca—appointed during the November Session of the Maryland Assembly, 1786, to prepare an address to the people on the issue of paper money, delivered their final draft on January 16, 1787. The House ordered that "the said address be signed by Mr. speaker, and that 1800 copies thereof be immediately published, and 100 copies sent to each county, and that it be published in the Maryland Gazette and Baltimore Journal." The message appeared in the *Maryland Gazette* on January 25, 1787, and in the *Maryland Journal* on February 2, 1787, as "An ADDRESS of the HOUSE of DELEGATES of MARYLAND, to their CONSTITUENTS." A subsequent London edition appeared in the same year.

3. Interest of Congress *domestic* debt for 1786, 1,606,566 dollars.

Suppose the proportion of this state one tenth, is 160,656 dollars, equal to £60,621 current money. Congress *domestic* debt consisted of continental loan-office certificates, of which this state has liquidated (and funded by the consolidating act) to the amount of £80,517:4:9, the annual interest of which being £4,831:0:4, deducted from £60,621, leaves a balance of £55,789:19:8, which must also be paid in specie, unless this state can pay the balance of former requisitions, which Congress state (on 30th June 1786) at 965,851 dollars; in which case it may be discharged in certificates (called *indents*) granted for interest due on continental governmental securities. The *condition* of paying this balance of former requisitions, is absolutely out of the power of the state, and if it was in its power, we have no means to procure the continental securities.

4. The proportion of this state of the interest of Congress foreign and domestic debt, is really, and must *for ever* remain, until we obtain continental securities, at £137,057:12:2 specie.

5. To the civil establishment of 1786, Congress, by their requisition of 20th October last, have called on this state to pay, before the 20th June next, 49,979 dollars, equal to £18741:2:6.

6. If this state can make no provision for the interest of Congress *domestic* debt, its proportion of Congress *foreign* debt, and civil establishment for 1786, will amount to £100,008:15:0 specie.

From this state it evidently appears, that this government ought, if possible, to raise above £100,000 for Congress for the year 1786, and that too without the lease provision for our proportion of the interest of Congress *domestic* debt.

The annual expences of our own government may be estimated at £16,000 specie. It is supposed that the whole, or the far greater part of our state debt, is funded by bonds for confiscated British property, except a debt we owe Messieurs Vanstaphorst of £45,700:4:7 current money, with interest to 1st September, 1786.

The property in this state *assessed* may be estimated at £10,000,-000 currency. If the whole demands were to be raised on the assessed property, it would require on every hundred pounds thereof about

	1:3:4
To this must be added the county tax, supposed	5:0
	£1:8:4

We deliberated whether the sum of £116,000 specie could be collected from you in the space of one year, and whether you could constantly and perpetually pay at least that sum annually.

In the course of our inquiry, as to your ability to pay such an annual perpetual tax, we took a general view of the present situation of your trade, and we also reflected on your private circumstances.

The imports since the peace are great, and a very considerable part of them consists of luxuries, and, from the best information we could procure, may be estimated at £600,000 current money.

The exports consist wholly of your produce, and we state them thus:

25,000 hogsheads of tobacco, at £15 current money per hogshead,	£375,000:0:0
700,000 bushels of wheat, or 140,000 barrels of flour, above consumption, at 6s.8d. per bushel,	133,333:6:8
Indian corn and lumber	30,000:0:0
	£538,333:6:8

These exports would require 31 vessels of the burthen of 400 hogsheads of tobacco each, and 35 vessels of 2000 barrels of flour each, navigated by 792 seamen and mariners, every vessel making two voyages to Europe within the year; and we have not above one-third of that quantity of shipping or mariners belonging to this state.

The debts due by you to Great-Britain before the war, we believe may amount to about £600,000 sterling.

The debts due to Great-Britain since the peace, is supposed to be about £400,000 sterling.

The debts due from you, *on interest*, to individuals within the state, may be estimated at about £350,000 current money.

The debt due from you to the state, on bonds for confiscated British property, and pledged to state creditors, is £275,600:3:1.

The great number of suits in the general courts, and in the several county courts, by British and domestic creditors, for the recovery of very large sums of money, convinced us of the inability of many of you to satisfy these creditors; and we know that above 800 executions were issued against the *state* debtors to the last general court, to compel the payment of the interest then due to the state.

It appeared to this House, that the arrearages of taxes, on the western shore, for 1784, amounted to £22,495:7:6, and on the eastern shore, for 1784, to £6,122:16:8½; and that the arrearages of taxes on the western shore, for 1785, amounted to £52,398:0:3, and on the eastern shore, for 1785, to £16,304:10:1½. Total of arrearages, for 1784 and 1785, £97,320:14:7. No return has been made by the commissioners of the tax for 1786, but the amount may be estimated at £100,000.—The whole of the arrearages of taxes, therefore, now due, are £197,320:14:7.

It is represented to this state by the board of treasury, in their letter of the 30th November, 1786, that the *surplus* of the receipt by Congress, from all the states, beyond what was necessary to defray the charges of the government, in the course of two and an half years, that is, from the 31st December, 1783, to the 30th June, 1786, was only 39,032 dollars, to be applied towards the discharge of the specie engagements unsatisfied in 1782 and 1783; and the board observed, that unless the several states adopted, without delay, a more efficient mode of supplying the general treasury than hitherto adopted, the confederacy of the states, on which their existence, as an independent people, too probably depended, *must inevitably be dissolved.*

The result of our opinions on this inquiry was, that you could not discharge your *private* and your *public* engagements; and that you must neglect your *private* obligations, or your *public* duty. For if you paid your *debts*, you would thereby be unable to discharge your *taxes*; and if you paid your taxes, you must thereby be rendered unable to discharge your debts. Your honour, welfare and safety, required that every exertion should be made to support the union. We thought it imprudent and useless to lay on you *further* taxes, unless some *expedient* could be devised to assist you in the payment of them, and also in the discharge of your private debts.—In every state there ought to be as much circulating money as will represent all the property and labour bought and sold for cash; and the current money of every country ought always to be in proportion to its trade, industry, consumption, alienation *and taxes.*—If government wants to borrow from, or to increase the taxes on, its citizens, it is necessary to use all possible means to augment the quantity of money in circulation, in proportion to the sum wanted on loan, or to be raised by taxes. We are convinced that there is not a sufficient quantity of circulating specie in this state to answer the purposes of commerce alone, because the chief produce of the country, tobacco and wheat, cannot command a reasonable and proper price; because lands, houses and negroes, will not sell for one half their actual value; and because specie cannot be borrowed unless at an exorbitant premium (from 20 to 30 per cent.) to carry on trade or manufactures, to build vessels, or to cultivate or improve our lands. It is difficult to ascertain the amount of specie in circulation in this state, and not less difficult to determine what quantity is necessary as a medium of commerce. We do not consider the trade of the state, at this time, in a more flourishing condition than before the war; and we do not think at any time before that period, that the circulating specie exceeded £200,000; the objects of commerce far exceeded that sum, and the residue was supplied by paper money and credit. We know that in 1776, above £238,000 in bills of credit, emitted by the old government, and above £200,000 issued by the conventions, were in circulation, and passed until August 1776, at par with specie. From this fact we draw these inferences, that the trade of this state, before the war, required a large sum of paper money to supply the deficiency of specie; and if our commerce is nearly the same at this time, as before the war, that even for that purpose the same quantity of paper may be emitted; and that if taxes increase the demand, the sum may be augmented according to such additional demand. There are no mines of gold and silver in this state, and therefore we can only procure those metals by the export of the *produce* of our lands, as we have no *manufactures*. The balance of trade being against us, for that cause we export, and do not import specie. As there is certainly not a sufficient quantity of gold and silver for a *medium* of *trade*, and for the *purpose* of *taxation*, we were of opinion, that a part of the *solid* or *real* property of our citizens, equal to the deficiency, might be *melted* down and made to circulate in paper money or bills of credit.

To explain and familiarize this idea of melting down and circulating *real* property in paper, we would suppose that the real property belonging to the citizens of this state is actually worth 15,000,000*l*. specie, that they owe for the public debt 1,000,000*l*. and the circulating gold and silver is only 200,000*l*. Gold and silver is the common standard to measure the value of all commodities, and are called the *representatives* or *signs* of wealth: It is evident that fifteen millions can discharge one, but if all the £200,000 could be collected by *taxes*, there would remain a balance of £800,000. How shall this balance be paid? Your property is worth above fifteen times that sum, and yet you must be *insolvent as to taxes*, if no mode can be devised to procure some representative of this property, *other* than gold and silver, which from its nature can circulate and answer *in taxes* the purposes of coin. The pressure of taxes, is less intolerable from the amount, than the scarcity of a *medium* in which to pay them. Gold and silver is not only the *medium* of *trade*, but also of *taxes*. We think there is not near enough of these metals for the *former*, and we are confident none of them for the *latter*. Our attention, therefore, has been given to devise some *medium for taxes*; and none occurs to us so proper and necessary as a paper money, and we reasoned thus; if lands, the most permanent and valuable of all property, can be mortgaged, and notes, or bills of credit, issued on such security, such notes, or bills of credit, would be the *substitute* or *representative* of such land, in the same manner as gold and silver is the representative of land and all other property; and these notes would possess all the qualities of a circulating medium of trade, as well as coin, and must have a real and intrinsic worth, as long as the lands, on which they issue, retain their value. Gold and silver has been called the *high way*, which carries the produce of a country to market. We think, in like manner, paper money (if there is not sufficient of those metals) may be the vehicle to convey the property of the state, by *taxes*, into the public treasury; and, in our opinion, this paper money will answer *that purpose* as well as gold and silver. Many of you who owe taxes have real property, but no specie; you have land, which is as much actual wealth as gold and silver; you cannot pay your land in taxes, or sell it for specie, but at a loss of one-third or one half its real worth; if you could on a mortgage of part of your land obtain what would answer for taxes, you would readily borrow.—We doubt not your inclination to contribute part of your property to support the federal union, and your own government, if you could be furnished with the means.

We have before stated, that the proportion of the annual interest of Congress *domestic* debt, (after deducting the interest of the sum liquidated by this state) amounts to £50,762:17:11¾. It is self-evident, if this government can pay no part of this interest, that it will be impossible for us ever to discharge the principal, with such an annual accumulating interest. At this time the final settlements, and other securities, issued by Congress, bearing interest, may be purchased from six to eight for one. It is apparent, that less than £200,000 specie, at this time, (and most probable for a considerable time hence) will purchase above £1,000,000 of liquidated continental securities. It appears to us, therefore, prudent and wise to make great exertions to procure the *means* of purchasing these securities in their depreciated state. The governments having lands to sell, have procured with them great quantities of these securities; it was *one* of the great objects of our proposed emission, to apply part of the sum received in taxes, or part of the sum not circulated on loan, to this purpose; if, as we expect, our paper should maintain its value at par with specie, or with a very little or trifling difference, it might either purchase these securities, or tobacco or flour, which might be exchanged for them. We also expected, that part of the £100,000 not appropriated for loan to individuals, would be borrowed by several of our counties, for the purpose of laying out and making the capital roads, by which the produce of the back country is brought down, and exported from George-town and Baltimore town, a great and necessary business, and which calls loudly for legislative assistance.

On this review of your circumstances, public and private, to enable you to pay such taxes as the exigencies of the federal union and your own government required, and with a view of furnishing the means to secure a quantity of continental securities, we proposed to emit bills of credit to the amount of £350,000 current money, and to circulate £250,000, part thereof, on loan at six per cent. interest, on ample landed security of above double the value.—We appropriated £100,000 for loan to the inhabitants of the several counties, for 30 days after the money was ready for loan, (according to the property and taxes of each county) the sum to the largest county being £11,500, and to the smallest £1,700.—No loan to be less than £50, and not more than £500 to the same person. After the expiration of the 30 days, any money not lent out as appropriated, to be lent to any inhabitant of the state, in sums not less than £50, nor more than £1000; and not more than £1000 to the same person.—If this £100,000 was lent out, six months thereafter, the treasurer was authorized, with the approbation of the governor and council, to appropriate and lend out the further sum of £50,000, in the same manner. If this sum was also loaned, three months thereafter, a further sum of £50,000 might be appropriated, with the like approbation, and lent out in the same manner; if this sum was also borrowed, three months thereafter, a further sum of £50,000 might be appropriated, with the like approbation, and loaned in the same manner. The bill provided, that not more than £200,000 should be in circulation at the same time, unless the governor and council should be fully satisfied, that the loaning a further sum would not in any manner affect the value of the sum then in circulation. The bill directed, that the six per cent. interest, and one twentieth part of the debt, should be paid annually, and that one half of the interest, and the one-twentieth part of the debt, should be annually sunk, and the other half of the interest should be lent. The bill declared, that the emission should *not* be a *tender* in law or equity, for any *past* or *future* debt for money, unless so agreed by the parties; and that the emission should not continue in circulation more than ten years; the bills of credit were to be received in payment of *all taxes and duties* due since March 1784, or to be imposed during the time the said bills shall remain in circulation; and in payment of all county assessments, salaries of officers of government, officers and attornies fees, &c. &c. but not in payment of five per cent. duties when imposed by Congress.—This is the substance of the bill; further particulars are contained in the abstract we directed to be published for your information.

By this scheme, not more than £250,000 could be put into circulation in the space of 12 months; and a debtor for £100, (if he paid his interest and one-twentieth part of his debt annually) at the expiration of nine years, would pay £36:19:6, and he would owe the state £63:0:6. By this plan, if £100 is lent, and one-twentieth part thereof and six per cent. is paid, annually, and the one-twentieth, and one-half interest, is sunk annually, at the expiration of nine years, the one-twentieth will bring into the treasury £41:11:3; the six per cent. will bring in £49:17:5; there will be sunk £66:10:0¼ of the principal; there will remain in circulation only £33:9:11¾; there will be £91:8:8 principal and interest paid in; there will be due to the state, with the accumulated interest, £83:7:5¾; and the state will gain £49:17:6; and if the debtor and his securities should all prove to be worth nothing, the state could lose only £8:11:4 of the original sum of £100. This will appear by the paper annexed, No. 1.—The paper annexed, No. 2, will also shew a true state of the emission of £250,000, agreeably to the plan of our bill, the sum sunk and in circulation, every year, and the profit to government.

This House intended to suspend the collection of the arrearages of taxes (before stated to be £197,320:14:7) until £100,000 of the emission could be fully in circulation, on loan, in every part of the state; and at no time would the paper money in circulation be equal to the amount of the taxes. We also intended to impose on you, for the supplies of 1787, a tax not exceeding 30∫0 for every hundred pounds worth of your property, and to continue the same for several years; and to cnable you to pay this tax, we intended, by purchasing your produce, to circulate among you the amount, or nearly the amount of the taxes, after paying the expences of this government. We hoped and expected, that you would readily submit to this taxation, and cheerfully exert yourselves to pay it, when furnished, in great measure, with the means, and when you must clearly see, that by such exertion you would relieve yourselves from a *perpetual* burthen, or a continental bankruptcy.

You will discover, from a deliberate attention to your affairs, that you are in a most critical and dangerous situation, and that some expedient ought to be immediately adopted, that affords some prospect of relief. If we remain inactive, and neglect to take decisive measures, certain political ruin must soon follow. No mode occurred to us so proper as an emission of paper money, and you will see, that the scheme has only a great national object in view, and has no relation to private persons, debtor or creditor; nor can it, in any manner, affect private dealings. The emission passing at par with coin, will be received by creditors in general; and will also answer all the purposes of domestic commerce. We think the emission will not depreciate, because the paper is circulated on a pledge above twice its value, and therefore the borrower will not part with it under its nominal worth; and because the value of all commodities, even of gold and silver, depends on the quantity and *use or demand* for them. We are of opinion, that if any government should direct its taxes to be paid in paper money, it would thereby acquire a certain value, even though the term of its final redemption should depend altogether upon the pleasure of the government; if issued on *private* security, and receivable in taxes, it may add to its value in the opinion of the public. By the plan, the uses created for the paper exceed the quantity in circulation, and the *taxes alone* can easily employ and absorb the whole; and the sum annually decreases very considerably, by the sinking annually one-twentieth of the capital, and one half of the interest.

The senate have differed in sentiment from us, and are opposed to any emission *on loan.* They have submitted the reasons for their opinion to your consideration, as we now submit ours, and you will give them such weight as you think they deserve. It appears to us, that the senate have assigned but one objection to an emission of paper money *on loan,* to wit, that it will depreciate: They have enumerated a great number of causes in support of their opinion, but it can only be a matter of judgment, to be determined by the event after trial. It is very clear to us, that if the money should depreciate, it cannot, in any manner, injure individuals; and we are not able to discover how the depreciation supposed (say five, ten, fifteen, or even twenty per cent. for argument sake) can injure our government. Let it be *admitted,* that £100,000 brought into the treasury by taxes, should purchase tobacco and flour only worth £80,000 in gold and silver, this deficiency must be made up by a further tax, but the state will neither be richer or poorer. Suppose a man owes two silver dollars for his tax, for which he must give three bushels of wheat, if no paper money; but if there is, he can procure two paper dollars for two bushels of wheat; will he increase or diminish his property by this circumstance? Why should paper money in this state depreciate more than in New-York or Pennsylvania, if emitted on as good a plan as in those states? In New-York the paper is issued *on loan, on land security,* and it passes at par with gold and silver, unless for the purchase of these metals for exportation, when the difference is two and a half per cent. In Pennsylvania their paper is issued *for taxes,* and passes current, except in the purchase of specie, in which case a difference is made from five to ten per cent. Both these governments are acknowledged to be in the most flourishing circumstances as to trade and wealth, and the most happy consequences have flowed from their paper emissions, both to the public and the individual.

It is objected by the senate, that our bill takes away the specie tax of 10s. which was applied to the use of congress, and also the supplies of specie arising from duties, two-thirds of which were appropriated to congress.

We admit, that our bill directed the emission to be taken in payment of the said tax, and of the said duties; and in reply to these objections, and to all the arguments used to shew that a paper emission will deprive congress, and this state, of specie supplies, we observe, that the system of taxation which we have hitherto adopted, is declared by congress to be *totally ineffectual,* and, if pursued, must endanger the existence of the confederation. This state, on examination and inquiry, is found, on the system hitherto pursued, among the most deficient in complying with the requisition of congress. Although the paper emission was made receivable for taxes in all cases, yet in all probability a considerable sum would be necessarily paid in gold and silver, because the demand of money for taxes and duties for fees of office, fines, forfeitures, and licences, exceeds the quantity of paper which will be in circulation at any one time. And with the paper thus paid for taxes, under the management of a proper revenue officer, the produce of our country might be purchased up, and supplies procured of gold and silver treble the sums produced by our former systems of taxes and duties.

It is objected also by the senate, that our bill introduces a tax of paper money for ten years, and suspends all taxes in specie for that period. This is a very mistaken construction of our bill. The emission is receivable in all taxes, and when received it lies in the treasury subject to the disposition of the general assembly. From the express terms and provisions therefore of the bill, the circulation may cease at any period the general assembly shall think proper. The senate in their message express their desire of an emission for the purpose only of purchasing liquidated continental securities. This proposal from the senate we could neither agree to, nor confer on, without giving up the privilege of originating all money matters, which privilege is granted to, and exclusively vested in us by the constitution. We have already explained that *one* of the *principal* objects of the emission proposed by us was, to obtain the *means* of procuring these continental securities. There is this manifest difference between the emission proposed by us, and that proposed by the senate. By our plan the money was *first* to circulate *on loan,* and every man, having land in fee, would have an opportunity of borrowing. By the proposal of the senate, the money was only to be taken out by the holders of the continental depreciated securities, and every person wanting this money for taxes, could only borrow from them. Every objection from depreciation applies with greater force to an emission only to redeem final settlements, than to an emission to answer *all* the purposes of taxation, and the payment of officers and lawyers fees, which alone would require a great part of the sum in circulation. It appeared to us, that acceding to the scheme of emission to purchase final settlements, though it might greatly benefit the *adventurers* in these securities, would not answer any great *public* purpose, and if it could, that it might be better effected by the emission on our plan; and it also appeared to us, that if we agreed to this scheme, it would effectually prevent an emission *on loan* for several years.

Having thus devised a system to relieve you in the payment of your taxes, and by the said system opened a loan-office, as the best means in our power to enable the industrious and enterprising to pursue their labours with spirit, vigour and effect, we turned our attention to the situation and circumstances of debtors. The plan on which the paper emission was proposed to be issued, left it optional with the creditor to take or refuse it; there was no legal obligation or force to take it on the principle of a tender for private debts: It was therefore eventual only, that this emission would afford any relief at all to the debtor; if happily it did not depreciate, the creditor no doubt would then take it, and consequently the debtor would thereby be relieved.

But the combined pressure of debts and taxes bore so hard upon the debtor, that we conceived some sure and certain relief ought, if possible, to be devised and adopted. Our courts of justice, it appeared, were filled with lawsuits, and it was generally admitted that there was not enough of gold and silver to pay taxes, much less to pay both taxes and private debts. In deliberating on the subject we found it both delicate and difficult. While we felt a real concern for the debtor, whose distress was in many instances occasioned by the calamities of the late war, and heightened immediately on the peace by the necessary imposition of heavy taxes, to pay off the national debt contracted during the war, we could not but be sensible at the same time of the critical situation of the creditor, whose engagements and prospects might be defeated by a suspension of debts. The treaty too was a circumstance which very much embarrassed and perplexed us.

On a review of our laws as to the legal remedy the creditor had against the debtor, we found he had his election to take the body of his debtor, or his lands, goods and chattels. If he took his execution against the property of the debtor, the law authorized an appraisement of it on oath, and obliged him to take the property at such appraisement, but the election as to species of property was given to the creditor. The law, which made this provision on execution against the goods and chattels of the debtor, was an act passed in 1716 under the old government, and by the statute of fifth of George the second, extended here, and adopted before the revolution, lands were put on the footing of goods and chattels as to executions for debts.

On this review we conceived, that if executions against the body could be suspended for a time, and the creditor obliged to take substantial property for his debt at its actual worth, a relief would be given to the debtor, and as much attention preserved to the creditor and treaty as circumstances and the necessity of the case would admit. It appeared to us, that in most cases the debtor had enough of solid property to pay his debts, his distresses and difficulties arose from the acknowledged scarcity of gold and silver, and the impracticability of commanding it on a public sale of his property in any proportion to its real worth, and in such cases the creditor to avoid the taking of property under the act of 1716, took out execution against the person of the debtor, and locked him up in a gaol; the debtor, to relieve himself from the distresses, horrors and calamities of imprisonment, had no other means left but by a public sale of his property for gold and silver.

As the difficulties of the debtor arose principally from the present scarcity of gold and silver, and not from a want of sufficient property of the debtor, we framed a bill suited to the necessity of our affairs, giving it a duration only of one year.

By this bill, to the abstracts of which we refer you, the debtor in all cases may, on execution issued against him, discharge the same by property to be valued by sworn appraisers: But lest such property might prove no satisfaction to the creditor from any particular circumstances he might be under, the bill, provided, that on all judgments, whether upon actions brought, or hereafter to be brought, if the creditor shall forbear to sue out execution, the debtor shall forbear to discharge the debt by property.

This bill is a system not adopted of choice; it is not devised as a fit or proper system for a permanent administration of justice, between creditor and debtor; we do not approve of it as such, or bring it forward to your view to be considered in that point of light. Such a system permanently established, would never suit a commercial country, nor operate either as an effectual or perfect administration of justice. We have adopted it on the principles only of necessity, resulting from the present embarrassed circumstances of the people, occasioned by the scarcity of gold and silver. It is a system merely calculated to meet the difficulties of the present times, and its duration was therefore temporary and limited to one year only. Considered on this ground, we trust it will meet with your approbation. But this bill also was rejected by the senate.

The Appeal of the senate, and of this house is *now* made to you as to the propriety and necessity of an emission of *paper money circulated on loan, for the purpose of enabling you to pay the heavy but necessary taxes for the support of your own and the federal government*; and we wish you to express your sentiments to both branches of your legislature. Under the present circumstances of our trade, and the heavy incumbrance of your debts to the state and individuals, we are of opinion, that you cannot annually pay, and that too constantly and perpetually, the sum of £116,000 in *gold* and *silver*. As the imposing taxes on you must always originate in this house, we were apprehensive if we laid such heavy taxes on you, payable *only in gold and silver,* which we think is very scarce, and bears no proportion to the amount of taxes, that you would compare us to the Egyptian task-masters who compelled the Israelites to make bricks without straw. If you entertain a different opinion from us, and think you can pay the necessary taxes *in gold and silver,* be pleased to signify your pleasure, and we will immediately proceed to pass laws for the collecting the sums necessary for the support of this government, and also to defray your proportion of the charges of the federal union.

Signed by order of the House of Delegates,

THOMAS COCKEY DEYE, *Speaker*

The Reply of the Senate
JANUARY 20, 1787

STATE OF MARYLAND
BY THE SENATE, JANUARY 20, 1787

GENTLEMEN, With inexpressible regret we perceive, by your message of the sixth of January by Mr. Bowie, that you have determined to adjourn to the 20th of March, and leave the material business of the session unfinished, after setting upwards of eight weeks at a heavy charge to the public.

Although we have been officially informed, that the continental treasury is empty, and the necessity of raising troops has been urged by congress, you have not passed an assessment bill to bring any money into the state or continental treasury, nor have you taken any measures to comply with the requisition of congress for raising a troop of horse.

EDITOR'S NOTE: The Senate committee—Thomas Stone, Charles Carroll of Carrollton, John Henry, George Gale, and Richard Ridgely—appointed to prepare a response to the appeal of the delegates, delivered its final draft to the Senate on January 20, 1787. The Senate unanimously endorsed the message and sent it to the House. Later that same day, January 20, the delegates responded: "The length of your message, and the communication of it within a few hours only of the proposed time for closing the session, prevents us from making full observations upon it. We shall only say, in reply, that we have paid every possible attention to the public affairs of the union, and the interest and happiness of our people. You have thought proper to overrule every material system proposed by us for these purposes, and have brought forward nothing effectual in their stead. The people must decide upon our conduct and yours, as to the utility, policy and rectitude, of the systems respectively proposed; and, we trust we can meet our God and our country with consciences as quiet and undisturbed as your own." The Senate's message appeared in the *Maryland Journal* on February 6, 1787.

An act of the commonwealth of Virginia for appointing deputies to meet at Philadelphia in May next for revising the federal government, and correcting its defects, was early communicated to this legislature: In consequence thereof your house proposed to appoint deputies, which we acceded to, and a conference took place to ascertain the powers to be given to the deputies. A report was made by the conferrees, which has been agreed to by the senate.

As this proposition originated with you, and the measure is confessedly necessary and important, we are not a little surprised that you have resolved to adjourn, without making this appointment. Although it may be urged, that this deputation may be made at the session proposed by your house to be held in March next, time enough for the deputies to meet at Philadelphia in May, yet it must be obvious, that the other states, perceiving that the legislature of this state has adjourned without making the appointment, may conclude that the measure has not met their approbation. This inference may create suspicions destructive of that unanimity which is admitted, by the wisest and best men in the United States, to be absolutely necessary to preserve the federal union.

The neighbouring states of Virginia and Pennsylvania have discovered their sense of the importance of this meeting, and their expectations of its effects, by appointing some of their first characters to assist in the deliberations.

We cannot account for your postponing the consideration of these great and interesting subjects, and your adjournment to the 20th of March, unless it be to appeal to the people upon the bill for an emission of paper money, which we rejected. This appeal tends to weaken the powers of government, and to disseminate divisions and discord among the citizens of this state, at a crisis, when the energy of the one, and the union of the other, are more than ever necessary. Appeals to the people, upon a diversity of opinion arising between the two branches of the legislature upon any public measure, are unprecedented. The framers of our government have no where intimated the propriety of one branch appealing to the people from the proceedings of the other. Every man of reflection will readily perceive, if this practice should prevail, that the public business will no longer be conducted by a select legislature, consisting of two branches, equally free and independent, calmly deliberating and determining on the propriety of public measures, but that the state will be convulsed upon every difference of opinion between those branches, respecting any question which either may think important. Thus the checks wisely established by the constitution, will in time be destroyed, force instead of reason will govern, and liberty must finally yield to despotism; for the same causes, all circumstances being similar, will produce here the same effects which they produced in the ancient republics of Greece and Rome. It must also be obvious, that the members of your house being more numerous, and more dispersed throughout the state, than the members of the senate, they will have greater opportunities of influencing the people, whose sense is to be collected, in so short a time, and before the merits of the question can be freely and fully discussed. Hence it is probable, that in most cases of difference between the two houses, the majority of the people will be induced to adopt the sentiments of the delegates; in consequence therefore of such appeals to the people, the senate will be deprived of that freedom of debate and decision, which the constitution meant to secure to that branch, and every benefit which might result to the state from that freedom, will be precluded. In such a situation, the powers of the senate would be annihilated, and although its name and semblance might remain, its real utility would cease.

We consider ourselves bound by the most sacred and solemn engagements to preserve inviolate every part of our constitution, and will not remain silent under measures which may tend to subvert our free and happy government.

If appeals are to be made, where is the line to be drawn? The present is a case of policy, blended with justice, but if appeals are proper in such case, why not in a case of justice only? And if so, and the sense of a majority, however collected, is in all cases to govern, then there are no rights in this state which are secured against the opinion of such a majority, full as well qualified to decide upon questions of justice and right, as upon political regulations. The bill which we have rejected declares, that the bills of credit shall not be a tender, we presume, upon the principle, that it would have been unjust. Suppose the people, upon the present appeal made to them by your house, should instruct the general assembly to make the bills of credit to be emitted a tender in all cases; this instruction, however unjust the object of it might be, even in your opinion, would be conclusive, according to your doctrine, and the general assembly would be obliged to comply with it, notwithstanding both branches might be fully satisfied that a clause to that effect would be impolitic, as well as iniquitous.

To some perhaps, who do not look forward to consequences, these appeals may appear flattering; but others, not unacquainted with the history of free governments, will recollect, that measures calculated to obtain the favour of the people, very often produced tumult and confusion, which generally terminated in the destruction of equal law and liberty. We are confident our fellow-citizens are warmly attached to this government, that they will view with equal concern and distrust, all acts in any degree tending to weaken and endanger it, and cautiously avoid engagements calculated to fetter the free deliberations of the legislature. Printed anonymous instructions, stating that the senate have appealed to the people upon the emission of paper money, are now circulating, when in truth no act or proceeding of this house, in the least countenances a supposition that we wish to disturb the public tranquillity by a measure so likely to produce heat and division. It would be well for you to consider, that although the rejected bill may be such a favourite as to induce the majority of your house to hazard dangerous consequences to force it upon the senate, yet when once fair argument is declined, and an appeal is made from the dictates of judgment to the voice of numbers, freedom of discussion and decision will be taken away, and that some of the present majority of your house, by a similar practice on some future occasion, may be reduced to the same situation in which they are now endeavouring to place the senate.

These observations are not dictated by any apprehension in this house, that there is a majority of the citizens of this state in favour of an emission of bills of credit upon loan, on the terms, and for the purposes, contained in your bill. We are satisfied, that the objections to the bill are unanswerable; and that if the sense of the people could be fairly collected, the majority would be against the measure: We are also convinced, that the majority would increase, if time were given to discuss, understand, and form a right judgment on, the subject. Without venturing to combat our reasoning in a constitutional manner, you propose to adjourn to a time so very short, that it is impossible a deliberate consideration of the question, and a free interchange of sentiments between the citizens, can take place. To decide justly, the judgment should be free from all biass. The passions are too apt to mingle with the decisions of large collected bodies of people; when so assembled, even the most moderate are liable to be inflamed by declamation, and hurried into measures inconsistent with their real welfare.

Several bills have been passed this session by your house, and rejected by ours, respecting which an appeal may be made to the people with as much propriety as upon an emission of paper money. As the reasons for the rejection of these bills may not be known, and motives different from those which influenced our conduct may be assigned, we think proper briefly to state our objections to the bills alluded to. The bill for the relief of debtors, violated the first principles of justice and legislation, by infringing the contracts of individuals, and by making a partial discrimination between public and private debtors. The bill, it is true, was to have continued one year only; but the objectionable principle of a legislative interference with private contracts, is as fully established by a continuance for one year, as for ten, and if we were to form our judgment from the preamble of the bill, we should be led to suppose, that the establishment of the principle, and not the intended and temporary relief, was chiefly in view. If once the general assembly should adopt the practice of intermeddling with the contracts of individuals, it would render the courts of justice of little or no avail, and by releasing parties from the obligation of their contracts, would introduce such uncertainty in private dealings, as would destroy all confidence between man and man, put an end to credit, and deprive the industrious citizen of one of the great advantages of civil government.

The bill to repeal the act for establishing permanent salaries for the chancellor and judges, we rejected as contrary to sound policy, and the declaration of rights. The established salaries we do not consider as profuse, even in our present circumstances. "The independency of the judges is essential to the impartial administration of justice, and is one of the best securities of the rights and liberties of the people." Although the judges hold their commissions during good behavior, their independency cannot be complete, while their conduct, as it may please or displease either branch of the legislature, may procure an increase or diminution of their salaries. The saving of a few hundred pounds ought not to be put in competition with an object of so much importance, especially as it cannot be made without a violation of a public engagement, and by with-holding a part of that recompence, which is but barely adequate to the services of men who devote their time and labour to the public, and have justly merited the regard and confidence of their country, by a faithful discharge of duty.

The following reasons have determined us to reject the bill "for the more easy and effectual setting off and providing for the discharge of the interest due to the creditors on the consolidated fund, and to explain and declare the law in future concerning debtors to that fund." State creditors under the consolidating act are entitled to receive in specie, the annual interest engaged to be paid them by that act, and are not bound to receive interest warrants in lieu of specie. These warrants will no doubt be a relief to those who have purchased confiscated property, and whose bonds are lodged in the treasury, and pledged by the consolidating act to the public creditors for the payment in the year 1790 of the principal sums due them, and of the annual interest to accrue thereon in the mean time, so far as the said consolidated funds shall be adequate to, or may be pledged for, such payments; but these interest warrants will not be equal in value to specie of the same amount, and consequently the public creditors will not receive what was engaged to be paid them by the consolidating act.

Another objection, still more forcible, lies against this bill. These interest warrants are made receivable in payment of any assessment, tax or duty, due to the state. Too great a proportion of the public assessment is now payable in certificates, and we are unwilling to adopt any measure which may increase that evil, and obstruct the influx of specie into the treasury, in discharge of taxes. The receipt of certificates into the treasury would lessen the capital of the state debt, and the interest warrants, proposed to be issued by the bill, might prevent the accumulation of interest, but they will not afford any relief to the federal government, which has called upon some of the states, and among others upon this, to raise troops, and have solicited loans of money for equipping and paying them, and have pledged the federal revenue expected to be raised in the course of the present year from the several states for the payment of these loans. The latter part of this bill takes from the courts of justice the decision upon contracts between the state and purchasers of certain confiscated property, and declares, that the operation of the contract shall depend upon the purchaser's construction of the law, a rule equally new and exceptionable.

We rejected the bill for the relief of insolvent debtors, not that we are averse to a bankrupt law, but because the proposed regulations differed so widely from those we think just and expedient, that it would have required more time to amend the bill, and model it into a good system, than could be spared, when objects more pressing and important engrossed our attention.

We have truly stated the reasons which induced us to reject the bills herein mentioned. We humbly hope the rectitude of our intentions will justify us before God, and we doubt not the reasons assigned will fully vindicate our conduct to those of our fellow-citizens who will examine them carefully and with temper. Our characters ought to exempt us from the reproach of duplicity; no part of our conduct can warrant the imputation, or justly subject us to the suspicion of having an interest separate from that of the people, or of being impatient of equal liberty. Some of us have been in the senate for ten years. A new election has lately been made, and a majority of the old compose the present senate. From this re-election and continuance of the same persons in the same trust, we may, without vanity, infer, that the conduct of the late senate has been generally approved, and that no suspicions are entertained against the present. We therefore flatter ourselves, that we possess the confidence of the people. If, for a steady adherence to principles we conceive intimately connected with the prosperity of the state, that confidence should be withdrawn, we shall regret this unmerited change of sentiment, but we should certainly deserve to forfeit the esteem of our fellow-citizens, if, accommodating our conduct to the opinions of others, we betray a want of sufficient fortitude, even to risk temporary disapprobation to secure permanent happiness to this country. We cannot consent to close the session without pressing upon your candid and serious attention the important subjects referred to in this message, and expressing our opinion, that the legislature is bound to attend to these subjects, and to adopt the proper means for carrying them into execution. A spring session will be attended with great inconvenience to individuals, and an unnecessary expence to the public; to defray this expence, additional taxes must be laid upon the people, who are represented by you as unable to pay those taxes which cannot be dispensed with, but at the hazard of all order and government. We are ready and willing to accede to any measures which shall appear to us calculated to promote the public welfare, give strength to the confederacy, and stability to our government; and we exceedingly lament, that the harmony of the two branches of the legislature, so necessary to promote these important purposes, should be interrupted; but, gentlemen, if you are determined to adjourn without finishing the public business, we shall have the several matters before us dispatched, so that an end may be put to the session this evening, and we shall hold ourselves acquitted before our country and the world, of the evils which may result from a measure we can neither prevent or approve. By order,

J. DORSEY, clk.

A Proposal from Anne Arundel County
FEBRUARY 8, 1787

TO THE PRINTERS OF THE MARYLAND GAZETTE

SIRS, The following draught of instructions has been proposed to the voters of Anne-Arundel county, it has already been signed by numbers, and is now submitted to the consideration of the people at large.

WE, the subscribers, inhabitants of   county, are impelled by a sense of duty to ourselves and fellow-citizens, to declare fully our unbiased sentiments on the principal matters committed in the address of the house of delegates. On a mature examination of the proposed plan of an emission, we do not conceive it calculated to extricate us from our embarrassments, or to produce any considerable good consequences to the government. We believe indeed, that paper money cannot be made to answer the salutary ends proposed. The diminution of taxes is merely nominal and fallacious; because, whatever revenue is by this scheme derived to the state, must ultimately come from the pockets of the people. As to burthens imposed under the name of taxes, if, on the one hand, a paper money enables the people to bear them with more facility; on the other hand it diminishes the real supplies of government, and enhances the public debt. Admitting even, that these positions are erroneous, experience hath taught us to dread the evils which have flowed from recent emissions. The difficulties under which we labour are magnified. Although serious, they are by no means such as to authorise expedients pregnant with certain mischiefs, and affording, at best, deceitful palliatives. From our present difficulties we may be delivered by a little economy and industry on our part, and the prudent management of the legislature in restoring public and private credit. The confidence of the people is government's best resource. A confidence between individuals would strengthen each others hands, and again put into circulation that medium which society has been deprived of by improvident laws.

There are cases, indeed, which call upon the legislature for immediate redress. We cannot, without the deepest concern, behold property wrested from our neighbours, and sold at less than half the value. The bill *for the relief of debtors* changes the nature of past contracts, and suggests a mode ruinous to creditors, repugnant to justice and good faith, disreputable to government, and fatal to our commercial interests. Instead of that bill, we would suggest a law obliging debtor and creditor to enter into a reasonable composition, proposed by either party, placing the one on a certainty of receiving his due at stipulated periods, and securing the other against suits before the expiration of the term.

To our immediate representatives we suggest this hint, and we entreat them to abandon that system which indirectly the people are advised to force upon the senate. On this head we declare, that we venerate a constitution under which we enjoy equal rights, and the greatest degree of liberty consistent with government. In the unhappy disagreement between the two branches of the legislature, the senate has our approbation; but, at the same time, we applaud the zeal and good intentions of the house of delicates [sic].

We lastly declare our opinion, that until some fatal period shall arrive, when the ends of government shall be perverted, and liberty manifestly endangered, the people cannot constitutionally interfere with the deliberations of the senate. Whenever exigencies shall require the people to make their own will the law, there will be no longer the constitutional legislature consisting of two distinct branches. Even the will of the people may not in truth be regarded, but under that pretext the ambition of a few individuals will be gratified. The whole fabrick of the constitution will be dissolved, and we shall plunge into a state of anarchy and confusion, from which we shall be fortunate indeed, if a frame of government shall arise superior to the present.

Samuel Chase to His Constituents
FEBRUARY 9, 1787

TO THE VOTERS OF ANNE-ARUNDEL COUNTY

GENTLEMEN, As one of your delegates I hold myself responsible to you for my conduct, and bound to obey your instructions, in every case, in which you please to give them; or to resign my seat. I observe in the Maryland Journal, of this day, a draught of instructions, which are asserted to be now circulating among you for subscription. I esteem it my duty to caution you against putting your names to a paper, which, in my opinion, contains an explicit and absolute *surrender* of one of your greatest and most invaluable rights and privileges, as freemen,—the *right* of instructing *either*, or *both* branches of your legislature, on any subject that materially concerns your welfare, happiness or safety. These instructions have *two* objects in view; *one* to prevent an emission of paper money on loan, to be received in taxes; and the *other* to establish a principle, that the people of this state have *no right* to instruct *the senate*, on any matter, however it may effect [sic] the prosperity, peace, or safety of the government.

As to the *first* object of these instructions, an emission of paper money. I know your sentiments, and have no reason to believe you have changed them; if you have altered your opinion, be pleased to inform me; and I will give up my *private* judgment, and endeavour to carry into execution your pleasure.

As to the *second* object of these instructions, "that you cannot *constitutionally* (that is, without a breach of it) interfere with the deliberations of *the senate*, (or in other words instruct that body, on any subject however important and interesting to you) *until* the ends of government shall be perverted, and liberty *manifestly* endangered," I earnestly solicit you most seriously to deliberate and consider the subject, before you give your approbation and sanction, to such a doctrine.

The framers of these instructions have assigned no reasons to induce you to adopt their opinion; and on so important a subject the sentiments of no man ought to have any further respect or influence with you, than what arises from the reasons adduced by him, and your confidence in his integrity, knowledge, experience and sincerity. The house of delegates are under a very different impression from the proposers of these instructions. In their address to you, they declare, "that they esteem themselves *responsible* to their constituents *for their conduct*, and that on all subjects that materially concern their welfare or happiness, they are to be *consulted*; and their opinions freely and fairly delivered ought to govern their deliberations." They also declare, "that they hold BOTH branches of your legislature bound by the instructions of the people, whenever they please to give them."—I should imagine that the opinion of *unknown* individuals, if weighed in the scale against that of your house of delegates, would instantly kick the beam.

The instructions proposed to you for your assent, do not controvert the *right* of the people to instruct the members of the *house of delegates*; it only maintains the position, that the people have no right to instruct the *senate*. By only denying the right of instructing the senate, it seems to admit the right of *control* over the house of delegates.

If the people cannot *constitutionally* (that is, without a violation of it) interfere with the deliberations of the senate, during the *five* years for which they are elected, I apprehend it must necessarily follow, that they cannot interfere with the deliberations of the house of delegates during *the year* for which they are chosen. It seems to me, that every reason urged to exempt the senate, from any dependence on, or control of, the people, will apply with equal, if not greater propriety and force, to exempt the house of delegates. All *lawful* authority originates from the people, and their power is like the light of the sun, native, original, inherent and unlimited by human authority. Power in the rulers or governors of the people is like the reflected light of the moon, and is only borrowed, delegated and limited by the grant of the people. The right of the people to participate in the legislature is the foundation of all free government, and where that right is not enjoyed, the people are not free; this right is the genuine parent of representation, and from this right proceeds a government, like ours, by representation. Both branches of our legislature derive *all* their power from the people, and *equally* hold their *commission* to legislate, or make laws, from the *grant* of the people; and there is no difference between them but *only* in the *duration of their commission*. Their authority proceeds from the same source, and is co-equal, and co-extensive. It appears to me, that the *mode* of choice by the people can make no difference in the *political relation* between the people and the house of delegates, and the people and the senate;—the *former* is elected immediately by the people themselves in person; and the *latter* is chosen by *deputies* appointed by the people for that purpose. The two branches have only a *derivative* and *delegated* power. The people create and vest them with *legislative* authority to be exercised agreeably to the constitution;

and therefore *both* branches must be equally the *representatives, trustees* and *servants* of the people, and the people arc cqually thc *constituents* of *both*. If the senate are under *no* control of the people, *in any case*, neither are the house of delegates. The *legislative* power by our form of government is granted to *two* distinct bodies of men, to operate as *checks* upon each other; and thence the evident necessity that *each* body should be entirely and absolutely free and independent *of the other*; but *both* bodies must be subject to the instructions of the people or *neither*. If there was but *one* branch of legislature, as in Pennsylvania, would it be independent of *all* control from their constituents? I have before observed that our government is a government *by representation*. The people appoint *representatives* in the senate and house of delegates to transact the business of making laws for them, which is impracticable for them to do in person. From the nature of a government by *representation*, the *deputies* must be subject to the will of their *principals*, or this manifest absurdity and plain consequence must follow, that a *few* men would be *greater* than the *whole* community, and might act in *opposition* to the *declared* sense of *all their constituents*.

The doctrine that the representatives of the people are not bound by their instructions is *entirely new* in this country, and broached since the revolution, and was never heard of but within these few weeks. You all remember that, under the *old* government, you claimed, and *frequently* exercised the *right of instructing* your members in the lower house of assembly. This right, and the exercise of it, was never questioned under the proprietary government. Astonishing to me, that any man should dare to doubt, much more deny, this right under the *new* government!—You also recollect that you claimed *no* right to instruct the upper house of assembly; and I conceive for this reason, because *they* were *not* elected by *you*, but were appointed by the proprietary; and were, in truth, *his representatives*. By our constitution *you* do appoint the senate, and they are, and have *uniformly* claimed themselves to be, *your representatives*. If they are *your* representatives, they are bound by *your* instructions, or you destroy the very idea of *election*, and of delegated power. To *represent*, is to speak and act *agreeably* to the opinions and sentiments of the persons represented, in the same manner as they would do, if *personally* present; of consequence therefore, to speak and act *contrary* to the declared will of the persons represented, is not to *represent*, but to *misrepresent* them.

The right of electors in England, to instruct their members in the house of commons, was never controverted, says a late writer, "until the system of corruption (which has since arrived to so dangerous a height) began to predominate in that kingdom; *then* it was, that arbitrary ministers, and their prostituted dependents, *began* to maintain this doctrine, *dangerous to our liberty*, that the *representatives* were *independent of the people.*" Before that time the constant language in the house of commons was "whose business are we doing? How shall we answer this to *the people?* What will the people of England say to this?" &c.&c.&c.

Our law books, and treatises by Sydney, and many other celebrated writers on the English government, inform us, "that not only particular members, but the whole body of the house of commons often refused to grant money, or to agree to requisitions from the crown, *before they consulted with their constituents*; and that they often adjourned for *this* purpose. The English history affords innumerable instances of instructions by the electors, in that nation, to their members in the house of commons; and this practice, for above 150 years, proves the sense of the people in that country, of *their right* to instruct, and that their representatives were bound to obey them.

We also find that the members of the house of commons frequently declared, in debate, "that their *duty* to their electors *obliged* them to do as *directed.*" Many of the greatest patriots the English nation ever produced, have declared their opinion that, "it is the *duty* of the representatives of the people *implicitly* to obey the instructions of their constituents." A late judicious writer thus delivers himself, "our *representatives* in parliament are not the bare likeness or reflection of us, their constituents; they actually contain our power, and are, as it were, the very persons of the people they represent. We are the parliament in them; we speak and act by them; we have therefore a *right* to know what they *say* and *do*; and should they contradict our sense, or swerve from our interest, we have a *right* to remonstrate and *direct* them; by which means we become the regulators of our *own* conduct, and the institutors of our own laws, and nothing material can be done, but by *our* authority and consent."

This doctrine that the *constituents* have no right to instruct their *representatives*, in the language of the two patriots, Sir John Barnard, and Sir William Windham, in the house of commons, "is not only a *new* and *wicked* doctrine, but it is the most monstrous, and most slavish doctrine, that was ever heard, and such a doctrine as no man will dare to support within these walls."—A celebrated American writer observes, "when the right of the people to instruct their representatives is taken from them, they may justly complain, as Demosthenes did for the Athenians.—That the *representative* has now *usurped* the *right* of the people and exercises an arbitrary power over his *antient and natural lord.*" This writer remarks, "that no instance can be produced in which the people have abused this right, nor is there any reason to believe they will ever do it; they act from what they *feel*; and when that feeling is *general*, it must be *real*." The virtuous and great Mr. Addison observes, "that the nobility and *gentry* have many *private* expectations, and *particular* interests, that hang like a false bias upon their judgments, and may possibly dispose them to sacrifice the good of their country to the advancement of their own fortunes; whereas the gross of the people can have no other prospect in changes and revolutions, than of public blessing, that are to diffuse themselves through the whole state in general."

I can find but one author who has ventured to assert, that a member of the house of commons is not bound by the instructions of his constituents. Judge Blackstone has delivered this opinion, and he founds it on a *fiction*, that *after* the person is elected he becomes the representative of the *whole* kingdom, and not of a particular *part*. The sophistry of this argument is sufficiently manifest; and if true, it would only follow that all the members would be bound by the instructions of a majority of all their constituents. Judge Blackstone is against voting by ballot, in the house of commons, "because the conduct of every member is subject to the future *censure* of his *constituents*, and therefore should be openly submitted to their inspection."—A late writer observes on this opinion of Judge Blackstone, "if the members of the house of commons are not obliged to regard the instructions of their constituents, the people of this country choose a set of despots every seven years, and are as perfect slaves as the Turks, excepting at the time of the general election;" and remarks, "that he laments that a writer, whose admirable work will be read as long as England, its laws and language remain, should be so sparingly tinctured with the true and generous principles of liberty."

By our constitution the general assembly are authorised to appoint delegates to represent this state in Congress; and you well know, that in very many instances, (some of them of the greatest consequence) the general assembly have claimed and exercised the right of instructing them, as to their conduct in their representative capacity. This power is not granted to the legislature by the constitution, and can only be supported on the principle, that the trust is *delegated* to them by the legislature, and therefore they must have a right to direct their conduct.

It is not unworthy of notice, that the proposed instructions most graciously allow the people to interfere with the deliberations of the senate, "when the ends of government shall be perverted, and liberty *manifestly* endangered." Where is this exception to the power of the senate to be found? Who is to judge when the senate shall pervert the end of their institution, and endanger the public liberty? The people I presume. Such a limitation as this on the power of the senate is useless;

for if they may act without any control, until our liberties are in *manifest* danger, it may be too late to resist; and we then could only execrate our own folly and blindness in submiting to such a restriction of the power of the senate. The right in the people to resist their rulers when they attempt to enslave them, is paramount, and not derived from the form of government, and it supposes a subversion of the government before it can be rightfully exercised; but the right of the people to instruct the legislature is necessarily implied in the establishment, and is the very essence of our government; and is to be exercised in the support and execution of it, according to the nature and principles of it. "Whenever government assumes to itself a power of opposing the sense of a *majority* of the people, it declares itself a proper and formal *tyranny* in the fullest, strongest and most correct sense of the word."

If it should be said, that it is no where declared in the form of government, that the people have a *right* to instruct their legislature, I would observe—that it is not prohibited; and that all power not granted by the people remains with them. I conceive this right of instructing commenced with the establishment of our government by *representation*, because it is necessary to that freedom, which is the essence of it; and is founded in the laws of justice, which are eternal and immutable, that those who are to feel the effects of any measure, should direct in the conduct of it, otherways they will be wretched tools and slaves.

It is one question, whether the citizens of this state (entitled to vote for delegates and electors of the senate) have *any right, agreeably to the constitution,* to instruct *the senate,* in *any case* that materially concerns the prosperity, peace and safety of the state; and that the senate are bound to act according to the instructions freely and fairly given by a *majority* of such citizens; and it is another and a very different question, whether the people shall exercise *this right* in any particular case, or on any particular occasion. The *existence* of the right is of the greatest and last importance of the people; the *exercise* of it may frequently be of very little consequence, or wholly improper and unnecessary.

I cannot believe that a majority of the senate, in their legislative capacity, will ever maintain, that they are not bound by the instructions of a *majority* of the people of this country, freely and fairly given. They are pleased to say, "that our government may, with a peculiar propriety be called *the government of the people;*" but if they are above any control of the people, *in any case,* I think with much greater propriety, our government may be styled a government *by the senate;* and in such case our liberties must finally yield to despotism—An unlimitted *negative* will soon include an absolute *affirmative.*

Impelled by a sense of duty, I have thus thought proper to put you on your guard, lest you should be taken by surprize, and subscribe a doctrine, which, in my judgment, if submitted to, will in time subvert your free government and erect a tyranny on its ruin——I am, Gentlemen, with every sentiment of respect and esteem, your obedient servant,

Baltimore-Town   SAMUEL CHASE

William Paca to the Citizens
FEBRUARY 15, 1787

TO THE CITIZENS OF MARYLAND

I HAVE READ with a good deal of concern the message of the senate on the proposition from the *house of delegates* to adjourn to the 20th of March, and I think it is indelicate with respect to the delegates, injurious with respect to the people, and repugnant in its principles to our bill of rights, constitution and government.

The advocates for liberty and the rights of mankind maintain, that all rightful government originates from the people, is founded in compact only, and introduced and established for the welfare and happiness of the whole. The government of this state stands upon that foundation, and the bill of rights expressly recognises it.

Declaration of rights, sect. 1. "*That all government of right originates from the people, is founded in compact only, and instituted solely for the good of the whole.*"

As the people then of this state were the founders of our constitution and government, and their object and design was their general welfare and happiness, the powers and authorities, which they communicated and transferred, must be limited and founded by such object and design; and the persons exercising such powers and authorities must be the *trustees* of the people, and as such *accountable* for their conduct, and this principle too the bill of rights expressly recognises.

Sect. 4. "*That all persons invested with the legislative or executive powers of government are the* TRUSTEES *of the public, and as such* ACCOUNTABLE *for their conduct; wherefore, whenever the ends of government are perverted, and public liberty manifestly endangered, and all other means of redress are ineffectual the people may, and of right ought, to reform the old or establish a new government; the doctrine of nonresistance against arbitrary power and oppression is absurd, slavish, and destructive of the good and happiness of mankind.*"

Both branches, then, of the general assembly being the *trustees* of the public, a very important question arises, who are to *judge* whether they execute the *charge and trust* thus committed to them with fidelity and according to compact, and the object and design of it? It is evident such a power to *judge* must exist *some where*; because, "*when the ends of government are perverted, and public liberty endangered, the people may, and of right ought, to reform the old or establish a new government.*" And indeed all limitations and bounds set to public authority would be mere mockery, unless a power was established some where to *judge* whether such limitations and bounds are kept and observed.—

To the question stated I answer, the *people* are the *judges*; for "who ought to be the *judge* whether the *trustee* or *deputy* acts well and according to the *trust* reposed in him, but he who *deputes* him, and must, by having *deputed* him, have still a power to discard him when he fails in his *trust*?"

The advocates for *despotism* in all countries treat this idea with contempt; What! say they, shall the *tinker* and *cobler* be the *judges* of *kings, senators* and *delegates*? Shall the *multitude* and *mob* sit in judgment upon the *public virtue* and *honesty* of *kings, senators* and *delegates*? Shall a rabble—such vile creatures—such contemptible things —whose force of intellect consists in the mere *voice of numbers*, empty sound, a crack or burst of air—vox et praeterea nihil—Shall *they* be the *judges* whether *kings, senators* and *delegates*, execute the *public trust* as *honest* men and as *honest trustees*? And shall *they* exercise the *supreme authority* of dismissing such illustrious spirits, the vicegerents of Heaven, from *public trust*, whenever they in their judgment shall think them *dishonest* or public *thieves* instead of public *guardians*?— In this strain the flatterers and sycophants of *great men* have reasoned and wrote against the right of *judgment* in the people, and against all *popular* security or barrier of public liberty: among these *prostituted* characters we find JUDGES, BISHOPS, and LORDS temporal; for, elevation in office, and wealth and titles, and political rank and dignity, have no influence at all in making men *good* or *honest*. And so extremely infatuating is power, that men who possess it, cannot discover this flattery or prostitution of character; they form high notions of themselves, grow proud and haughty, and conceive that the Supreme Being have marked them out as *favourite* spirits, and not only given them a *superiority* of *power* over their fellow citizens, but a *superiority* also of *sense* and *virtue*. They who are invested with *legislative powers* are most subject to this *pride* and *self-conceit*; and although thousands of their countrymen have a just knowledge of the principles of government and the rights of mankind, and all are competent judges of their own good and evil, their own feelings, benefits and sufferings, yet they consider an appeal to the *judgment* of fellow citizens as an appeal to the *tinker* and *cobler*, and as a diminution of their power, and a degradation of their consequence, rank and dignity. But this right of the people to *judge* whether their *trustees* execute the *trust* committed, with fidelity and according to compact, and the object and design of it; and whether they make the good and welfare of the people the *rule* of their conduct, and the end of their deliberations; and this *supreme authority* of the people to resume the powers of government whenever they find dangerous designs entertained against their liberties, the *public trust* violated, and the powers of government abused—has been ever admitted and maintained by every patriot and friend to the rights and welfare of mankind. These principles "Mr. *Locke*, lord *Molseworth* [*sic*] and Mr *Trenchard*, maintained with their pens; Mr. *Hampden* and lord *John Russel* with their blood; and Mr. *Algernon Sidney* with both."—And in the sentiment and style of a distinguished writer, I will venture to add,—"they are not only the principles of speculative students in their closets, or of great but unfortunate men, whom their zeal and virtue have led to martyrdom for the liberties of their country and welfare of mankind, but they are likewise the real principles of our *present actual government*,"—the principles of the *American revolution*, and the principles on which the *senators* and *delegates* of this state hold and exercise their power and authority.

But it is objected that this right of judgment and supreme authority can never be exercised but "*when the ends of government are perverted, and public liberty endangered*;" and the writer of instructions published in the last Annapolis gazette proposes that the people should subscribe the following declaration, viz

"*We lastly declare our opinion, that until some fatal period shalt arrive when the ends of government are perverted and liberty manifestly endangered the people cannot constitutionally interfere with the deliberations of the senate.*"

Thus spoke and wrote in a former day a distinguished champion for *absolute power*; on which doctrine Mr *Locke*, the great advocate for the rights and liberties of mankind, thus remarks; "to tell people they may provide for themselves by erecting a new legislature, WHEN by *oppression, artifice*, or being delivered over to a foreign power, the old is gone, is only to tell them they may expect relief when it is *too late*, and the evil is *past cure*. This is in effect no more than to bid them first be *slaves*, and then to take care of their *liberty*; and when *chains* are on, tell them they may act like *freemen*. This, if barely so, is rather MOCKERY than RELIEF, and men can never be safe from *tyranny*, if there be no means to escape until they are perfectly under it; and therefore it is that they have not only a right to GET OUT of it, but to PREVENT it."—

The right to *judge* must therefore *perpetually* exist, and may be exercised *on all occasions*; but the *supreme authority* to dissolve the old government and establish a new one, I admit, can only be exercised when redress of grievances cannot be obtained, or designs are *entertained* or *executed* endangering or destructive of public liberty and happiness.

But it is objected, that this right of the people to *judge* of the conduct of their *trustees* cannot extend to an interference with *the deliberations* of the general assembly; that the people have no right to instruct *both branches* and bind them by *such instructions.*

I would fain know of the senate and their advocates, whether *public oppression* is not a perversion of the ends of government? And whether the imposition of taxes, for example, in *gold* and *silver* beyond the circumstances of the people, and the quantity in circulation, is not *public oppression?*

As the people are *judges* of what is public oppression, public injustice, or a perversion of the ends of government; what, I would ask, are the people to do, if exercising their right of judgment, they should be of opinion that the imposition of taxes, to the amount of the public demand, and the exacting them in gold and silver, is a *public oppression?*

Perhaps I may be told that the people should apply to the general assembly for redress by *petition* and *remonstrance,* and that such an interference is perfectly *constitutional,* as it leaves both branches *at liberty* to exercise their judgment to reject or grant the application.

But suppose the application rejected. What then? I maintain the people have a right to *instruct* both branches and *demand redress*; for they are the *constitutional judges* of what is *public oppression*; they are the *constitutional judges* of what *acts of violence or neglect* pervert the ends of government; they are the *constitutional judges* of what ought to be the conduct of both branches on a representation of *grievances* and *public oppression.* And if they are the *constitutional judges,* their judgment and *instructions* are final and *conclusive.*

There is no power, but the people, superior to the *legislature*; and the *legislature* are the *trustees* of the people and *accountable* to them; and therefore it is that the people only are the *constitutional judges* of *legislative* or *public* oppressions—And hence the right of the people to *interfere* with the deliberations of both branches of the *legislature* by *remonstrances* and *instructions.*—

The senate put the case of instructions requiring what some of the members might think *unjust* and *iniquitous.* In the case put, such members in my opinion ought to do one of two things, either execute the instructions, or resign thcir trust.—

The senate, and the friends of the senate say the people ought not to *force* upon the senate the bill for an emission of paper money on loan. This is strange language for *trustees* to use towards their *constituents*. Is it a *force* upon the *deputy* for the *principal*, apprehensive of injustice or oppression, to instruct his *deputy* to take measure to prevent it? If the *deputy* dislikes the instructions of his *principal*, is it not his duty to execute them or resign? Would it not be *extremely impertinent* in the *deputy* to tell his *principal*, I will neither execute your instructions nor resign? And could it be said that the *principal* acts with *force*, if under such circumstances of obstinacy and perverseness, he insists that *his deputy* should do one or the other, under the peril of being dismissed? No man can seriously think so.

The address of the house of delegates to the people the senate consider as an *appeal*; and this *appeal*, they say, tends to weaken the powers of government, disseminate division and discord, raise convulsions, destroy the checks wisely established by the constitution, subvcrt liberty, and introduce despotism—

And what is this address which the senate call an *appeal*? One would imagine from the severe comments and remarks which they have made upon it, there was something in it of a very dangerous tendency indeed! And yet this address is nothing morc than an account of transactions rendered by *trustees* to their *constituents*. Thc addrcss gives information of the federal debt, both foreign and domestic, states the demands and requisitions of congress for the current year, the expences and charges of our own government, the circumstances of our trade and commerce, the amount of our private debts and arrearages of taxes, the quantity of gold and silver in circulation, the impracticability of raising, by taxes, the sums wanted for the exigencies of government, the necessity of some systems to relieve the people in payment of their taxes and private debts, the measures adopted by the house of delegates, the reasons by which they were influenced, and the senate's dissent to these measures; and then considering the senate's first message as an intended justification of their conduct to the people, the address joins issue upon it and requests the sense of the people to be expressed to both houses.

I see nothing in the address but what I have stated. If the senate's doctrine be true, then it follows the house of delegates are never to address their constituents on *public affairs*, especially if these affairs have bccn *agitated* by both branches and a difference of opinion entertained. And I take it for granted the doctrine equally applies to the senate.

Let us consider, for a moment, this doctrine. Both branches are the *trustees* of the people, and *accountable* to them for their conduct; but yet neither branch, according to this doctrine, must render an account to the people by *an address*, nor give them information of what is done or doing by their *trustees*. If either branch should *neglect* its trust, or *violate* its public duty, yet the other branch must not inform the people of it; because to do so is to *appeal* to the people, and the house of delegates being more numerous, would be more able to *misrepresent* and *dupe* the people, and so get them on their side against the senate; and this would destroy the consequence and *independency of the senate*. Both branches must therefore hold their tongues, and not tell tales on each other to the people. However injurious and dangerous the conduct of either branch may be to the liberties of the people, yet all is to be *hush!* and the people are to find it out if they can; no information can *constitutionally* come from their *trustees*; for this would be an *appeal* to the people. And, on the principles of this doctrine, the doors of both houses ought to be shut, and the practice of keeping journals of the votes and proceedings ought to be abolished, and the liberty too of the PRESS as to the proceedings of the *legislature* ought to be taken away; because if the people were to know what passes, they might, perhaps, be *against* the senate; and, if the senate were *wrong*, the people ought not to know it; and, if they should know it, they must put a padlock upon their lips, and not *talk* or *speak* of it, or *express* their sense of it; for this would destroy the *independency* of the senate, disseminate division, raise convulsions, destroy liberty, and introduce despotism.

It is well known, that our public affairs are in the most critical and desperate way. An unhappy difference prevailed between the two branches, with respect to the measures which ought to be taken. Both branches are independent; neither is obliged to give way to the other— While they differ in opinion, no supplies can be raised, the government must be at a stand, and possibly may be dissolved.—Under these circumstances, was it wrong or improper for either branch to state this difference of opinion to the people, and to request their sense or judgement as to the measures, which ought to be adopted, whether the systems proposed by the senate, or those proposed by the house of delegates? Nay, is it not the public duty of *trustees* to state to their *constituents* such difficulties as impede the execution of their *public trust*? And what other method can possibly be suggested of removing the present impediments, to all further legislation, as to supplies, than for both branches to abide by the *sense* of their *constituents*?—"In a controversy, says Mr *Locke*, between a prince and *some* of his people,

where the law is silent or doubtful, and the thing be of great consequence, I should think the proper *umpire* in such a case would be the
body of the people, *who lodged the trust!*"

But if the address of the house of delegates be an *appeal*, the
senate's first message is also an *appeal*, and the first appeal that was
made. The address can only be considered as an appeal, because it
states to the people the subject in controversy between the two
branches, vindicates the conduct of the house of delegates, and submits
to the people the reasons which influenced the passing of the bills for
a *paper emission* and for the *relief of debtors*. This address was in
consequence of the senate's first message accompanying their negative
to the paper money bill; and in that message they went into a variety
of arguments to justify their dissent; and they state their object for
doing it to be—*to lay before the people*, their *constituents*, the reasons
which influenced their dissent. This message was *printed* by order of
the senate in *hand bills*, at the public expence, and circulated among
the people, for *their consideration*. The house of delegates considered
this message *as an appeal* to the people, and calculated to justify the
senate's conduct *before the people*; they therefore addressed the people
by a *public address*, calculated on the like principles of information,
defence, and justification—and although the house of delegates only
followed the example of the senate's first *message* and *appeal*, yet their
Honours, speaking of the *address*, are pleased to say, "we consider ourselves bound by the most sacred and solemn engagements to preserve
inviolate every part of our constitution, and will not remain silent under
measures, which may tend to subvert our free and happy government"
—How extremely modest and genteel men can be when they are
senators!

But appeals by *trustees*, to the people, their *constituents*, say the
senate, are only calculated to obtain *favour* of the people—modest
indeed!

And appeals to the people are appeals from the *dictates* of *judgment* to the *voice of numbers*. Modest again!

"No governments, says lord CAMDEN, ever care to acknowledge the
people to be against them. For whatever may be the case with the
opinions of the multitude in abstruse and refined matters, which but
little concern them, nor do they much trouble themselves about; yet
the end, and therefore the touchstone and trial, of all governments
being their welfare and happiness, there is hardly *common modesty* in
affecting to *despise* and *refuse* their sense concerning their own good
and evil, their own feelings, benefits, or sufferings. It is, in these things,
the *voice* of the *people* is said to approach the *voice* of their *maker*.

The SYCOPHANTS of GREAT MEN, endeavour therefore to throw, on the *artifice* and *influence* of *individuals,* all discontent and dissatisfaction of the public."

I do not contend that the people ought, on *all public matters,* to interfere with the deliberations of the legislature by *remonstrances* and *instructions;* the right ought to be exercised only on *great occasions;* and, I think, none greater or more important, than when a difference of opinion, subsisting between the two branches, suspends the powers of legislation and prevents those measures, which are necessary for the *public safety and happiness.*

I own, the people, in the exercise of power, may *possibly* go to extremes and become *licentious;* but I maintain, that *senators* and *delegates* may *possibly* go to the like *extremes* and become *oppressive* and *tyrannical.* And the history of mankind teaches, that public mischiefs, disorder and convulsion, do not so often happen from the *wantonness* of the *people* and their dislike to legal government, as from the *insolence* of *rulers,* and their tyranny and oppression and *contemptuous* treatment of humanity, and the *public voice* of distress.

It is idle to say, that the right of judgment, which I contend for, and the authority of the people to *instruct* the legislature, destroys the *independency* of the SENATE, and lays a foundation for anarchy and confusion. For let government be of what nature it may, a *monarchy, aristocracy* or *democracy;* let our rulers be *kings, senators* or *delegates;* cry them up as much as we will, speak, write and publish their abilities, integrity, patriotism, wealth and connexions, call them "The sons of JUPITER," say "They are divine and sacred, descended or authorised from Heaven," yet if those *rulers, kings, senators, delegates, Heaven-born spirits* or GODS, should look down with contempt on *earth* and *mortality,* and should sport and trifle with the rights of humanity, and in their frolicks and gambols should be guilty of *public injustice* and *oppression;* and when applied to for redress should be *insolent* and *contumacious;* I am inclined to think, the people would pay but little regard to the *forms* of government, or to the pretended virtue, patriotism and divinity of such rulers, and would *resume* and take back into their own hands, the powers which they gave and transferred; and on the principles of the *American revolution,* would maintain that LIBERTY and HAPPINESS, which they are entitled to by nature and nature's GOD.

PUBLICOLA

"A Constituent" to the Printers
MARCH 8, 1787

TO THE PRINTERS OF THE MARYLAND GAZETTE

THE DISAGREEMENT between the two branches of our legislature, and the measures pursued in consequence of that disagreement, call for the serious attention of every citizen of the state. An appeal is made by the house of delegates on the subject of this difference. The question which gave rise to the appeal, though of considerable consequence, is far less important than the appeal itself. An emission of paper money to the amount, or indeed to more than the amount, required by the house of delegates, and upon terms the most favoured by the supporters of that measure, although it may be attended with pernicious effects, yet cannot, it is hoped, produce those lasting evils that must result from a measure which, should it succeed, and be formed into a practice, will give an effectual blow to the constitution itself.

Even favourers of an emission feel some surprise at the conduct of the framers, and supporters of that scheme. Instead of a hasty appeal to the people, why did they not enter into a discussion of the subject with the senate upon the principles of the appeal, and in reply to their message? Merely to assert, as the appeal does, "that the message of the senate contained nothing in it, but what related to the depreciation of the paper, and that the senate had enumerated a great number of causes in support of their opinion, but that in the opinion of the appealers, this was a matter of judgment to be determined by the event," I say, merely to assert this, without inquiring into the causes, and stating to the people their reasons in opposition to them, does by no means establish the propriety of such a trial. Men of prudence regulate their conduct by probable events, supported by reason and experience. Hazardous experiments are ever rejected by the considerate and wise, in favour of remedies less doubtful in the event, although perhaps more silent, and slow in their operation.

But this might have been deemed unnecessary. For with respect to taxation, it is declared by the appeal to be a matter altogether immaterial, whether the bills of credit depreciate, or not. The words are these, "It is very clear to us, that if the money should depreciate, it cannot in any manner injure individuals; and we are not able to discover how the depreciation supposed (say five, ten, fifteen, or even twenty per cent for argument sake) can injure our government." With respect to the former part of this position, a question is put a little lower down in the appeal, which intimates this circumstance to be a benefit, rather than an injury. Thus, "suppose a man owes two silver dollars for his tax, for which he must give three bushels of wheat, if no paper money, but if there is he can procure two paper dollars for two bushels of wheat; will he increase or diminish his property?" This question offers a flattering prospect. Let us look into it. The legislature for instance, calls upon the people for taxes to support the government, and to discharge its debts. A tax of two silver dollars in the hundred, we will say, is necessary for these purposes, instead of receiving these into the treasury, the state will get but two thirds of the real sum called for, provided paper is paid. For considering both, in the expression of the appeal, as representatives of the property, the difference between them, according to the state of the question, is as two to three. Well. By a preceding paragraph a deficiency is admitted in the annual supplies, and it must be made up, says the appeal, by a further tax, that is in effect, I apprehend, the person, who paid two paper dollars for his last year's tax, must make it up to two silver dollars in the subsequent one. Thus a portion of the last year's burthen must be added to the weight of the present. Now let us repeat the question. "Will a person, thus circumstanced, increase or diminish his property?" If the deficiency is to be made up by an equal tax upon the whole, and some have paid in the full tax, *really*, in specie, and others, *nominally*, in paper, there may be some substance in the question. But, I trust, the general assembly can never have it in view to countenance such inequality. If not, the person, who is to make up his last year's tax, I am of opinion, will deem the increase rather ideal. Unless incurring a debt may be said to be increasing his property; which indeed may have some truth in it in this case, if we consider the fate of arrearages heretofore. In fact the sentiment appears pretty general, if we may judge from common practice. But when the affairs of those people, who adopt this mode of increase, come to be wound up by themselves, or others, the balance is too often found, to the sore regret of their creditors, to be on the other side of the account.

"Let it be admitted, says the appeal, that £.100,000 brought into the treasury by taxes, should purchase tobacco and flour only worth £.80,000 in gold and silver, this deficiency must be made up by a further tax, but the state will neither be richer nor poorer." In reply to this observation, I will ask the following question: Suppose the necessity of the state requires a supply of £.100,000; suppose to satisfy this requisition the treasurer receives only the sum of £.80,000; with respect to that year, is not the state unable, that is too poor, by £.20,000 to discharge necessary demands? But the deficiency is in the pockets of the people. Well, when a tax equal, we will say, to fifteen shillings specie is laid, and the people, by the application of paper money in the payment, discharge only a portion, say two thirds, of the real tax required, it will become necessary, even by the admission of the appeal, to make a further addition of one third, or five shillings specie, to the next year's requisition. If in the lowest state of the tax an arrearage happens, would it not be madness to expect, that when the tax is increased by former dues, that arrearages will not increase also? If so, when is each year's deficiency to be paid up? At what stage are arrearages to stop? If they are attendant on every new tax imposed, government, I trust, in the midst of imaginary riches, will find itself steeped in actual poverty.

"The state will neither be richer, nor poorer!" If there be an annual addition to the debts of the state, and to the interest on them, will not every increase of the same be a new incumbrance? Here let it be remembered, to prevent state cavils, that by much the greatest part of the debts already incurred, and that will be incurred, must necessarily be external. I imagine our government can never have in view the event of a bankruptcy, to obtain a general clearance; if not, the more its debts are increased, the greater proportion of its property it will take to discharge them. And all, or the greatest part of this, must fall into the hands of strangers, and of course, be so much deducted from the general wealth of the state, and of its citizens. Arrearages of taxes carry no interest. Debts incurred in consequence of them receive a yearly addition from this circumstance. The means therefore relied on to discharge these debts, must fail in that respect, even supposing, and this can scarcely be supposed, that the whole of them will be fairly collected and lodged in the treasury. Now let me ask, with what propriety can it be said by the appeal, that those deficiencies will be made up by further taxes, and that the state will neither be richer nor poorer in consequence of this circumstance?

Notwithstanding the appeal holds out an idea, that the depreciation of the bills of credit is a thing immaterial in itself, as to taxation, yet we observe a desire to impress a belief, that they will not depreciate. For in the project for melting down the solid and real property of the citizens of this state, and circulating it in paper money, "the bills of credit, says the appeal, will be the substitute of such solid property, in the same manner as gold and silver is the representative of land and all other property, and these notes would possess all the qualities of a circulating medium of trade, as well as coin, and must have a *real intrinsic* worth, as long as the lands, on which they issue, retain their value."

There does not appear to me to be a necessary connexion between the "must have a real and intrinsic worth" and the security pledged for the redemption of these bills. The lands mortgaged may be sufficient for the redemption of twenty times the sum in circulation at the end of the term of emission, but whether at that period there will be gold and silver enough in the treasury, by virtue of the above security, for this purpose, and if so, whether this gold and silver will be applied to that use, or be diverted to some other purpose, are circumstances so uncertain, that the paper from a view to the security, instead of possessing a real *intrinsic* value, I fear much, will have but a faint representative one. The real and intrinsic value of a thing, in common language, is the established fixed value of a thing in itself. Gold and silver money, though the representatives of wealth, are said to have a real intrinsic value, that is, a value in themselves, independent of that circumstance; for not being confined to that use alone, they are equally, or nearly, as valuable for other purposes. Can this be said of paper money? Is there one valuable purpose in life to which it can be applied independent of its ideal use? Bank bills and bankers notes in England have, in effect, an intrinsic value, because you can, upon producing them, obtain what they represent; and it is owing to this circumstance alone that they have. Will our bills of credit have this effect upon sight? It would be a glorious sight. We might then boast, without a fable, that the golden age had returned.

The appeal says, "suppose the depreciation at five, ten, or even twenty per cent for argument's sake." If by this is meant a sudden depreciation to any one fixed point, there to remain without alteration, there may be some reason in the position. But let common sense, let experience determine (and surely our experience will afford full information,) whether such a case is, in the most distant degree, probable. The depreciation must necessarily be by stages, every intermediate one of which, between the imposing, and the application of the tax, will proportionably lessen its value, and of course be injurious to the same, by rendering the annual supplies, inadequate to the purposes for which they are imposed, and thereby occasioning a rapid accumulation of debt.

The appeal does not undertake to eliminate the quantity of specie in the state, but alleges, that there is not a sufficiency in circulation to answer the purposes of commerce alone, "because the chief produce of the country, tobacco and wheat, cannot command a reasonable price, because lands, houses and negroes, will not sell for half their actual value, and because specie cannot be borrowed unless at an exorbitant premium, from twenty to thirty per cent."

As to the preceding part of the foregoing assertions, with respect to the price of wheat and tobacco, if they do not command a reasonable price at this time, I am apprehensive, another reason, and perhaps as good a one, may be assigned for that effect, as the one given in the appeal. That paper money was formerly as good as gold and silver, is undoubtedly true; but that it has not been the fate of bills of credit, for some years past, to enjoy that reputation, is equally true, and by consequence, the possession of them has not been held in so high estimation, as it formerly was, or as that of gold and silver. Those who were so provident, as to retain the latter in their hands, during the late continual fluctuation of the former, experienced the good effects of such conduct. On the contrary, those who pursued a different plan, severely felt, and sorely lamented, the part they had taken. This is still fresh in the memory of all of us. What then is the natural consequence? Why says a thirfty, considerate man, an emission of bills of credit is likely to take place, which will most probably experience the fate of former emissions. I have gold and silver in my chest. That I know cannot suffer by any change. Therefore fast bind, safe find. This will be the reasoning both of those who are in, and of those, that are out of debt. The former will reflect, that perhaps he may find an easier way hereafter to discharge his public, and private dues, than by parting with his hard money for that purpose; at least he is willing to try it. The latter may be of opinion, that should he part with it, it may not be in his power to replace it, with what is of equal value. Thus each will contribute to lessen the circulation. This has actually been the effect of the expectation of an emission of bills of credit. During the circulation of the different species of paper, with which this, and the other states, were not long since overwhelmed, we know that scarcely a piece of gold, or silver coin was to be seen. Upon the decrease, and cessation of that currency, gold and silver began to find their way into the commercial, and other dealings of men. The farmer, the planter, and the miller, were all sensible of this. The articles they carried to market commanded a generous price, and that in cash. It is but very lately that this has ceased to be the case. In the place of cash credit is introduced. The merchant and trader, if possessed of specie, are desirous, like the rest of their neighbours, to keep it for a good market, or, if they part with it, to take advantage of the present scarcity. It is in vain to say that the paper will not be a tender, therefore cannot be injurious to any one. The necessities of men will oblige them to take it in most instances. Those who cultivate the earth, cannot keep its produce on hand. They must take what they can get, or suffer the fruits of their industry to perish in their possession. The actual circulation of paper for many years expelled gold and silver from all the transactions of men. The late and present expectations of another, or other emissions, has had that operation in a great degree. And as long as this continues or whenever the measure is carried into effect, the same consequence must accompany that situation, or result from this event.

That lands, negroes, and houses, will not sell for half their value, is rather owing to the imaginary worth we affix to these articles, than to their real value, estimated according to their produce. But satisfactory reasons, of a different kind from that in the appeal, may be assigned for a decrease of value in these articles, supposing it to be the case. Upon the breaking up of the war, vast prospects of profit were opened to adventurers in the mercantile line, which, though they have proved declusive [sic], drew all the cash into that channel, that could be procured. The great advantages that were offered in the purchase of public securities, employed all the specie, that could by any means be scraped together by those who engaged in this adventure. The slow and moderate profits arising from lands, negroes, and houses, had nothing alluring, whilst such objects as these were in view, therefore they attracted but little of the cash in circulation. But this situation was extraordinary. Those scenes were already closed, or closing fast. Our affairs were returning into the old channel. Gold and silver began to have a general circulation in the country as well as in towns. The farmer and the planter began to feel the change; and I am sorry to say, only began; for the wisdom of our present politicians is now exerted, and has been for some time, to deprive them of that sensation as speedily, and effectually, as they can accomplish it, and they may boast of having succeeded already, at least in part. The high premiums, that have been given for specie, may be accounted for by the same reasons, with this additional one, the uncertainty creditors are under of receiving the full amount of their loans. This I hope, will prove an idle fear; but surely there are grounds for it. He who has smarted under the lash, will use every means in his power to withdraw himself from the full effect of the blow.

Considerable arrearages of taxes have been urged as a proof of the scarcity of a circulating medium, but other and more obvious reasons may be adduced to account for this effect, viz. the remissness of the collectors in the performance of their duties; frauds committed by them with respect to monies received; money collected and appropriated to their own use, never accounted for, and that probably never will be accounted for; repeated laws and resolutions passed in favour of these defaulters. When such causes as these exist, why need we go in search of others to account for an empty treasury, and heavy arrearages? It is generally said, and I believe the fact to be so, that there is no inconsiderable number of the citizens of this state, who have not paid a single tax since the commencement of the war. Some are deficient one, some two, and some a greater number of years. And the most of these are not of the lower class of people, but such whose circumstances would well enable them to pay, but who preferred the indulgence to the receipt of the collector, which he has been willing to grant in return for former favours, or in expectation of future services. The poor and industrious class of people have in general paid up their taxes. An emission, in this instance, is not therefore calculated for their benefit, but will rather have a contrary tendency, as they have already discharged their public dues to the full and *real* amount of the taxes that have been called for by government; nevertheless one of the pretences for an emission of bills of credit is, the relief of the poor in this particular. This pretence is popular, and may appear specious, but has nothing in it solid or substantial.

The bill provided, says the appeal, "that no more than £.200,000 should be in circulation at the same time, unless the governor and council should be fully satisfied that the loaning a further sum would not in any manner affect the value of the sum in circulation." Suppose the governor and council were of opinion that a further loan would affect the value of the bills of credit then in circulation, and of consequence determined that no more should be issued on loan. This might delay an increase of the circulating sum until the next session of assembly; but can we believe that it would not then be done, when the appeal declares it to be immaterial as to the government, whether the bills of credit depreciate or not, and plainly intimates it to be beneficial to the individual if they should? The opinion of the senate might in this case too differ from that of the house of delegates. But the opinion of the senate will be of little avail, should the mode now adopted by the latter to carry their measures meet with success.

However plausible the scheme for reducing the paper in circulation annually, by sinking one half of the interest, and one twentieth of the principal of loans, may appear, there is one circumstance, mentioned in the appeal, which I apprehend will defeat the happy effects that are expected to flow from that project. I mean the annual deficiency of supplies, or in other words, the poverty of the treasury. Let us imagine a case, which is by no means improbable, that money is wanted for some of the purposes of government, viz. for the purchase of produce to raise specie for congress, and that there is not a sufficiency in the treasury for this use, without applying the aforesaid interest and twentieths, perhaps not enough even with this addition. This, I say, is not an improbable case. Should it happen, what will become of the sinking fund? I don't imagine there is much difficulty in answering this question. Present necessities must be satisfied, if possible, and the plan of raising paper money to purchase articles to be resold for specie, with the train of losses and expences attending its operation, will alone create a necessity sufficient to absorb all the paper that it will be in the power of the legislature to levy upon the people; at best it will leave but a very scanty portion for the other purposes of government. Adieu! then to the sinking funds.

I have said, that the question, which gave rise to the appeal of the house of delegates, though of considerable consequence, is far less important than the appeal itself. I mean not to enter into a discussion of the question respecting the *right* that either branch of the legislature may have to appeal to the people for instructions on subjects, whereon the two branches cannot agree, nor respecting the *right* the people may possess of instructing either part, or the whole of the legislature, in all cases where they may deem their instructions necessary. It will be sufficient to shew, that the *practice* of appeal by either branch will be productive of considerable mischief, and will in the end destroy the constitution itself. I have made use of the term, practice, because where that mode is adopted I see nothing to limit its application, nor can it be discovered to what objects it will be confined. We may therefore conclude, that appeals will be made in all cases of difference between the two branches of the legislature, at least in all those cases that may be deemed important by one of them.

This custom, we observe, has originated with the house of delegates, and it is easy to foresee that it will remain with that body. The members of that house are considered as the more immediate representatives of the people, and it is considered that they know their interest better, and have it more at heart than the members of the other branch. The senate is viewed as an aristocratic body, as composed of rich men, and therefore are supposed to have a distinct interest from the main body of the people. In all differences between the house of delegates and the senate, these ideas being constantly inculcated, it will require no great degree of the spirit of divination to foretel[l] which will, at least, generally prevail.

The constitution says, that the legislature shall consist of two *distinct* branches. Nay, it seems so desirous of preserving this distinction, that from a consciousness that a privilege confined to the house of delegates, viz. "of originating money bills," might be made use of to destroy the independency of the senate, it declares in strong and expressive terms in the eleventh section, "that the senate may be at *full* and *perfect* liberty to exercise their judgement in passing laws, and that they may not be *compelled* by the house of delegates either to *reject* a money bill, which the emergency of affairs may require, or to *assent* to some *other* act of legislation, in their conscience and judgment injurious to the public welfare, the house of delegates shall not on any *occasion*, or under any *pretence*, annex to, or blend with, a money bill, any matter, clause, &c. &c. &c." This section shews the desire, the *anxiety*, I may say, of the constitution to preserve the independency of that branch of the legislature to which it relates, and which might have suffered by the abuse of a privilege that was confined to the house of delegates alone.

A *full* and *perfect* liberty to exercise their judgement in passing laws, is by the constitution deemed a matter so essential, and of such magnitude, that no *pretence*, no *occasion* whatever is admitted as a plea with the other branch sufficient to deprive them of the exercise of that right. What is the object of the appeal of the house of delegates? Is it not, in fact, to control the senate in the full exercise of their judgment; I address myself to men of plain understandings. A quibble may impose upon the ignorant, or satisfy the casuist. But men of a different complexion, whatever professions may be used, are not to be convinced by bare assertions, or by flimsy arguments.

Should this mode prevail. Should the full and perfect liberty to exercise their judgment (I repeat the words of the constitution, for there cannot be stronger) be taken from the senate, what will be the consequence? Men of indpendent spirit will never accept of or retain a seat in a body where they cannot exercise their understandings, or declare their opinions with freedom. Of such men alone will the senate be composed, who will submit to any compliances, and who can adapt their opinions to any occasions. The distinction required by the constitution will be at an end. There will, in fact, be only one branch in our legislature. We have often seen and felt the benefit of two.

Were it however to happen, that the senate, notwithstanding this practice, and being constantly over-ruled in their opinions, did still retain a spirit of freedom in their debates and determinations, this, instead of producing any good effect, would probably be attended with the greatest evils. The state will be kept in continual agitation by the differences of the two branches of the legislature; personal animosities; quarrels amongst neighbours; divisions in families; and often bloodshed, would be the consequence. Government, which is instituted to preserve union and tranquillity amongst men, will become the source of division and disorder. Every new appeal will be the parent of new disturbances, which will be the worse, as the minds of men had been fretted by former opposition.

These are evils, and evils likely to result from that situation of affairs. But what is said on the other side? Shall the senate be a body independent of the people? Shall they know no restrictions but what their own wills impose? Shall they have it in their power to ruin the state, and shall the people be without relief or remedy? Such questions often terrify, and generally impose upon weak minds. The alarm conveyed by them looks like danger, but it is only the danger of sound.

Should the ends of government be perverted by either, or both branches of the legislature. Should they or either of them become (I mean the *real*, not the *imaginary*) oppressors, instead of protectors of the people, I trust there is that sense and spirit in the citizens of this state, that will enable them to discover and urge them to resent every attempt to injure or oppress them, and to provide against future dangers and abuses.

When the people of this state delegate a power to particular men to make laws for their government, which persons by our constitution are to be the most *wise, sensible* and *discreet* men in the society, it may reasonably be supposed, that by that constitution it was intended the people at large should not interfere with the body thus appointed, at least in the ordinary course of legislation. The bill of rights has reserved a right to the people in extraordinary emergencies to resist oppression, which undoubtedly they would be entitled to do, even without any particular reservation in the constitution for that purpose. From the complexion of the whole clause in which this reservation is made, I think it appears, that the framers of the constitution esteemed the interference of the people in *legislative* and *executive* matters, at least improper and unnecessary, but in cases mentioned in the clause, viz. when the ends of government are perverted, and liberty manifestly endangered. The distinction is founded in wisdom. In matters of opinion, upon which the ordinary business of legislation must turn the people at large cannot be supposed to be competent judges. In those cases that forcibly strike the senses, and operate upon the feelings, all men are equally qualified to decide.

Let us suppose that the practice of appeals should take place. Can we imagine it will be confined to those cases alone, wherein the ends of government are perverted, or liberty manifestly endangered? Those who have been present at the transaction of public business in either branch of the legislature must have observed, that although the intention of the members may be always directed to the public good, yet their tempers are not always free from passion, or their minds from prejudice. A bill for an emission of paper money, and the other bill mentioned in the appeal may, upon a candid and dispassionate inquiry, be deemed such acts as do not affect the ends of government, or endanger liberty. Yet we find the people are addressed on those subjects. Any other bills may go through the same process that those have done, and thus the people may be called from their ordinary occupations to give directions to those, who they themselves have declared to be the most wise, sensible and discreet amongst them, on subjects that they have never considered, or had an opportunity of considering.

In a legislature like ours, framed *entirely* of the representatives of the people, undistinguished by titles, interest, or rank, from their constituents, and regularly returning, at fixed periods, into the common mass of citizens, governed by the same laws, and enjoying the same privileges, one would imagine, that there cannot arise an occasion, which can render them opposed to the interest, and inimical to the welfare of their country. In legislatures composed *partly* of the representatives of the people, and *partly* of those, who, in their legislative capacity, are independent of them, there may at times be occasion for the interposition of the people. For there being two, or as in the British constitution, three distinct branches, and only one of them taken from the common body, and depending on them for their existence, the others forming bodies, not only independent on the people in this respect, but distinguished, and *separated* from the rest of the society by prerogatives, titles, honours, and considerable privileges; in such governments, I say, there may often be occasion for the intervention of the people, to watch over their own representatives, and to guard them against any undue authority, or influence in the other branches, which might prove prejudicial to their general interest, and dangerous to liberty. But in our constitution, there is no such body. Arguments therefore drawn from a practice in governments like these, are totally inapplicable to us. Authors are quoted on this occasion. But they are quoted with the same taste, and propriety, as such arguments are advanced

I am sensible, that to question even the propriety of the interference of the people in any case, be it what it may, in matters of legislation will be deemed an attempt on liberty. All the topics used in the most desperate and dangerous cases, will be urged in opposition to such a sentiment. Revolutions of government in favour of, or against liberty, will contribute to furnish means for the purpose of opposing a doctrine so pernicious. But, in the midst of this clamour, let it not be forgotten by the citizens of this state, who now live under a free government, and who are desirous of preserving the constitution, *as it now is*, that they cannot more effectually reduce this to the situation of the worst of governments, than by throwing such a weight into either branch of our legislature, as will overbalance, or countenance such conduct in one, as will destroy the effect and independency of the *other*.

A CONSTITUENT

Thomas Stone to the Printers

MARCH 28, 1787

TO THE PRINTERS

I TAKE the first opportunity, which ill health, and necessary attention to professional business, have admitted, to reply to such
parts of two publications in the Maryland Journal, under the title of
"extracts of letters from Annapolis," as seem calculated to throw an
unmerited odium on the members of the senate, who were concerned
in submitting a proposition to the people of this state.

The writer of the pieces alluded to, makes the following suggestions:—That the proposition was *drawn* by Mr. Carroll and me, and
agreed to by the other members of the senate—that it was artfully
penned, with intention, that if generally signed by the people, it might
be construed to establish the position, that the senate (and also the
house of delegates) are *independent* of the people, and not bound by
their instructions *in any case*; but if the the proposition was rejected by
the people, the senators then intended to take shelter under the pretence, that the proposition only meant to declare that the senate is
independent of the house of delegates."

It is not very material by whom the proposition was *drawn*, as all
the senators present agreed to it, and it cannot be doubted, but that all
were as competent judges of the meaning, as the two who are supposed
to have been the draughtsmen, but it would seem, from the manner in
which the proposition is stated to have been *produced*, that the writer
referred to intended an inference should be made, that the two senators
artfully worded the proposition so as to admit of a construction *not
perceived by the other senators*, who are represented to have *assented*
only, without having any other share in the business; this representation
is mere supposition, and is altogether different from the fact, for there
was not the smallest concert between Mr. Carroll and me in this transaction; we had not, to my knowledge or belief, any conversation or
interchange of sentiment, previously to the meeting at Mann's tavern,
upon the subject of a proposition to be submitted to the people; nor
was any proposition, declaration or instruction, drawn by *us*—We
did not see each other except in public in the senate, or in committee,
when we were too much engaged in the pressing business of the session,
to confer on other subjects—The following is a true narrative, to the
best of my recollection and belief, of what lead to, and happened at,
the meeting at Mann's tavern. The general assembly having adjourned

very late on Saturday night the 20th of January last, it was thought necessary that a meeting of the senators, then in town, should be held the next morning, to determine on the best mode of dispersing the messages of the senate, and to consider if any thing else was necessary to be done by the senators, as individuals, before they parted. The senators met on Sunday morning, according to an appointment for this purpose,* and *after a short conversation among the senators, and their sentiments being given upon the subject of a proposition to be submitted to the consideration of the people, I drew up what appeared to be in substance conformable to the opinion of the senators;* the draught was examined by all the senators present, and amendments were made in it, I think, by two members of the senate, and after amendment, it was agreed to without objection by any one—I do not recollect that Mr. Carroll, of Carrollton, dictated or wrote any part of the proposition, he copied it from the rough draught, which I believe was interlined, and part erased by the amendments which had been made to the original draught—the copy was read, and delivered to the printer by Mr. Carroll, in the presence of the other senators, with a request that it might be printed, ready to be sent with the senate's messages, and so far from the proposition, being the result of deep consideration, with intention to deceive, I believe the whole time taken up in settling the mode of circulating the messages, and framing and copying the proposition, did not exceed one hour.—The proposition agreed to is as follows:

"We the subscribers attached to the present form of government, and esteeming it proper and necessary to preserve every part of it, are of opinion, that each branch of the legislature ought to be free, and at full liberty to exercise their judgment, upon all public measures *proposed by the one to the other.*["]

The circumstances which took place before the adjournment of the assembly, ought to be taken into consideration, to form a just opinion of the design with which this proposition was made to the people, by the senators.—It is well known, that upon the bill for an emission of paper money being dissented to by the senate, the house of delegates determined to adjourn, and to address the people—printed instructions to be signed by the people, in favour of the bill, directed to both branches of the legislature, and stating that both had appealed to the people, were dispersed by the friends of the bill, as the senators

* *I did not perfectly remember whether I drew up any proposition before I went to Mann's, or whether the first proposition drawn up at Mr. Mann's was by me or Mr. Gale. Upon application to Mr. Carroll, of Carrollton, for his recollection of this part of the fact, he has given it as above stated; and I have relied on his memory for the part of the fact stated in italic. From the circumstances he mentions I have no doubt but the fact was as stated.*

were informed; a majority of the delegates having passed the bill, *they* did not want instructions to regulate *their* conduct, the only sensible end to be answered, by obtaining instructions in favour of the measure, was to *oblige* the senate to agree to a bill, which they had unanimously dissented to—the senate considered this proceeding of the house of delegates as an appeal to the people by one branch of the legislature against the other, they stated the dangerous tendency of such appeals, and the consequences to be apprehended from them—they knew that by the constitution the senate and house of delegates were equally free and independent of each other, and they wished to prevent a practice, which, by throwing the whole powers of legislation into the hands of the delegates, would render of no avail the provision of our constitution. With the messages in which these matters are stated, the proposition was intended to be circulated; and it was designed by it to collect the sense of the people on this point, whether the two branches of the legislature should, as heretofore, be left at liberty to exercise their judgements on measures proposed by the one to the other, or whether the people would introduce the practice of appeals, to oblige the dissenting branch, to accede to the measures proposed by the appealing branch. —The proposition contains the sentiments which the senators conceived were proper to be expressed by the people upon this subject; and it was supposed, that if the people signified their opinion to the legislature in the terms of the proposition, it would be considered as a *direction* from the people to the *legislature*, and would restrain the *practice of appealing* to the people upon a disagreement between the two houses; but at all events it was important to know the sense of the people on this subject, because if appeals, and instructions in consequence of them, were to become a part of ordinary legislation, it would be more wise, in all doubtful cases, to take the sense of the people *before* any formal determination, rather than to subject either branch to the odium of having acted contrary to the sense of the people, by collecting their opinion *after* a decision; besides, it would be obviously proper, upon this mode of conducting legislation, to make regulations for taking and signifying the sense of the people.

It is said by the writer alluded to, that "the *declaration* of the senators having no exception or explanation, is clearly an assertion that each branch of the legislature is free from *all control*"—to me it appears, that the proposition contains an explanation so pointed, that it cannot fairly be taken to mean any thing different from what I have explained to have been the intention with which it was made—the first part of the proposition is, that each branch of the legislature ought to be free, and at full liberty to exercise their judgment on all public measures— then follow the words "proposed by the one to the other," which *by pointing to the case* in which the opinion of the people was desired, shews that it was the intention of the framers to check the practice of appeals (which it apprehended was intended to be introduced contrary to the wishes of the people) by obtaining the opinion of the people, that both branches of the legislature ought to be left at liberty to exercise their judgment, *under the circumstances stated*—the concluding words shew likewise that it could not be the intention of the framers, that the proposition should be taken or construed as a negative or surrender of the people's right to instruct the legislature;—had this been the design, what was the use of these words? They were certainly put in for some purpose, but according to the above mentioned writer's construction, they stand for nothing, and by the same mode of construction, the most innocent sentence may be made to speak blasphemy.—I do not pretend that the proposition is drawn with all the accuracy with which it might have been, if more attention had been given, to convey the intended ideas with such precision as to prevent every possible misconstruction; all I insist on is, that hastily as the proposition was drawn, it is sufficiently plain to exclude any supposition that it was meant to decide any question respecting the rights of the people, and I never had an idea that it could, by any rational creature, be considered as a denial of the people's right to control the legislature; nor do I believe, that any other senator ever entertained an opinion that it could possibly bear this construction.

It is said by this writer, that the declaration of the senators, and the draught of instructions by judge Hanson, are in *reality* the same. To me there appears to be a substantial and striking difference between them; the draught of instructions *denies* that the people have constitutionally a right to interfere with the deliberations of the senate, unless the ends of government are perverted, or liberty manifestly endangered, and declares, that "whenever exigencies shall require the people to make their own will the law, there will be no longer the constitutional legislature consisting of two branches," which plainly imports, that the people have not a right, under *our constitution*, to direct the legislature to pass a particular law in any case. The proposition of the senators does not determine the *question of right*, and by leaving the two branches of legislature at liberty under *particular circumstances*, means only to declare, that it would be improper for the people to exercise the power of directing either branch to accede to the measures of the other, under *these circumstances*; now the *existence of a right*, and the forbearance to *exercise that right in particular cases*, are perfectly consistent ideas; the latter may be agreed to, without a denial or surrender of the right—The exercise of, or forbearance to use, a right, is a matter of prudence in those who may possess it, which does not in any degree affect the existence of the right; but a surrender or a denial of a right, by those who have the power of determination, puts an end to the right, if it be of a nature capable of being destroyed by such means.—If a denial of a right, and a declaration that the right, if it exists, ought not to be exercised *under particular circumstances*, to give efficacy to an inconvenient practice, be one and the same thing, then there would be grounds for the writers assertion; but if they are altogether different, then he has erred in the conclusion by him made, that the proposition and instructions are in substance the same.—The misconstruction which this writer has given to the proposition of the senators, cannot be more strikingly shewn than by pointing out the difference between it and the instructions; for if these two instruments *substantially* differ (as the writer has admitted that the instructions are plain and explicit) he must also admit that the proposition was not *intended* to mean the same thing that the instructions import.

I do not remember that I ever gave an opinion upon the question, whether the legislature were bound to pass particular laws, by the instructions of the people in favour of such laws, nor do I mean either directly or indirectly to give an opinion on such question in this address. If ever it should be my duty to pass an opinion upon this subject, I shall do it according to the best of my judgment, without being influenced in forming or declaring the opinion I may think just, by a consideration of the power or weakness of those who may differ with me.

It must be admitted, that the existence of a right in the people to instruct the legislature, is consistent with a negative *by the people* to the practice of appeals by *either house*, upon a difference of opinion between the two branches of legislature—The exercise of such right by the people, freely and of their own accord, leads not to the same consequences which it is apprehended the practice of appeals would produce.—The great body of the people, left to form their opinions freely and without bias or prejudice, are said never to err, but this infallibility has never been ascribed to any select branch of legislature; and I believe it will not be contended, that a perfect freedom of forming an unbiased opinion, will take place among the people, after a decision upon the question has been given, by their immediate representatives, who must be admitted to possess much greater weight and influence among the people than the senate.—When once the opinion of the house of delegates is known, and the people are *called on* to affirm or reject this opinion, the decision of the representatives will in most cases greatly influence the sentiments of the people, and may induce them to form opinions, different from what they would have done, if the weight of this influence had never been applied, and it appears to me, that a measure recommended by the delegates, must be most disagreeable to the people indeed, if instructions in its favour cannot be obtained.—I do not mean by these observations to point to the measures upon which the two houses of assembly have differed, or to the men who have advocated or dissented to these measures; I reason from what appears to me to be the nature of things, without taking into view any particular present objects.

Independent of the observations I have made from the wording of the proposition, and the circumstances under which it was made, the nature of the subject is sufficient to shew, that it never could be *intended* to be set up as a negative or surrender of the rights of the people; for it must be clear, that the inherent or constitutional rights of the people cannot be destroyed or surrendered *in this manner*, if the declaration or proposition was ever so explicit; but the circumstance of the instrument being *doubtful*, would of itself be sufficient to defeat the end, which the writer supposes was meant to be attained by it. I want terms sufficiently strong to paint the ridiculous figure any senator would make, in attempting to set up the proposition, which has been stated, as a negative or surrender of the people's rights to dictate to both branches of the legislature.—So far from the proposition being made with design to settle the question of the people's right to instruct, that this question never was, to my knowledge, discussed in the senate, or at the meeting at Mann's tavern—I never intimated, nor did I to my recollection ever hear any other senator declare, any thing which indicated an intention of opposing the will of the people, and if the senate, or any of its members, were to set themselves in opposition to the great body of the people of this state, I should think them rather objects proper to be confined for insanity than dreaded as tyrants.

It may be contended, that supposing the conclusive words of the proposition restrict the preceding general words, yet that the effect of the proposition taken altogether, would be to *deny or destroy the right of the people* to interfere whenever the circumstance of a difference between the two houses happened.—I answer, that as it is clear, from the circumstances under which the proposition was made, the nature of the subject, and the language used, that its *object* was to restrain a practice of the *legislature,* and not to affect the *rights* of the people; it never could have been fairly set up by the senate as a *negative to these rights* in any case, because this would be to make a proposition intended for one purpose, to serve for another and different purpose. —There is no doubt but senators, if they were inclined to expose themselves to ridicule, might set up constructions the most absurd, and claims most visionary, but I go upon the supposition, that acting like men endowed with some share of reason, they would not found a claim upon an instrument which all mankind would agree gave not the least colour to the pretension.

With the design and for the purpose I have explained the proposition to have been made, it was rational, and if agreed to, would have effect. For the purpose and with the design imputed by this writer, it was both ineffectual in its nature, and absurd in its composition; let the candid and sensible determine which construction ought to be made.

It is said by this writer, "That when men of erudition express themselves in a vague indeterminate manner, their candour and intention may be justly suspected." This appears to me to be a very harsh sentiment; and I do not remember to have met with it before, except from a writer in the Baltimore paper, sometime ago, who alleged, that the lawyers who were concerned in drawing laws, ought to be suspected of intending to produce disputes, and by which they get fees, *because* the expressions in our laws were doubtful and vague—many circumstances ought to concur, none of which exist in the present case, to justify so severe a judgment against any fellow citizen, upon a ground so slight as want of precision in expressing ideas—Laws are penned by men of erudition, they frequently are doubtful; it will not follow that the legislature, or any member of it, intended to deceive or create disputes.

The proposition does not intimate, nor was it intended to convey, the idea that it was the *design* of the house of delegates or any of its members, to destroy the present constitution, or any part of it—The injury to part of the constitutional legislature, was apprehended to be the consequence of a practice the senators wished to restrain; and therefore the preservation of every part of the constitution, was properly connected with the mode to be adopted for discountenancing the practice—Every one in the least acquainted with the history of mankind must know, that precedents are often set by men without any improper motive; and yet such precedents have produced great mischiefs, by being applied by others to purposes not designed by those who originated them, and often contrary to their unavailing opposition.

Several circumstances are mentioned in the pieces alluded to, of which I know nothing, and therefore shall not notice; nor do I think it necessary to say any thing to the *shelter* and *subterfuge* which the writer has been pleased to *make* for the senators.

Whether I am a friend or an enemy to *public liberty and the principles of the late revolution*, I must submit to be determined from my public conduct; if this will not decide the question in my favour, it cannot be expected that my *professions* will have much weight, and I do not apprehend the suggestions of others will have influence to induce an unfavourable opinion, if contradicted by my actions.

As it was my duty to be informed of our constitution and the rights connected with and derived from it, I have used every endeavour in my power to acquire this knowledge; and if I am still ignorant, it is my misfortune, not my fault; it is freely confessed, that I am ignorant of many things which I have endeavoured to know. And I should be wanting in candour not to declare, that every day's experience convinces me of the fallibility and weakness of my judgment; but that I ever designedly injured, or attempted to deceive, the people of this state, cannot be admitted, because it is not true.

I neither profess power or influence, nor do I desire them; so far from looking to a permanent public station, and wishing to annex to it independent powers, and of course troubles and difficulties, that I consider the office I now hold to be much too arduous and weighty for my abilities, and I feel that it imposes on me a burthen the greatest of my life, and shall rejoice when the time arrives, that I can, with propriety, quit a station, in which I am not so vain as to suppose I can render services to the public in any degree equal to the sacrifice of quiet, health and interest, which necessarily attends the execution of public trust by a man in my situation.

As an American I deeply regret the divisions which have taken place among men intrusted with public concerns in this and other of the United States. Would to Heaven it was in my power to remedy an evil, which every well informed friend to this country must see and lament; that I have always endeavoured to compose differences, and have not in any degree contributed to those which now distract the councils of this state, is true; but this is poor consolation to a man who is bound to live in, and anxious for the prosperity of, a country, where those who ought to unite, are endeavouring to wound and destroy each other, while those who are in principle its enemies, with exulting pleasure are viewing the contest, and are ready to seize any favourable opportunity to involve the whole in ruin.

Annapolis   T. STONE

Alexander Contee Hanson to the People
APRIL 1, 1787

TO THE PEOPLE OF MARYLAND

I AM TOLD, that the *thinking* part of mankind have condemned me for publicly asserting and maintaining, that, until the ends of government shall be perverted, or liberty manifestly endangered, you ought not to interfere with the deliberations of the senate. They acknowledge the truth of the position, but they apprehend danger from bringing the question into controversy. To me this censure seems not to have originated from *deep* thinking.—The address of your delegates had asserted the right of instructions in the fullest extent and in the most positive unequivocal terms. Both enemies and friends of the paper system had offered their draughts for subscription. It is probable that a majority of the people will be found opposed to an emission. But, had not the right of binding the senate by instructions been denied, the proceedings on this occasion, might hereafter be cited as a precedent. The silence of the senate on this point is truly to be commended; because *their* denial of the right would have afforded a pretext of charging them with an intemporate [*sic*] thirst of power—They had already been accused of contemning the rights, wants, and sentiments of the people, and of being actuated by an overbearing and aristocratic spirit. Whether or not they possessed powers for the general good, was a question which they thought improper at this season for themselves to discuss. On these several accounts, it was my duty, as a guardian of the constitution, and not particularly interested in the question, to protest against what I thought a most dangerous innovation.

A second class of political reviewers have passed on me a more severe sentence. They have declared, that disputes about the right are perfectly immaterial; that, let the meaning of the constitution be what it may, the senate is bound to respect the opinions of the people; that the people, not being able to legislate advantageously for themselves, ought in most cases to leave both branches entirely free; that after every thing that can be said or determined, whenever the great body of the people shall think proper to exercise their *power*, the *right* will be out of the question. To all these positions, except the first, I readily agree. I cannot admit, that it is nugatory to settle the question, whether, agreeable to the constitution, the people may oblige either branch to pass a particular bill. So long as the people shall be impressed with an idea that they can, at any time, *constitutionally* control and direct the legislature, they may think it their duty so to do; and they will be applied to for that purpose, whenever men of popular talents shall be disappointed in their favourite scheme. Those circumstances therefore will be more likely to take place, which might end in a dissolution of the government—I mean an attempt to bind the senate by instructions, and the senate's refusing to act against their own judgments. But, let the people be thoroughly convinced, that they cannot control the legislature without a suspension or dissolution of that government, which almost every man has sworn to maintain, and he that applies to the people, except on occasions of the last importance, will be deemed no better than a promoter of sedition, or what St. Paul calls "a pestilent fellow."

The doctrine of the binding force of instructions has been adopted upon a mistaken idea, that it is connected with the principles of the English and American revolutions. In England there was supposed to be a stipulation between the governing and governed, which was broken by one of their kings. On that occasion, the people, without essentially changing their forms, transferred the supreme executive power to other hands. In America, even the forms of government have been changed, and the revolution, in every respect is complete.—We resented the attempt against our freedom, we threw off the fetters of dependence, and we adopted such modes of government, as we thought most suitable to our circumstances.

In Maryland, as in her sister states, there is that, which has been much talked of by speculative writers, and has never before existed, unless in a few doubtful instances quoted by Mr. Locke. We have a real compact, entered into on behalf of the people by their genuine representatives, chosen for that express purpose. The whole power of legislation is committed to two distinct bodies of men, *without the assent of both* which, no proposition can be passed into a law. There is however a special reservation, that whenever they should become unmindful of their trust, or pervert the ends of their appointment, or in other words, shall violate their contract, the people may either set aside, or reform the constitution. It is an avowal of the true principles of independence; and it is intended for your direction, if at any future disastrous period an attempt shall be made to enslave you, or to take away any of your constitutional rights; *provided always, that you have no other means of redress.* By express stipulation therefore, is vested in the people that right which they inherit from nature, and which they might vindicate without the stipulation.

The right of the people to bind their representatives, chosen under this compact, is quite a different thing. If it exists at all, it must, as well as that, be founded on the constitution, or be inherent. It is mere sophistry to allege, that a lesser right is involved in the greater; because that greater right cannot be exercised without a suspension, or a dissolution of the government, and this lesser right is to be exercised, whilst the constitution remains in full force and vigour.

No man has been yet hardy enough to construe any part of the declaration or the form of government into a positive recognition of this right. But, although in making ample provision for the appointment of representatives, the constitution has not said a word about it, there are some men, who have supposed it involved in the right of suffrage—

In the beginning, it was enough for me to shew, that even admitting a right of binding your immediate representatives, it would be incompatible with the institution of two distinct branches for you to have the same right of binding the senate. On this head, I shall make no additional remark, except this very striking one. No law can be passed by the legislature, until a bill be proposed by one to the other. Now if the people can direct both branches when, in consequence of your instructions, a bill is originated and proposed by one, the other's right of dissent is taken away. The doctrine therefore so materially contravenes positive provisions, that the framers would have at least made an exception in its favour, had they intended or conceived that the people should possess it.

It may seem extraodinary that a man, writing on so important a subject, should have had no recourse of authority. The truth is, I conceived my arguments too powerful to need the unfair aid of mighty names. It does not indeed occur to my memory, that any writer before myself has examined the case of a legislature, consisting of two distinct bodies of men, deriving their authority immediately, or ultimately, from the act of the people. My proposition has been stigmatised with the epithet of newfangled. It may indeed be called *new*, because it is a simple denial of an affirmative proposition, never advanced until the late unlucky disagreement.

The writer of a short essay in Mr. Goddard's paper of March the 2d, has examined the right of instructions generally. He has done it in a manner so simple, concise and masterly, that no man who reads it with a sincere desire of attaining the truth, can withold his assent from any thing it contains. Being inserted as a fugitive piece, containing nothing but plain good sense, and the author being unknown, it may probably, by this time, be almost forgotten. I would recommend a perusal of it to every man who entertains a doubt respecting the subject.

I did not, at first, take notice of an essay under the signature of Publicola; but I understand that the author's confident assertions, and the great names he has mentioned for authorities, have even staggered men in the right faith. He has informed you, as I collect from the whole of his piece, that Mr. Locke, lord Molesworth, and Mr. Trenchard, have maintained with their pens the right of binding by instructions; that Mr. Hambden and lord John Russel have maintained it with their blood, and that Mr. Algernon Sydney has maintained it with both. In a popular harangue, this assertion might not surprise. Com-

EDITOR'S NOTE: The essay to which Hanson referred appeared in the March 8 issue of the *Maryland Gazette* and is reprinted above as the "Constituent" article.

mitted to writing, published to the world, and open for examination, there is no excuse or palliation for it, except that which Publicola would disdain to offer.

In Mr. Locke's two celebrated treatises of government, I can find nothing to countenance the opinion, that in a government by representation the people have a right to prescribe a particular law. He considers the natural unalienable right of interfering, when the ends of government are perverted or liberty manifestly endangered, in the same light as I have done, except that he does not go quite so far with respect to the legislature's gratifying the wishes and sentiments of the people. Would any man, after reading Publicola, conceive, that Mr. Locke concludes his book with the following words?

"When the society hath placed the legislative in any assembly of men to continue in them, and their successors, *with direction and authority for providing such successors*, the legislative can never revert to the people, whilst that government lasts; because having provided a legislative with power to continue for ever, they have *given up their political power* to the legislative, and cannot resume it. But if they have set limits to the duration of their legislative, and made this supreme power in any person or assembly, only temporary; or else, when by the miscarriages of those in authority, it is forfeited; upon the forfeiture, or at the determination of the time set, it reverts to the society; and the people have a right to act as supreme, and continue the legislative in themselves; or erect a new form; or, under the old form, place it in new hands as they think good."

I demand whether this be not a most pointed authority against Publicola's doctrine.

I have most diligently examined Mr. Algernon Sydney's discourses on government; I find in one of those the following words:

"We always may, and often do, give instructions to our delegates; but the less we fetter them, the more we manifest our own rights, for those, who have only a limited power, must limit that which they give; but he that can give an unlimited power, must necessarily have it in himself." P. 453.

In his page 451, is the following more remarkable and more intelligible passage.

"Every county does not make a distinct body, having in itself a sovereign power; but it is a member of that great body, which comprehends the whole nation. It is not therefore for Kent or Sussex, Lewes or Maidstone, but for the whole nation, that the members chosen in those places are sent to serve in parliament. And though it be fit for them, *as friends and neighbours* so far as may be to hearken to the opinion of electors for the imformation [sic] of their judgments, and to the end that what they shall say shall be of more weight, when every one is known not to speak his own thoughts only, but those of a greater number of men, yet they are not strictly and properly obliged to give account of their actions to any, unless the whole body of the nation, for which they serve, and who are equally concerned in their resolutions, could be assembled. This being impracticable, the whole punishment, to which they are subject, if they betray their trust, is scorn, infamy, hatred, and an assurance of being rejected, when they shall again seek the same honour. Although this may seem a small matter to those who fear to do ill, only from a sense of the pains inflicted, yet it is very terrible to men of ingenuous spirits, *as they are supposed to be* who are accounted fit to be intrusted with great powers."

These are the only material passages in Mr. Sydney relative to the subject, and these do not suit Publicola's purpose. Mr. Sydney's plain meaning is this: "Constituents may indeed instruct, or communicate their opinions, or give advice, which their representatives may follow, or otherwise, as they shall think proper, taking care to consult the general good, and incurring certain disgrace if they shall not act right."

To say, that this extraordinary man fell a martyr in support of the right contended for by the delegates, would betray either ignorance, or an opinion that ones adversaries are ignorant, and that the rest of the world are also ignorant, or will not choose to contradict a man endowed with superior *"powers."*—The assertion, or rather the intimation, conveyed from the whole of Publicola's piece, respecting the great Mr. Hambden and lord Russel, is no better grounded—Of Mr. Trenchard and lord Molesworth, I know very little; but I will venture to say, that neither has maintained the right of constituents to direct absolutely their representatives.

If the memory of the unfortunate Sydney be dear to all true patriots, and if all such, who are men of erudition, are acquainted with his writings, how comes it, that the distinguished writer in the Annapolis paper, of February 23d, can find no author, except *judge* Blackstone, who has denied, that a member of parliament owes implicit obedience to the directions of his constituents. From this writer's very quotations, he must have been sensible, that other eminent men had long since denied it. Perhaps he will take *"shelter"* under the distinction between *author* and *speaker*. He quotes Sir John Barnard and Sir William Wyndham; but does not say on what occasion was uttered, or in what book may be found, that furious indecent proposition, "that the *freedom of representatives* is not only a new and wicked doctrine, but the most monstrous and most slavish doctrine, that was ever heard, and such a doctrine, as no man will dare to support within these walls." Neither of these two gentlemen ever uttered it, and there is a monstrous misrepresentation, whether wilful, or otherwise, I cannot dive into men's hearts to determine.

On the 13th of March, 1733-4, a motion was made in the house of commons, for leave to bring in a bill for repealing the septennial act, and for the more frequent meeting and calling of parliament. After much debate, Mr. Willes, at that time attorney-general, and since a most eminent chief justice of the common bench, spoke against the motion; and, in the course of his harangue, delivered the following sentiments:

"That we all have a dependence on the people for our election, is what I shall readily grant; but after we are chosen, and have taken our seats in this house, we have no longer any dependence upon our electors, at least, in so far as regards our behaviour here. Their whole power is then devolved upon us; and we are, in every question that comes before this house, to regard only the public good in general, and to determine according to our own judgments. If we do not, if we are to depend upon our constituents, and to follow blindly the instructions they send us, we cannot be said to act freely; nor can such parliaments be called free parliaments. Such a dependence would be a most dangerous dependence. It would in my opinion, *be more dangerous and of worse consequence than a dependence upon the crown*; for, in a dependence on the crown, we can see no danger, as long as the interest of the crown is made the same with that of the people; which every man must allow to be the case at present; whereas the people of any county, city or borough, are very liable to be misled, and may be often induced to give instructions directly contrary to the interest of their country."

Sir John Barnard, (as he well might) professed, that this doctrine appeared to him to be new. Sir William Yonge supported Mr. Willes, denying that the doctrine of independence was either new or extraordinary. The fact was, the latter part of Mr. Willes's speech had given offence; and Sir William Wyndham, at the same time that he condemned it, made a kind of apology for the learned speaker. His words are these:

"What the worthy gentleman under the gallery (Sir John Barnard) took notice of was *an expression* that fell from the learned gentleman, (Mr. Willes) I dare say without design. He said that we were to have no dependence upon our constituents. He went further. He said it was a dangerous dependence. Nay he went further still, and said it was *more dangerous than a dependence on the crown. This* my worthy friend took notice of, and, with his usual modesty, called it a new doctrine. It is Sir not only a new doctrine, but it is the *most monstrous, the most slavish doctrine that was ever heard, and such a doctrine as*

I hope no man will ever dare to support within these walls. I am persuaded the learned gentleman did not mean, what the words he happened to make use of, seem to import; *for,* though the people of a county, city or borough, may be misled, and may be induced to give instructions contrary to the true interest of their country, yet I hope he will allow, that, in times past, the crown has been oftener misled; and consequently we must conclude, that it is more apt to be misled, in time to come, than we can suppose the people to be."

For this *historical* account, I am indebted to the 3d volume of Chandler's debates, and shall leave it to my readers to make the proper reflection.

On the first subject of the binding force of instructions, I confess that Sir Edward Coke, Mr. Sydney, Judge Blackstone, Mr. de Lolme, and Dr. Franklin, are the only authors I have perused, who before the present dispute have maintained the negative. But my reading is extremely confined, and I possess not the faculty of intuition. My reading is indeed so limited, that I have never seen a single book asserting, either directly or indirectly, that in a legislature by representation, the people may prescribe laws, and their delegates are bound to obey. The *lex parliamentaria* has a chapter on the right of electors; but neither in that, nor any other chapter, is the point even mentioned. I again call for any known book on the English constitution or law, or for even a resolve of the house of commons, in support of the doctrine.

I know that members of parliament have some times retired for the purpose of taking their constituents opinion. On certain occasions it is said, the whole house has done so. This appears from Sir Edward or lord Coke's institutes. There may be sometimes great propriety in this conduct. The happiness of the people being the true end of all just government, an attention should ever be paid to their sentiments and feelings. That a representative should yield them a blind obedience, you perceive, on a singular occasion, has been denied by some men in the British house of commons; and it *was not then* supported by others. Perhaps it never was. It is denied by Mr. Sydney,* one of the greatest advocates for equal liberty that England ever produced. It is denied by judge Blackstone, not so remarkable indeed either for professions, or deeds of patriotism, but of the first reputation for science and integrity, and not particularly concerned in the question. Before the present constitution was even in embryo, his arguments wrought a thorough conviction in my mind; and I have never yet heard ought but declamation and sophistry to refute them.

* May the illustrious spirit of Sydney forgive that injury, which from the misinformation of Publicola, I lately offered to his memory!

But leaving the constitution of England and the opinion of its writers out of the question—in all governments by representation, the people are said to possess an inherent right of directing and binding their delegates. I have consulted the most approved modern writers of all countries on the law of nature and nations. In these I find, in my favour, a great variety of general positions, which the limits of a newspaper will not permit me to transcribe. They uniformly state the rights of the people, as I have done. In not one of them, can I find any support of the right in question. Say then, that you disregard all authority and listen only to reasons, from whatever quarter they shall come. This is exactly as I wish; and I trust, that by this time, you are disposed to examine the question with coolness and candour. Read then the essay* which I have before recommended, and attend to the following considerations.

When the legislative power is in the people at large, it is truly the government of the people, or a strict democracy. When the society enters into a solemn compact, prescribing modes of election by the people, whereby a select body or two, or more select bodies, shall be for ever kept up, to legislate for the people, this is another form of government. It is the government by representation. But if notwithstanding this compact remain unbroken, the people may deliberate for themselves, and prescribe laws; it is again the government of the people, confounded with the government of representation, or properly no regular government at all. It is indeed possible, that a government by representation may exist, with an express article of the compact, that in certain cases, the sense of the people shall be taken in a manner prescribed, and shall lay the foundation of a law. But to say, that without this positive provision, in a government by representation, the people may still deliberate and prescribe what must be obeyed, and that notwithstanding the regular government shall, at the same time subsist, is to say, that a thing is, and is not, it is to say, that a government by representation *only*, in spite of the most solemn compact, cannot exist. It is, in short, to utter the most inexplicable nonsense, inconsistency and absurdity.

That the people in a government by representation, cannot, on any particular occasion, legislate for themselves advantageously, is owing to the same reasons, that, in the beginning, recommended the government by representation, in preference to the government of the people at large. In no case, can the people be all gathered together at one

---

* Perhaps it may be necessary for me to remove indelicate suspicions. That essay was by many ascribed to me. I declare, that I know not who was the author, and wish much to be informed.

spot. It is agreed on all hands, that men in a remote corner of the state cannot so well judge, what will suit the society, as when they are convened at the capital from every part, and hear all that can be urged on every side. It is agreed likewise, that men in general, cannot, in any place, so well judge as those, who are selected from their fellow-citizens, on account of superior talents, and devote their attention to the public affairs. It cannot be denied, that undue influence will ever be exerted in obtaining what is called the people's sense; and it is impossible, that every man can be qualified to decide nice questions of policy.

It is alleged, that, if your representatives are independent in their votes, they will become your masters.—Strange it is, that no medium can be found between implicit obedience and arbitrary sway! The several constitutional restrictions on the power of the legislature, and the mode of appointing your representatives, have not surely been attended to. For violating their duty, they cannot expect, at the end of the year, otherwise than to be dismissed with disgrace; and, as a part of the people, they are themselves to sustain, in the beginning, the mischiefs originating from the bad laws they enact. There is no power in the state capable of corrupting either branch of the legislature—Whilst left at perfect freedom to act as a check upon each other, your liberties can incur no risk, unless you can suppose them guilty of undue combination; and then that fatal period has arrived which demands your interference. I should not be surprised if the patriots in England, beholding the baneful influence of the ministry, obtained by barefaced bribery and corruption, should sometimes contend for a doctrine, which might if established by law prevent some of the evils, arising from the improper duration of parliaments; but there is no good reason whatever for establishing this doctrine in Maryland.

The most certain way of examining all propositions is to trace the consequences of their admission. My proposition cannot be wicked, because, if admitted, it will promote ORDER and GOOD GOVERNMENT, and can do no harm. It cannot be slavish; because it will tend to preserve unimpaired our free and happy constitution. There is however enough to justify my calling the opposite doctrine wicked, slavish and absurd. It is wicked, because if established, it must introduce disorder, riot and arbitrary sway—It is slavish, because it tends to confer the height of power on a single branch, and thereby to encourage the most fatal designs.—And it is absurd, because it would render the constitution a jumble of inconsistency and contradictions.

Annapolis   ARISTIDES

"A Constituent" to the House of Delegates

MAY 3, 1787

TO THE HONOURABLE THE SPEAKER OF THE
HOUSE OF DELEGATES

THE PROPRIETY of addressing the following lines to you, Sir, will appear from the nature and importance of the subject on which they treat. You are placed at the head of one branch of our legislature; of that branch, whose attention the ensuing remarks may most properly lay claim to. The more immediate representatives of the people, are by many supposed to be the more immediately interested in their concerns. I shall not contest the point. At present I feel myself willing to acquiesce in it, and therefore adopt this mode of divulging my sentiments on a question, and matter as interesting as any that can be proposed, or happen, in an established government; I mean the interference of the collective body of the people in the affairs of legislation. Without troubling you, Sir, with further preamble, I shall immediately enter on the subject.

Doctor Swift, in one of his Irish tracts, exposes the absurdity of those writers, who were daily publishing their thoughts on the affairs of Ireland, and who extracted their reasons, and examples from the histories of other countries, applying them to a nation, totally different from these countries, in government, situation, and circumstances. In another tract he says, "of the like nature are innumerable errors committed by crude and short thinkers, who reason upon *general* topics, without the least allowance for the most important circumstances, which quite alter the nature of the case."

The former of these observations I shall venture to apply to those writers, and talkers amongst us, who are constantly quoting the practice of the people of England, and the sentiments of those authors, who have confined their speculations to the British government, and of course are only applicable to the particular case, and situation of that country.

The authors who have treated of the British constitution, have attributed all the danger, to which that government is exposed, to those branches of the legislature, who do not receive their delegation from the people; that is, to the influence they may obtain over their representatives, by means of which, they will be able to carry matters according to their wishes, and having from their exalted situation in the state, a separate interest from the commonalty of the nation, they will use this influence to increase their grandeur, and benefit themselves to the injury, perhaps to the ruin of the main body of the people.

Lord Bolingbroke carries this idea with him throughout his remarks on the history of England, and frequently repeats it in his dissertation on parties. To this source he refers all the dangers arising to that constitution. In the earlier part of the English history, that is, soon after the Norman conquest, he observes, "that the king, the barons, the clergy, were all in reality enemies to public liberty. Their party, were so many factions in the nation, &c. &c." This opposition of interest between the people, and those branches of the legislature, who were independent of them in their legislative capacity, and the continual attempts of the latter, at, and before that period, and frequently since, especially in the reigns of the house of Stuart, to carry those points, which were favourable to their particular, but unfavourable to the general interest and liberty of the nation, required the strictest attention of the people to their affairs, and continual watchfulness over their representatives, lest they should be made a party in their measures. Notwithstanding every caution on their side, this was sometimes effected, as we observe in the reign of Richard the 2d. "who procured a packed parliament of men imposed on the shires and towns by his authority, wholly managed by court favourites, and which kept all its endeavours to destroy the liberties and privileges of the people." The consequence of which was, that having no hopes from parliament, they flocked to the first standard, which was set up against the king.

More than one instance of this kind occurs in the history of England. Those branches of the constitution, and more particularly the kingly one, having views inconsistent with the general good and welfare, have made repeated attempts to enlarge their authority, and to erect their grandeur, upon the debasement of the commons. The constant warnings that have been given by patriots and writers on these subjects; the dangers they have exposed; their calls upon the people to be upon their guard, recommending and supporting their occasional interposition, has arisen from this, "that there was a power, or powers at work, who having interests and views opposed to theirs, were concerting measures, which, if they succeeded, their liberties and rights must certainly fall a sacrifice.["]

We know that by the constitution of Great-Britain the king has not only an equal authority in matters of legislation, with the other branches of parliament, but that the whole executive power is lodged in his hands. He is also the head of the church, and the fountain of honour. Appointments to offices, to titles, and to clerical dignities, with his other prerogatives, renders him a person so formidable, that he may well be esteemed a danger to the government over which he is placed.

The nobility, who with him are distinguished from the rest of the citizens of the state, though not with equal pre-eminence; who derived their distinctions from him, and who are daily increasing, and may be increased on special occasions, to promote monarchical, or aristocratical designs, for they are frequently allied; the nobility, I say, with the dignified clergy, who form no inconsiderable part of the house of lords, may become instruments in his hands to effect the worst of purposes, for that may truly be esteemed the worst of all purposes, which has for its aim, the sufferings and debasement of many, to promote the grandeur, or pleasure of a few.

I speak the language of one, who is interested in the fate of the governed, whatever may be said by those, who pronounce themselves patriots, or the patrons of liberty. I am interested in equal freedom and equal rights, and I know that whatever tends to injure, or destroy a free government, injures or destroys both.

Under such a constitution as I have above described, (and such an one the British constitution is) let me be permitted to repeat the idea of these writers, that there is a necessity, a constant necessity, for the people to watch over, and occasionally to interpose in the conduct of those, whom they appoint to represent their part in the legislature of the government. Their liberty, their property depends upon the conduct of this branch. This branch is in constant danger of the influence of the other branches, who have often shewn themselves, and therefore may always be supposed to be, enemies to its freedom, and by consequence inimical to the interests of those who appoint it.

This, Sir, is true of the English government; but what has this to do with us? Have we a king armed with powers, equal to those of the king of England? Have we a house of lords created, and supplied with members, in the same manner, and having the same privileges as the house of lords in Great Britain?

These questions may be unnecessary, but the following one may not be so. Is either branch of our legislature possessed of, or does it pretend to powers, to authority, or privileges in any way similar to the above? Are they not both taken from the common body of citizens, and do they not return to their former situation, at the expiration of the periods of their appointment? If any little consequence, or dignity (for power is out of the question, except such as is conferred by the constitution) attend their station, are they not lost, when the members depart from office, and return to the degree of private citizens? It may be imagined by many, that even these questions are unnecessary. I myself should deem them so, had not, to say the least of it, a groundless alarm been given and attempted to be spread against one branch of our legislature. The motives of those, who have been instrumental in giving and spreading this alarm, I will not pretend to judge of; but of this I am sure, if these persons succeed in their endeavours, their success will prove more injurious to the constitution and government of the state, than any mischiefs they in their proper senses can apprehend, or that they can with any shew of reason point out, should the worst they pretend to fear, and expect, take place.

If there is a distinction made by the constitution, in favour of either branch of the legislature, it is made, Sir, in favour of the one, over which you preside. I allude to the privilege of originating money bills. This power if not exerted at all, or if not used in time, or improperly used, may prove of considerable injury to the government, and of course to its citizens. But this distinction, I have observed belongs to the house of delegates.

Let me suppose a case or two, which I sincerely hope may never happen, and of which there can be *little danger*, when we consider how abhorrent they are to the spirit of our constitution, every part of which inculcates the ideas of equality, and general good, and enjoins these observances on those, who may have any thing to do in the administration of public affairs. The cases I mean, are derived from the consideration of privilege, mentioned in the preceding paragraph.

Money, as Mr. Hume, I think, observes, is not one of the springs of government, but it is the oil, that keeps all the wheels in an easy, and even motion, without which they would soon be clogged, and the whole machine would become irregular, and disordered. Should that branch, which possesses the sole power of originating bills to levy money on the people, omit on some account or other, to prepare the necessary supplies in proper season, for instance in order to gain time to carry a favourite point; should a stop be put to all public business, let the importance be ever so great, or the occasion ever so pressing, if a particular measure proposed, was not immediately acceded to by the other branch; should these things, *however improbably*, happen, it is obvious that much mischief might arise to the public from such proceedings. There are few matters of any consequence transacted by the general assembly, with which the raising of money on the people, is not connected. The extent of that privilege is evident from this consideration. Let it be supposed, that* congress makes the most pressing application to the government for troops and money, to defend the frontiers of the states, which are plundered and wasted, and whose inhabitants are tortured and massacred, by a savage merciless enemy; let it be supposed *however improbably*, that that branch of the legislature, which has the keeping of the public purse, should neglect or refuse to untie

* *See the resolution of congress for raising a troop of light horse in the state of Maryland, 20 October, 1786.*

the strings of it, because an immediate acquiescence in some of its schemes or propositions does not take place; it is no difficult matter to conceive in such a case, the mischiefs that this conduct might occasion. But cases of this nature, Sir, are so *unlikely* to happen from an abuse of that privilege, that an apprehension of danger from this quarter, would be a needless concern.

The absolute difference I have endeavoured to point out, between our constitution, and that of Great-Britain, must necessarily impress on the mind of a citizen of this state, who reflects at all, ideas, and principles, suitable to that distinction, and the propriety of pursuing a conduct formed upon the peculiar circumstances, and situation of this constitution. We are now independent of that government in our persons. Let us be independent in our minds. A senseless clamour sounded upon principles, though granted to be true in themselves, the observance of which has become unnecessary with us, by the change that has taken place, nay, which would most probably be attended with pernicious effects, ought to be, and will no doubt be disregarded, and despised, by every reasonable, considerate man. What then, sir, must we think of the head or heart of that man, who feeling, or feigning a patriotic concern for the liberties and interests of his fellow-citizens, would involve his country in discord and confusion, or what might in its consequence prove as bad, would destroy the constitution, under the stale popular pretence of preserving and exercising the rights of its citizens? Should it proceed from a defective head, he might be pitied and pardoned; but a faulty heart would deserve neither commiseration, or mercy. If there be so deluded, or so abandoned a character, let those who know him, make the application.

I am aware of the noise that has been, and will continue to be sounded in the ears of every listener, against the doctrine I support. But if he will reflect as well as listen, the delusion must quickly vanish. A general assembly composed of freemen and equals, not elevated above their constituents, but by their own deliberate choice, and that only for short periods, unprivileged by distinct personal rights or rank, can never in a mind untainted by prejudice, and not distempered by faction, be compared to a British parliament, headed by a British king. Principles and practice in the one government can only in such minds be adopted, as a rule of conduct in the other.

But let us, Sir, take this subject up on a more general scale. The foregoing remarks are confined to a particular case. Reasons that are applicable to every government, and that arise out of the nature of the thing ought, and will be with men of sense, and political integrity, decisive.

Mr. Locke in his treatise on civil government, describing the nature and extent of legislative power, says, "that it is the supreme power of the commonwealth, and that nothing has the power of law but what it shall appoint *pursuant* to its *trust*. This power is limitted to the *public good*. A power to *preserve*, and not to *destroy*," proceeding upon these principles, he says, "that in a constituted commonwealth, (by which he means all established governments) there can be but *one supreme* power, which is the legislature, to which all the rest are, and must be subordinate. When this power *abuses* its trust, so as to become dangerous to the *safety* and *security* of the people, there is a supreme power in the people, to *remove* or *alter* the legislature; and thus the community perpetually retains a supreme power of saving themselves from the attempts, and designs of any body, even of the legislators, whenever they shall be so foolish, or so wicked as to lay, and carry on designs, *against the liberties and properties of the subject*." In all cases where this may happen, Mr. Locke puts it upon the principle of self-preservation, that the collective body of the people can properly interfere. It is true he does not mention such acts of the legislature as have not this mischievous tendency; but from the whole of his arguments, it is apparent, that he meant to confine this power of the people to desperate cases; nay, he even supposes a dissolution of government, where they can with propriety exercise their supreme authority. In that situation they recover the delegated power, and may act as they think will be most conducive to their present and future welfare. But I will use his own words, "the community may be said in this respect to be always the supreme power, but not as considered under any form of government, because this power of the people can never take place, till the government be dissolved."

Now it may not be amiss, Sir, to make a short comparison between our own constitution, and the foregoing positions. The fourth article of the declaration of rights, which has been often quoted for a different purpose says, "that whenever the ends of government are *perverted*, and liberty manifestly *endangered*, and all other means of redress are ineffectual, the people may, and ought of right to reform the old, or establish a new government."

Mr. Locke says, "that where the legislative *trust* is abused, so as to become dangerous to the *safety* and *security* of the people, in that case they may *remove* or *alter* the legislature." So far it will be admitted on all hands, that they agree. But it is contested, that under the nature of a *trust*, the people have a right to interfere and direct their *trustees* in all cases where they shall be inclined so to do. It is observable in the above quotation, that Mr. Locke makes use of the word *trust*, and considers the members of all legislative bodies as *trustees*; but he draws no such inference from these principles. His inference, drawn from the nature, the use and extent of the power delegated is, that in every case, where the legislative body acts within, or does not exceed that power, the people cannot with propriety interfere, but that their right of interposition accrues upon such an abuse of trust, as endangers their safety and security. There is such a consonancy between the words and principles of the constitution, and those of this author, that it is evident to me the framers of it had him in view, when that article was drawn, and that the same spirit influenced them, that dictated his opinions.

On the subject of resistance, Mr. Locke compares the case of the legislature to that of a private trustee, who is *accountable* to the person conferring the trust, and concludes, that the people have in like manner a right to judge when those they depute, have violated the trust reposed in them, but he confines this to the case of resistance to *arbitrary power*. In the same chapter he says, "the power that every individual gave to the society, when he entered into it, can never revert to the individuals again, as long as the society lasts, but will always remain in the community; because without this, there can be no community, no commonwealth, which is contrary to the original agreement; *so also*, when the society hath placed the legislative in any assembly of men, to continue in them and their successors, *the legislative can never revert to the people whilst that government lasts*; because having provided a legislative power to continue for ever, they have given up their *political* power to the legislative, and *cannot resume* it. But if they have set limits to the duration of their legislative, and made this *supreme power* in any person or assembly, only *temporary*; or else when by the miscarriages of those in authority, it is forfeited; upon the forfeiture, or at the *determination*, it *reverts* to the society, and the people have a right to act as supreme, and continue the legislative in themselves; or erect a new form, or under the old form place it in new hands as they think good." Thus it appears according to Mr. Locke's doctrine, that when the collective body of the people have entrusted legislative power to an assembly to continue for ever, they give up their *political* power to that body, and cannot *resume* it, but when it is forfeited by miscarriages; nor can it ever revert to the people, whilst that government lasts. He makes the case the same with temporary governments so long as they endure; for upon their *determination*, or forfeiture, the *supreme power*, he says, *reverts* to the society. The power is exactly the same in both, whilst it continues, that is *supreme*, and only differs as to duration. But what does he mean by the word miscarriages? This we shall discover by comparing the present with a former quotation, of the same author. In this he asserts that the legislative authority is forfeited by miscarriages, and also, that this authority can never revert to the people, whilst the government lasts, therefore the miscarriages must be of such a nature, as to occasion a dissolution of government. What conduct then in the legislature is it, that occasions a dissolution of government? Why such a conduct, says he in a former passage, as is dangerous to the *safety* and *security* of the people.

Another question, Sir, occurs in this place, which is an important one. What is meant by the people's giving up their *political* power, and having no right to resume it? Their political power here, as I understand it, is their right of legislation. Well, if as according to Mr. Locke, this is given up, will they have a right to direct, and to require that their directions shall be obeyed? I will not pretend to be positive, but in my apprehension this if not a *real* resumption of the legislative power, as some people may perhaps imagine, ought at least to be called in the style of the civilians a *quasi*-resumption; and their effects, I apprehend, will be nearly the same. I confine myself to those powers of the legislature, which are constitutional. If these be exceeded or abused, the people have a power superior to instruction, a right of compulsion; the weight of which, I sincerely hope tyranny may ever feel, whether it appears in the shape of a monarch, or of a general assembly.

Mr. Locke probably reflected, for he was not a *crude* and *short* thinker, that there might be danger to a government from anarchy and licentiousness, as well as from an abuse of legislative authority. He meant to calculate his system, so as to prevent both. A constitution established on the principles of freedom and equality, not to be violated on the one hand, by those who were appointed to the execution of it, or to be infringed or rendered useless, by the rest of the society, might appear to him a scheme more beneficial to the whole, than that system, which being made secure on one side, was left open to invasion on the other.

Dr. Rutherforth, in his institutes of natural law, makes a distinction between the *constitutional* and *natural* rights of the people; which he applies to all governments however composed. This distinction he founds upon the opinion of Grotius. That body with which the sovereign power is lodged, or the legislature of the community, he considers as *independent* of the collective body of the people, so long as it continues to act in conformity with the constitution, and commits no violation of the rights of the citizens. I will cite his own words in his comment upon the opinion of Grotius. "The point that he, Grotius, wants to establish is, that unless in *perfectly democratical* societies there is in some *one* man, or in some *body* of men, within the society, a civil despotic power lodged, which though it is originally derived from the collective body of the people, is exercised afterwards so far *independ-*

ently of them, as not to be subject to any *constitutional* restraints from that body. Despotic power is a bad name indeed, because it is commonly used to convey the notion of what is arbitrary and tyrannical. But this bad meaning will be taken off, if we call it civil despotism, which is the civil power originally inherent in the community or collective body itself, but entrusted by their consent either express or tacit, with the governing part of each community." In this case he says, "the people have no constitutional right to *restrain* or *punish* those governors, who are entrusted by them with this power. *But then,* where the constitution is *broken,* or where the constitutional governors *pretend* to, and *make use* of, a power which does not belong to them, *a power of causelessly and arbitrarily oppressing the people,* which is no part of civil power; our author as far as appears, does not contend, that in these circumstances the people have no *natural* right of doing themselves justice. *And certainly* we ought very carefully to distinguish between a *constitutional* right in the people to *interfere* in the affairs of government, to *direct* or *restrain* the legislative and executive bodies in the exercise of the power, that is *entrusted* with such bodies, and a *natural* right in the people to maintain the constitution, as it was at first settled, when any attempts are made to *alter* it; to *resume* the legislative and executive power, when the constitution has been *broken*; or to defend themselves against all *unsocial* or *unconstitutional* oppression."

The only remark I shall make on the foregoing passage is this, that Grotius, and after him his commentator, extends the doctrine laid down to all kinds of governments, whether the supreme authority be lodged in *one* person, or in a *body* of men. There is an exception with respect to societies perfectly democratical. But the import of that exception is, that in those societies there is no *select* body, that possesses those powers. The reason is obvious, because in perfectly democratical societies, the people at large, or the collective body is the legislative power. This body is possessed of supreme power, but that power is not delegated, or exercised under any particular constitutional form.

To illustrate, and confirm these principles, I will cite one passage more, out of hundreds that might be produced, from the last mentioned author, and if I do not grossly misconceive his meaning, it will be considered, I think, pretty much to the point, "Whether the supreme governing body consists of a *single* person, as in monarchies, or of a *number* of persons, as in other forms of government; if we were to consider it as a *trustee* or deputy for the people, that holds the trust or deputation *precariously,* and has no right conferred upon it by being appointed to this office; the people would then be authorised judges of the behaviour of this supreme body; nothing, which they determined about its behavior, could be wrong; they might remove it from its office for every fault, or for every suspicion, or even without any fault or any suspicion at all. *But* the governing part of a civil society, whilst it is a *trustee* for the general benefit, *is not a precarious* trustee, that has no right of its own, and holds at the will of the part, which is governed. Its power is limited indeed by the purposes of social union; so that the people are not in subjection to it, and may lawfully resist it, when it counteracts these purposes. But it has a *right* to this limited power, and cannot be justly *deprived* of it without cause, or be *lawfully resisted in the exercise* of it."

Supported by such authorities as these, I think I maintain a good cause, when I allege, that the interposition of the people, to use the most gentle term, in the ordinary matters of legislation, is improper, and is only useful and necessary, when according to the words and spirit of our constitution, "the ends of government are perverted, and liberty manifestly endangered." The names of a Locke, and a Rutherforth, in the cause of reason and liberty, will surely outweigh the pompous, and often seditious harangues of a turbulent declaimer, the puny observations of a political scribbler, or the shameless assertions of a publisher of *spurious* extracts of letters.

But, Sir, it may be asked, for the most trivial questions are sometimes asked, are the people to stand tamely by, and see their rights violated, and their interests sacrificed? I answer *no*, they are not to stand tamely by, and see this doing or done. When they feel, or are fully convinced of this, they have not only a right, but it is their duty as men, and freemen, to rouse, and make the delinquents feel the full weight of their power and resentment. But before this be done, they ought to feel, or be fully convinced. A settled disposition in the legislature, or a part of it, to oppress, confirmed by acts, should be the beacon to warn them of their danger, and to light them to revenge.

Now, Sir, I appeal to the good sense, and to the cool reflection of my fellow citizens. Is ours a constitution of such a frame, as to keep them in continual alarm for their rights and interests, which those constitutions justly do, where the liberty of the people being constantly in danger, ought to be guarded by constant attention, and watchfulness? Or does our constitution require their interference, but when, according to its express words, "the ends of government are perverted, and liberty manifestly endangered?" I have repeated these words often. They cannot be too often repeated. They, at the same time, point out the evil, and direct to the remedy.

Mr. Locke's opinion of such a government as ours is, "that there is not much to be feared, where the assemblies are *variable*, whose members, upon the dissolution of the assembly, are subjects under the *common* laws, *equally* with the rest. When the legislature have made laws, the members being separated again, they are themselves subject to the laws they have made; which is a new and *near* tie upon them, to take care, that they make them for the public good." It ought not to be forgotten, that the authors last mentioned were the chief pillars upon which we supported the late revolution, and upon which our government is erected. To discard them now, when that is established, would be nothing less than to destroy the foundation, when the superstructure is raised, and upon which it can only be supported with credit and stability.

My intention, Sir, is to impress a veneration for the constitution under which I live. I wish to preserve the powers and independency of the whole legislature, and of each branch of it, entire and uninfringed. This wish, I trust, is the wish of a good citizen, and a good subject. And I know no other way of effecting this, than by keeping in view and practice the principles I have endeavoured to inculcate.

I shall make no comparison, Sir, between the senate and the house of delegates; nor shall I say any thing of the appeal of the latter body to the people. Although I think the measure wrong, I do not condemn those concerned in it. I have had the honour of serving with several of those gentlemen, and I am well satisfied they were actuated by the best of motives; the interest of the state. My view is to combat, and if I can, to eradicate opinions that I think mischievous. Should there be a single exception to what I have just acknowledged; should any part of this address affect any entertainer, or circulator of these opinions, it is not my fault. Perhaps upon fairly examining his own bosom, he will find me blameless. But, Sir, I have already intruded too much upon your patience. Let my apology be, and I know you will admit it, the importance of the subject. Believe me, Sir, with all due respect to your station, and person.

A CONSTITUENT

William Paca to Alexander Contee Hanson
MAY 10, 1787

TO ARISTIDES

IN YOUR LAST address to the people of Maryland, you have been pleased to take some notice of Publicola. The right of the people to instruct their delegates, had always appeared to me an essential safe guard of public liberty. I not only read of it as a speculative opinion, of individuals in their closets; but history told me of its being actually exercised in all countries, and all governments, where the people had a share in legislation, by delegates or representatives, and when I found you and a few others among us, asserting a different doctrine, I considered it as a dangerous attack upon the rights of my fellow-citizens, and therefore made some animadversions upon it.

But it was your duty, you say, as a *guardian* of the constitution, to protest against what you conceived a most dangerous innovation. This, Sir, seems to me to be another new-fangled doctrine. I wonder what it is that has made you a *guardian* of the constitution, to *protest* in *news papers* against what you may conceive to be *innovations*. I can find nothing of it in your commission as a judge, nor can I find it in your oath of office. But you may tell me, the oath of allegiance, which you also take, binds you to defend the government, against all conspiracies and combinations. If this be the ground on which you rest your title, to be the *guardian* of the constitution, to *protest* in news papers, why then every constable in the state, and every cryer of the courts, and the very door-keepers of the general assembly, are equally with you *guardians* of the constitution; for they all take the same oath of allegiance. In the exercise of your *judicial* authority, upon subjects *judicially* before you, no doubt you have great and extensive powers; but as to questions not before you *judicially*, you are only a *private* citizen. If however the title flatters and pleases you of being a *guardian* of the constitution, to *protest* in *news papers*, you may take it, and so may the cryer of your court, for what I care about it.

You were not, you say, particularly *interested* in the question. Now I think you were *particularly* interested; for if I mistake not, the peoples instructions were to have been given upon the bill for a paper emission; and by provisions of it, the *officers salaries* were to be paid in that money. You were as much disinterested upon the subject, as you were upon other matters, in which you have displayed your patriotism, by memorials and pamphlets.

But, except on *important occasions,* a man that applies to the people for instructions, will be deemed, you say, a *promoter of sedition,* or what St. Paul calls "a pestilent fellow." I would ask, who are to judge what are *important occasions?* I beg pardon; to be sure the *guardian* of the constitution to *protest* in *news papers,* must be the judge; and as you, Sir, have already determined, that the distresses of the people as to their taxes and debts, and the ways and means proposed for their relief were not a subject important enough to be laid before the people for their instructions, why then every delegate, who applied for such instructions, was a *promoter of sedition,* or what you say, St. Paul calls "a pestilent fellow." When judge Jeffries, that bloody monster, butchered and murdered the illustrious Sydney and lord Russel, and other patriots, his butcheries and murders were defended by perverting the doctrines of St. Paul; when bigots and zealots lighted up the flames of persecution, the stake, fire and faggot, were defended by the like perversion of the doctrine of St. Paul; and when members of the house of delegates are to be marked and branded, as *promoters of sedition* and *pestilent fellows*, we see a judge of the general court of Maryland mangling St. Paul in like manner, and making the like *pious* application of his writings.

Our constitution and form of government says, that our judges ought to be *learned in the law*, and provided with *liberal* salaries; but for men not *learned in the law*, no salary at all is provided. A *judge* who perpetually dabbles in politics, and spends his time in writing laborious notes, laborious memorials, laborious pamphlets, and other laborious publications, must find it, I think, very difficult to require and retain such a knowledge of the law as his station requires.

Of all men in the community, a *judge* ought to be most disengaged, from the agitations of private or public discussions. The character he sustains, decides upon the lives, property and liberties of his fellow-citizens and it is impossible to hold the scales of justice with a steady hand, when the judgment is shook by the assaults of prejudice and passion. Of all topics, I know of none so likely to enflame the minds of men, and raise their passions as questions touching the liberties of the people; and the records and annals of England tell us, that when *judges* once enter the lists as *partizans of power*, they soon become *prostitutes* upon the bench, and *fit instruments* to execute the most wicked and atrocious purposes.

You collect, you say, from the whole of my publication, that I asserted that "Mr. Locke, lord Molesworth, and Mr. Trenchard, maintained with their pens *the right of binding by instructions*; that Mr. Hambden and lord Russel maintained it with their blood; and Mr. Algernon Sydney with both." This collection of yours, Sir, is nothing more than the work of a prolific fancy; indeed there is so little ground for it, that I am almost led to think it a *wilful* misrepresentation.

Having fabricated an assertion for me, you then proceed to expose it. "In a popular harrangue this assertion might not surprise; committed to writing, published to the world, and open to examination, there is no excuse or palliation for it, except that which Publicola would disdain to offer." I have no objections to your exposing your own assertions and declarations; but to tell the people of Maryland, they are my assertions and declarations, is to depart from all truth and decency; and "there can be no excuse or palliation for it except that, which Aristides would disdain to offer."

I cited the illustrious names of Locke, Molesworth, Trenchard, Hambden, Russel, and Sydney, to maintain the following positions.

1st. That all legislative power is a *grant* of the people, and a *trust* for their welfare and happiness.

2dly. That the people are the *judges* whether this trust was properly or improperly executed.

3dly. That if they were of opinion it was not properly executed, they might go even to the extreme of resuming the powers of government, if *other* means of redress were ineffectual.

The great object of my publication, was to prove the propriety of the assembly's adjourning to take the *sense* and *judgment* of the people, upon the measures proposed by the house of delegates and rejected by the senate. It therefore became material to establish the principle, that the people are the *rightful judges* of the good or bad tendency of all public measures. To maintain this principle, I cited the above authorities, and I hope you will admit they are directly in point. I afterwards shewed, that the right of interference by *instructions,* was a natural and necessary result from the principle or *right of judgment.* Not that these patriots employed their pens and blood in defence of the *particular right of instructing,* but in defence of principles, from which I contended, the right of instructing resulted as a plain and natural consequence. And before I have done, Sir, I think I shall oblige you to confess it by fair argument.

But you have insulted it seems the memory of Sydney, and you have thought proper to beg pardon of his illustrious spirit. May the illustrious spirit of Sydney, you say, forgive the injury which from the *misinformation* of Publicola, you lately offered to his memory. I think the asking of pardon was the least you could do. But why is the blame to be put upon me? What *misinformation* did I give you? I absolutely deny giving you any; you again misrepresent me, and seem to forget the obligations of truth and decency.

It is remarkable however, that when you thought Mr. Sydney was in *favour* of the *right of instructing,* you immediately insulted him; he was then no doubt a *promoter of sedition,* or what you say St. Paul calls "a pestilent fellow." But when upon reading a passage in his writings, which you do not understand, you thought he was against the *right of instructing,* then you cut about, and extol him for a *great patriot,* and you bring him forward before the people of Maryland as an *illustrious advocate* for you. I believe, Sir, you must once more cut about, and consider Mr. Sydney, as you seem originally to have done, a *promoter of sedition,* or what you say St. Paul calls "a pestilent fellow;" for although Mr. Sydney did not fall a martyr upon the *particular point of instruction,* nor was quoted by me for that purpose, yet I assert he expressly maintains the peoples right to instruct, and tells us in the most explicit terms that the people of England enjoy this right, and have never parted with it by their own consent, nor suffered it to be taken from them by force or any other unjustifiable means.

But how is this possible you may ask, considering the passages you have cited from Mr. Sydney, and which you say are *all the material passages* upon the subject. I answer and say, you did not understand the passages you cited, and that there are *other material passages*.

Remember the question between us is not upon the *right* or *force* of instructions from a *particular* county, city, or borough, but upon the *right* and *force* of the *national voice* communicated and declared to the legislature by *memorial, remonstrance* or INSTRUCTION, from *every* county, city, and borough, or the *majority* of the nation. The adjournment of the house of delegates was, not to take the sense, judgement and *instructions* of a *particular county*, but to take the sense, judgment and instructions of *every county*. The right of judgment, which the people retain on the establishment of civil government, and which presides and watches over the legislative exercise of the powers communicated, and decides in all cases, whether these powers are properly or improperly executed, dwells not in the people of a *particular* county, city, or borough, but in the people of every county, city, or borough, or a majority of them.

As to the force of instructions from a *particular* county, city, or borough in England, different opinions have been entertained by different writers upon the subject. The representatives there for a county, city, or borough, are said by some to be representatives not only *for the county*, but for *the whole nation*. From whence it is contended that although a county, city, or borough may instruct, yet their instructions cannot be conclusive and binding, because they are *partial*. Others entertain a different opinion, and assert that each county has an *exclusive absolute right* of binding its own representatives by instructions, and reject the idea as a fiction that the representatives *of a county*, are the representatives of the *whole nation*.

The very ground upon which the objection is made that the people of a particular county have not an absolute conclusive right to instruct the representatives of that county, admits the binding force of instructions from every county, or the majority of the people; for the objection is that the representatives of a county being the representatives of the whole nation, instructions from a particular county, can only be the instructions *of the minority*. But put the case of instructions from *every county*, or from the *majority* of the people, and then the objection ceases, and the instructions are *absolute* and *conclusive*.

Among the number of writers, who are of opinion that the representatives of a county, are the representatives of the whole nation, is Mr. Sydney. And upon this principle it is that he considers the opinions of the electors of a *particular county* when communicated to the representatives *of that county*, as a proper interference for information; but not as an *absolute and conclusive instruction*. Take now the passage you cited:

"Every county, says Mr. Sydney, does not make a *distinct body*, having in itself a *sovereign power*; but it is a member of that great body which comprehends the whole nation. It is not therefore for Kent, or Sussex, or Lewes, or Maidstone, but the whole nation, that the members chosen in these places are sent to serve in parliament. And though it be fit for them as friends and neighbours, so far as may be to hearken to the opinion of the electors, for the information of their judgment, and to the end that what they shall say, be of more weight, when every one is known not to speak his own thoughts only, but those of a greater number of men, yet they are not strictly and properly obliged to give an account of their actions to any, unless the whole body of the nation for which they serve, and who are equally concerned in their resolutions could be assembled. This being impracticable, the whole punishment to which they are subject, *if they betray their trust*, is scorn, infamy, hatred, and an assurance of being rejected, when they shall again seek the same honour."

Mr. Sydney, it is plain speaks in this passage of the force of instructions, from the people of a *particular county*, to the representatives of such county, and considers such instructions not *absolutely conclusive*, because the persons chosen are not only representatives for the county, but the whole nation.

It is material to consider what led Mr. Sydney to make the remarks and observations in the passage cited. Mr. Filmer, a ministerial partizan had published a book in which he asserted, "that the people of England must *only choose*, and trust those whom they choose, to do *as they list*."

Mr. Sydney devotes a whole chapter in refutation of this very slavish position. He replies and says, "This is ingeniously concluded; I take what servant I please, and when I have taken him, I must suffer him to do what he pleases. But from whence should this necessity arise? Why may I not take one to be my groom, and another to be my cook, and keep them both to the offices for which I took them? What law does herein restrain my right? And if I am free in my private capacity, to regulate my particular affairs, according to my own discretion, and to allot to each servant his proper work, why have not I *with my associates the freemen of England*, the like liberty of *directing* and *limiting* the powers of the *servants* we employ in our public affairs."

If this is not an explicit assertion of the people's right to *direct* and *control* their delegates, I am mistaken indeed. And if our people have the like command over their delegates and representatives, as they have over their *grooms* and *cooks*, I think, Sir, you have egregiously mistaken Mr. Sydney, on the point of instructions. If A. and B. indeed have a groom or a cook, neither A. nor B. separately and exclusively can direct and limit his powers, but both certainly may; and so, if representatives of a county be representatives of a whole nation, the people of the county cannot separately or exclusively *direct* and *limit* the powers of such representatives. But why have not I, with my associates, the freemen of Maryland, the liberty of directing and limiting the powers of our delegates and representatives?

Mr. Sydney having placed this right of directing and limiting the power of public servants in the body of the people, proceeds to distinguish the government of England from the United Netherlands, in the mode and manner of exercising this right. He says, that every province, city, or canton, is a *distinct body*, having an *exclusive sovereignty* and therefore the delegates of a particular province, city, or canton, are absolutely bound by the instructions of such province, city, or canton, they being delegates only for such province, city, or canton. But not so he says, amongst us; every county does not make a distinct body, &c. and so goes on as already cited.

And why I would ask does every province, city, or canton, in the United Netherlands possess the absolute right of instructing their delegates? Because each province, city, or canton, is a distinct body, having a distinct sovereignty. And why does not every county in England possess this right as absolutely? Because each county is not a *distinct body*, nor a distinct sovereignty. But why shall not the freemen of England, the body of the nation, possess this right as absolutely as a province, city, or canton in the United Netherlands?—

Mr. Sydney then goes on and maintains, that this right of directing and instructing delegates and representatives was recognised and exercised by the people of Spain and France, when those governments admitted the people a share of legislation by deputies and delegates; and he tells us that this right (when he wrote) was used and practised in the states of Languedoc and Brittany, and in the diets of Germany. The histories of Denmark, Sweden, Poland, and Bohemia, he says, testifies the peoples right of instructing, and if this right does not still subsist in these countries, the people, he says, "must have been deprived of it by ways and means as best suit the *manners* of *pirates* than the *laws of God and nature*. And if England does not still enjoy the same right, it must be because she has been deprived of it by the same unjustifiable means, or by our own consent. But thanks be to God, we know of no people, who have a better right to liberty or better defended it than our own nation. And if we do not degenerate from the virtue of our ancestors, we may hope to transmit it entire to posterity. WE ALWAYS MAY AND OFTEN DO GIVE INSTRUCTIONS TO OUR DELEGATES, &c."

Could Mr. Sydney, Sir, express himself in a more explicit language, was it possible to assert the peoples right of instructing in more forcible and positive terms? What a striking difference do we see between his notions of this right and yours? To deprive a people of this right, he says, would better suit the manners of a *pirate* than the laws of *God and nature*. But you say to suffer the people to enjoy this right would be a *wicked thing*, because "*it must introduce disorder, riot and arbitrary sway.*" When this illustrious patriot speaks of England's maintaining and preserving this right of instructing amidst the storms and tempests that threatened her liberties, he breaks out in a transport of joy and gratitude, "thanks be to God, we know of no people, who have a better right to liberty, or better defended it than our own nation." But when you speak of the defenders of this liberty in the state of Maryland, you mark and describe them as *promoters of sedition*, or what you say St. Paul calls "pestilent fellows."

You see, Sir, you neither understand Mr. Sydney, nor his doctrines nor principles. You got hold of a passage relative to the *force* of instruction from a *particular county* and you applied it to the *national voice*. But Mr. Sydney, you find, asserts and defends in the warmest terms the *national right* of judging and instructing. This was the only point contended for by myself and the other advocates for the peoples right of instructing the SENATE. And this admitted, it follows that the house of delegates may rightfully apply for instructions, and that the people may rightfully give them, and when given they are equally conclusive and binding upon both branches of the general assembly.

I found the right of instructing upon the same principles that Mr. Sydney does; he maintains that delegates are *public servants*, deriving all their authority from the grant of the people, and that the people are therefore the judges, whether they employ that authority for their happiness or their destruction. "That the people are the judges, Mr. Locke, lord Molesworth, and Mr. Trenchard, maintained with their pens, Hambden, and lord Russell, with their blood, and Mr. Algernon Sydney with both." And that the people are the judges I too maintain, and thank Heaven I can do it without risking any fatal consequences; for while Aristides is the GUARDIAN of the constitution, what have I to fear from the head or heart of a *Jeffries?*

My position then is this, that the people of Maryland are the judges whether the general assembly in the exercise of the powers with which they are entrusted, employ them for their safety and happiness, or for their ruin and destruction; our declaration of rights and compact teaches this doctrine; for it expressly says, that the powers of legislation are a grant of the people; that both branches are the trustees of the people; that when their powers are abused and *all other means of redress are ineffectual*, the people may then resume them.

If the people are the judges, it follows, that every proceeding and measure of the general assembly is a proper subject for their consideration and judgment. And thence it is that we have a journal of our proceedings in both houses printed and published at the public expence. And if the people are the judges, then the measures proposed the last session by the house of delegates and rejected by the senate, were also proper subjects for their examination and judgment.

The question Sir, between us is now brought to a point. Suppose the people deliberating upon these systems had been of opinion, that their welfare and happiness required the adoption of them, and that rejection would endanger or destroy the public safety; I ask, what were the people to do under such a *national* sense and judgment of these systems.

It has been said, that although the people are the judges, and may form such an opinion and judgement; yet our compact and form of government, puts a padlock upon their lips, so that they cannot speak, and a fetter upon their hands, so that they cannot act, for *one year* with respect to the house of delegates; and for *five years* with respect to the senate. But when these periods are determined and the time is come for a new election, then the people may—I beseech you what? Why, after they have lost their country and its liberties and become slaves, by means of being padlocked and fettered during the above periods, they may *then* speak and act like *freemen*; they may then *discontinue* those members who have already struck the blow, and completely destroyed them.

But you may say that this is not your doctrine, for you admit that when the ends of government are perverted, the people may immediately interfere. I presume you also admit, that the people are the judges what are the ends of government, and what measures of the legislature are a perversion of them. Suppose then the people had been of opinion that the senate's rejection of the measures proposed, endangered their safety and happiness, and thereby perverted the ends of government, what were they to do under such an impression and conviction? If you admit they might immediately have interfered by memorial, remonstrance, or instruction, it is all I contend for; for whenever they can *rightfully* interfere, their instructions must be conclusive, and they can rightfully enforce obedience to them.

Government was made for the happiness of the people; they are the judges whether the powers of government are employed for that purpose. This right of judgment admitted, I ask, how can a legislature rightfully over-rule the national voice upon a subject affecting the national safety and happiness, communicated and declared by memorial, remonstrance, or instruction? If the people are the judges, their judgment and voice must be conclusive, if not conclusive, then the legislature is despotic.

You do not, Sir, seem to me to have a proper idea of what is meant by the *supreme power* of the legislature. It is *supreme* only while it is employed for the happiness of the people; while it operates within this sphere, there can be no rightful interference from the people. But when this power is employed in the pursuit of measures, or enaction of laws, which the people think are *oppressive* and *injurious*, or in rejecting measures, which they think their happiness requires, then this power is not *supreme*, and the people may rightfully interfere, for such an interference combats only the measures of an *usurped* authority.

You demand to know whether the passage you cited from Mr. Locke was not a pointed authority against my doctrine? I answer, no, I wish you were better acquainted with Mr. Locke and his principles of liberty. I agree with him, that the supreme power of legislation can never revert to the people, but upon the *miscarriages* of those, into whose hands it is placed. But who, does Mr. Locke say, are the judges when such miscarriages happen? The people. And what if such miscarriages happen? Why the people may interfere; for in all such miscarriages the *supreme power* flies out of its sphere, and the peoples interference does not touch the *rightful*, but the *wrongful* exercise of it.

Whenever the people think the powers of government are improperly exercised, they may interfere two ways.

1st. By memorial and remonstrance.

2dly. By instruction and demand.

And their application or direction may be enforced two ways.

1st. By discontinuing the members on a future election.

2dly. By resuming the power of government.

The one or other mode of coertion may be adopted according to the exigency of the case.

But my doctrine, you say is *wicked*, and tends to introduce *riot* and *disorder*. Other partizans of power have said the same thing before you. But the principles, which I contend for, are established upon foundations too strong to be shaken by the feeble efforts of a judge, who, if we may believe his writings, neither knows nor feels what liberty is.

The *binding force* of instructions, you assert, has no connexion with the principles of the English and American revolutions. I never read a writer so confident in his assertions, and yet so often mistaken.

The binding force, Sir, of instructions is entirely founded upon the principles of both these revolutions. The principles were, that all rightful power is derived from the people, that it is to be exercised for their welfare and happiness, that the people are the judges, and when they think it is not so employed they may speak and announce it by memorials, remonstrances, or instructions; and if they are disregarded they may right themselves by discontinuing their members at a future election, or if the magnitude of the case requires it, by resuming the powers of government. It was upon these principles the people of England struck off the head of king Charles the first; it was upon these principles that America broke her connexion with Great-Britain, and became an independent empire; and it is upon these principles that we see you, Sir, a *judge* of the *general court* of Maryland, with a salary of £.500 per annum; and like a *blessed guardian* employing all the powers and faculties of your soul to destroy the best guard which the people have for their liberty, safety and happiness.

PUBLICOLA

Alexander Contee Hanson to the People
MAY 11, 1787

TO THE PEOPLE OF MARYLAND

ARISTIDES, having already, from the impulse of an honest zeal, appeared much oftener in print than an attention to his own interest would have permitted, perceives himself under the disagreeable necessity of appearing again. He was not suffered to discuss a great political question, without having his character drawn into the controversy. In return, he means not to touch either the public or private characters of his enemies, so far as they have no relation to the charges against Aristides. He might indeed submit his cause upon what has already been said, and what is otherwise known to his fellow-citizens. But as here is a possibility, that an unjust inference may be drawn from his silence, he proposes, at a more convenient season, to make some comments on the writings and other exhibitions of Publicola.—

Whilst he perceives a most stedfast determination to effect the ruin of himself and his house, he feels that undisturbed peace of mind, which results from a consciousness of having never by action, word, or thought, deserved the displeasure of his countrymen. Happy is he, that the rectitude of his whole conduct has driven his adversaries to such pitiable shifts! With all the eagerness of rancour, they have sought occasions to arraign him. In what has the pursuit terminated? He requests those who listen to the charge drawn from his political writings, to peruse these writings with candour and attention. With respect to the charges exhibited on a recent occasion, he requests you to mark the strange inconsistency between this and the former charge. He calls upon the world to assign one motive, he could possibly have, for destroying any of the guards to your liberty, safety and happiness. In defence of the equal rights and equal liberty, intended by the constitution, he has made those exertions, which he conceived his country entitled to, from every man in his situation. But it seems, a person in his situation should remain unconcerned, even when the state is thrown into convulsions; and his interference affords ground for another charge—

Already, my fellow-citizens, have the enemies of Aristides demonstrated, that an individual shall not with impunity, oppose their designs. What they have done affects him not *deeply*. To those, who think as he does, and who, notwithstanding, can with callous indolence behold the persecution of a man, whose crime is that of vindicating the constitution, he suggests the following considerations:

The great leading principle of a republic is the love of public good; and every man should feel himself a protector of the constitution. But if every effort to protect it must be attended with a certain sacrifice of private good, that which is the business of all, in a short time, will become the business of none. Unprotected and defenceless, your sacred constitution will be exposed to every assault; and a little time may afford cause for the advocates of arbitrary sway to exult in their favourite position, *that mankind were never intended to be free*. The great and stupendous revolution of America may then only serve to establish this position into a maxim. It will be then indeed (to use the words of an enlightened Congress) that "the last and fairest experiment in favour of the rights of human nature will be turned against them; and their patrons and friends exposed to be insulted and silenced, by the votaries of tyranny and usurpation."

Annapolis   ARISTIDES

Alexander Contee Hanson to the People
JUNE 9, 1787

TO THE PEOPLE OF MARYLAND

SOME TIME AGO, it was asserted, by the enemies of Aristides, that an officer of the government has no right to meddle with public affairs, except those which relate to his office. This position has given way to another more plausible. "A judge should dedicate the time, not employed in the administration of justice, to the abstruse study of his profession. He cannot otherwise be qualified, in all cases, to give skilful decisions. And, if he suffer himself to be drawn into the agitations of public discussion, he cannot hold with a steady hand the scales of justice." Let us contrast this doctrine with a celebrated law of an ancient brave enlightened people, whom the *Publicola* of all succeeding times have affected to admire. In the republic of Athens, instituted for the preservation of equal rights, and approaching as nearly as one could wish, to a perfect democracy, the man, who remained inactive during a civil commotion, was liable to be punished as a traitor. This law was intended to make each citizen feel himself a guardian of the public weal. The bearing an high office in the state would have been the worst of all defences for a man arraigned under this law; as his situation would have naturally induced his fellow-citizens to expect from him more signal services. But, mercy on us! how culpable amongst certain enlightened moderns is a judge, for assuming the title and office of a guardian of the constitution, and for protesting against innovations in a news-paper. A man of common sense however, when the duty of this guardian leads him to preserve his fellow-citizens from the dangerous impression of pestilent doctrines, will admit, that news-papers are of all others the most proper and convenient vehicles. Let me here propose a few queries to Publicola.

Has he never applauded the former exertions of Aristides?

Has he never commended the author for his seasonable, disinterested, and useful publications?

Has he, on no occasion, advised him to employ his pen, for the public information?

Before Aristides opposed the late paper system, did Publicola ever condemn him for an improper disposal of his time?

But to descend to a more particular inquiry,—Did not Publicola, in the most flattering terms of approbation, speak to Aristides of a publication in the session of 1784, by which Aristides had the credit of having prevented a committee from bringing in their report for an emission of paper?

When Publicola, from being the decided enemy of paper, on a sudden became as decided an advocate, it struck many men with wonder and amazement. But who was there, that considered Publicola's proposition as a signal for changing his own opinion?

The man, my beloved countrymen, who makes truth his guide, and your substantial good his object, must ever raise up enemies to himself. Publicola has called me the *partisan of power*. He seems to have adopted the cant under the former government. What power is there, to which Aristides pays his court? Is he labouring to augment the authority of the governor and council? And if so, how is it they can require him? Is it then the senate, whose authority Aristides would erect on the ruin of your liberties? Has he made any attempt to extend *their* privileges, augment their power or increase the duration of their offices? Has he ever ascribed to them alone the power of making laws? He well knows that the senate cannot even propose a *money* bill, and that, whenever they venture to propose any other bill, which is rejected by the delegates, there is an end of the business. *They* never think of appealing to the people, and thereby compelling the delegates to adopt their proposal. He must then, after all, be a partisan for the power of the delegates. He has maintained indeed, that, in passing or rejecting bills the two branches are on terms of perfect equality; and that the members of each branch are at full liberty to exercise their own judgments. Examine well the position, and say whether it can justify the charge.—That the position has ever been denied, he presumes is not, because it would tend to the establishment of undue power; but because, if both branches, as to the ordinary affairs of government, are under the control and direction of the people, one of them must become far greater than the other. From the nature of things, the people must, in most cases, decide in favour of their immediate representatives. The consequence will be this. No man of superior worth will prefer a seat in the senate, degraded thus from its constitutional importance. One branch will in effect become supreme; and the state may be ruled by a few men, combining from interest or ambition. Reflecting maturely on these things, you will view Aristides in his true character, not the base sycophant, and partisan of power, but *the real and not pretended* assertor of equal rights,—the determined foe to arbitrary sway. As well might Publicola be compared to Catiline or Cethegus, as Aristides to Sir Robert Filmer or Judge Jeffries. But on no occasion, if even detected and fairly exposed, would Aristides descend to illiberal abuse.

What a wretched thing is man, under the dominion of malignant passions! Publicola has even made some malicious insinuations respecting the professional capacity of Aristides. To a charge of this kind it is difficult to answer, without deviating from the received rule of propriety. I am happy however, that to you, my fellow-citizens, I can safely make my appeal. To whom has Aristides behaved with the insolence of office? To whom has he denied, or wantonly, or unnecessarily, delayed, or made a shameful traffic of justice? On what occasion has he failed to maintain his dignity? Whilst dependent on a precarious annual vote, was he ever dependent in his opinions? or did he ever yield to the improper influence of leading members? He defies the world to shew one instance, where he has not bestowed a becoming attention to the matter before him, or where his judgement has been biassed by fear, affection, prejudice, or partiality. He has ever felt too much anxiety not to use all proper means of information, and, at this moment, he reflects with a conscious pride, that his decisions have been universally approved by the intelligent, the impartial, and the disinterested.

On no occasion have I undertaken a task more irksome than the present. When assertion is substituted for sound argument, and pointed authority; when that assertion is mingled with invective, and slander is vented in general terms; when at one moment Publicola maintains almost the doctrine of Aristides, and, at the next changes his ground; when he uses words suited to mislead, and then taxes Aristides with indecency and falsehood for not conceiving him aright; the labour of pursuing him appears almost endless—There are some who will censure Aristides for honouring those disgusting effusions with his notice, whilst others will perhaps require a comment on every part.

It was impossible for common sense to consider the recent appeal of the delegates otherwise than as an attempt to force, at last, upon the senate a measure, which it had repeatedly and unanimously rejected. Aristides conceived every principle of policy and justice opposed to the plan; and the means of effecting it, should they succeed, appeared far worse than the measure itself. It was the general idea, that the sense of the people should be conveyed by written instruments or instructions. At the instance of several respectable men, he prepared a draught, expressing in the most decent respectful terms, a disapprobation of the plan, and defining the peoples general right of interference. Had there really existed a dispute between the two branches, necessarily and constitutionally to be decided by the people, it was certainly improper for either a senator or delegate to dictate either the form, or substance of the decision. The interference of Aristides, both as a matter of right and a matter of duty, was natural, proper, and consistent with his official character. But no sooner was his draught submitted to the public, than he was abused in news-papers, by Publicola, by the delegate of Anne-Arundel, by a scandalous anonymous letter writer, and by several others, not to be named. He then supported his opinions by a pamphlet, the success of which exceeded his most sanguine expectation. Trusting entirely to the force of his reasons, and taking up the question on the true construction of the constitution, he quoted no other book or authority of any kind. But, as many of you thought the opposite doctrine countenanced by the principles of several admired writers and patriots; and, as he had ever found authority more prevalent than reason, he determined to consult books, and quote authority. He had never perused the essays on government, of either Sydney, or Locke. From passages in Publicola's first address, he had supposed them advocates for the right of the people of England to control their representatives, and was utterly astonished to find both these writers pointedly in his own favour. He therefore published again, to detect misrepresentation, and to turn against his opponents those very authors, which vaguely they had quoted against him. Hence sprung the rage and clamour of Publicola. Like a foaming champion he has rushed forth, regardless of hazards, provided he could annoy the man who had neither wronged nor wished to wrong him, and who, at that time, was concerned for his delusion. He did not, however, think proper to answer the pamphlet of Aristides, nor the excellent essay in Mr. Goddard's paper. On a vain supposition, that Aristides had mistaken the meaning of Sydney,* he reproaches him with not understanding what he read. Examine the passage again.

"Every county does not make a distinct body, having in itself a sovereign power, but is a member of that great body, which comprehends the whole nation. It is not therefore for Kent, or Sussex, Lewes, or Maidstone, but for the whole nation, that the members chosen in these places are sent to parliament. And though it be fit for them, as friends and neighbours, so far as may be to hearken to the opinion of electors, for the information of their judgments, and to the end, that what they shall say may be of more weight, when every body is known not to speak his own thoughts only, but those of a greater number of men; yet they are not strictly and properly obliged to give an account of their actions to any, unless the whole body of the nation for which they serve, and who are equally concerned in their decisions, could be assembled. *This being impracticable,* the only punishment, to which they are subject, if they betray their trust, is scorn, infamy, hatred, and an assurance of being rejected, when they shall again seek the same honour, &c."

I still maintain my construction to be right. When Mr. Sydney asserts, that a thing cannot be done, he has more sense than to suppose the people have a right to do it. Is there ought in this, or any other passage to shew, that, if a majority of counties and boroughs should join in one letter of instruction, the whole house of commons would be bound implicitly to obey it? Aristides might here retort; but every body knows that Publicola and he are both learned enough to understand plain language.

---

* On the mistake occasioned by Publicola's first address, it was natural for Aristides to speak of Mr. Sydney, in terms of disapprobation. He was not fully apprized of Mr. Sydney's merit, on finding he had wronged him, it was natural for a man of candour to make a concession, although he could address only the manes of the injured patriot. To acknowledge voluntarily, an error, is the part of a liberal soul, and never yet dishonoured a character truly to be respected. But a proud, arrogant man, will commit an hundred wrongs, sooner than attone [sic] for one.

The dispute is not concerning the propriety of the peoples voluntarily offering their opinions, advice, or remonstrance. In times to come, perhaps these may operate as seasonable checks to arbitrary proceedings. When genuine, and fairly obtained, who is there will dare to despise them? When obtained in the manner lately essayed, on a subject, whereon the people in general never pretended to be competent to decide, who is there of a proper turn of mind that will hold himself bound to obey? Take the following passage from Mr. Hume, an author whose *political* essays have been ever greatly respected.

"The political controversy, with regard to instructions, is a very frivolous one, and can never be brought to any decision, as it is managed by both parties. The country party pretend not, that a member is absolutely bound to follow instructions, as an ambassador, or general, is bound by his orders, and that his vote is not to be received in the house, but so far as it is conformable to them. The court party again pretend not that the sentiments of *the people* ought to have no weight with each member; much less that he ought to despise the sentiments of *those* he represents, and with whom he is more particularly connected. And if their sentiments be of weight, why ought they not to express them? The question then is only concerning the degrees of weight, which ought to be placed on instructions, &c. &c."

I dare believe no man of the least consideration in England ever supposed, if instructions were not obeyed, that the people had a right to dissolve the government. The dispute in England is indeed frivolous; but our dispute is of a different cast; because Publicola expressly denies, that delegates or senators have a right to vote against them, or that the legislature can decline passing a law, dictated by a majority of counties. If you can adopt his sentiments, the consequence will be this. Either the disobedience of the legislature may produce convulsions in the state, or, by the instrumentality of the people, a single man of great popular talents, or a small combination of such men, may carry measures against the united wisdom of the legislature.

That I may not again innocently be charged with fabricating assertions for Publicola, take his own words.

"The right of the people to instruct their delegates had always appeared to me an essential safeguard of public liberty. I not only read of it, as a speculative opinion of individuals in their closets, but history told me of its being actually exercised in all governments, and all countries, where the people had a share in legislation by delegates or representatives."

If his meaning be, that in all governments, the legislature of which consists either wholly, or in part, of representatives, laws have been passed agreeably to the commands of the people at large, precluding the deliberations of the legislature, I demand a few instances. Can he give any instances whatever, where, in matters of ordinary legislation the people have interfered by positive commands? Is there any instance in history, where the right of the people to lay their commands has been recognized by the legislature? I have before called on my opponents for any known book on the English constitution, or law, or even a resolve of the commons, giving to instructions of the people the force of absolute commands. I repeat my challenge; and I challenge them to produce any approved book, asserting, that, in a government by representation, where there is an express compact delegating the powers of legislation, without an express reservation in the people, the legislature is notwithstanding bound by the instructions or commands of the people.

The sentiments of writers respecting other governments, Aristides has indeed always thought perfectly immaterial, in the construction of our own solemn compact, or constitution. For, after all that has been written, there never was a question more simple than the following: *Can the people of Maryland rightfully interfere in matters of* ordinary legislation, *and oblige each, or either branch, to pass a law contrary to their own judgments?* This question, in the outset I maintained to be determinable, only by the declaration of rights, and the form of government. These two instruments, taken together, constitute the great original compact, whereby the whole society has solemnly agreed, and interchangably plighted their faith, to be governed agreeably to its provisions. In this compact, nothing at all is said of instructions; but a good deal about *freedom of speech, liberty of the press, and right of petitioning.* Publicola does not assert, that it is impossible for the people, by any compact whatever, to delegate the whole power of legislation. He at last resorts to that shift, which I looked for in the beginning. It is (*so far as I understand*) to support his doctrine by a strained construction of the 4th article of the declaration.

"That all persons invested with the legislative or executive powers of government are the trustees of the public, and, as such, accountable for their conduct. Wherefore, whenever the ends of government are perverted, and public liberty manifestly endangered, *and all other means of redress are ineffectual, the people may, and of right ought to reform the old, or establish a new government.*"

The doctrine contained in this article, is evidently borrowed from Mr. Locke, who considers it as an express or implied article of all

* *By matters of ordinary legislation are meant laws, providing for the support of government, the administration of justice, the correction of manners, protection of property, regulation of commerce and finance; in short all laws respecting domestic concerns, which the constitution authorises.*

original compacts; whereas subsequent writers have more justly considered, that, for such infractions of the compact, by the government, the people are no longer bound; but may immediately exercise their power, in making a new compact. But, whether the right of interference, on the grand occasions mentioned in the article be founded on, or be superior to the compact, no writer of established reputation has ever construed it into a right of prescribing to the legislature, or considered the disobedience of the legislature to the mandate of the people as a perversion of the ends of government.

In support of my doctrines, I again refer you to Mr. Locke, whom Publicola has the modesty to tell me, I do not understand—

"When the society hath placed the legislative in any assembly of men, to continue in them, or their successors, with direction and authority for providing such successors: the legislative can never revert to the people whilst that government lasts; because, having provided a legislative with power to continue for ever, they have *given up their political power* to the legislative, and cannot resume it. But, if they have set limits to the duration of their legislative, and made this supreme power in any person, or assembly, only temporary; or else when by the miscarriages of those in authority, it is forfeited; upon the forfeiture, or, at the determination of the time set, it reverts to the society, and the people have a right to act as supreme, and continue the legislative in themselves; or erect a new form, or, under the old form, place it in new hands, as they think good."

I will now explicitly lay down the doctrine, from which I have never swerved, and which, I am persuaded, you will think resting on too solid foundations, to be shaken by the efforts of a man, who would make equal liberty consist in the peoples not being bound even by the government which they have chosen themselves.

1. When an actual original compact of government has been entered into by the people of any country, by themselves, or their representatives, chosen for that express purpose, that compact is binding, not only on the original framers, but on all persons, who shall thereafter become citizens of the state; every citizen has a right to have that compact inviolably preserved; and on all occasions, the true construction of it is to govern. All power indeed flows from the people; but the doctrine, that the power actually at all times resides in the people, is subversive of all government and law.

2. In Maryland, exists an original compact, containing a complete system of government, except where alterations have taken place, agreably to the regulations and principles, therein contained. This compact defines the rights of the people, and ascertains with precision, the powers delegated to the three several departments of government.

Wherefore *during the existence of the said compact,* there can be rightfully exercised no powers whatever, except those therein mentioned and defined.

3. By this compact, the whole power of legislation, restricted by certain regulations, is committed to two distinct bodies of men, chosen at frequent stated periods. Without the consent of both these, no law can be framed; and either may reject that, which is proposed by the other.

4. The happiness of the whole, being the declared end of this compact; and the power of legislation being delegated to promote the general good; the legislature is bound, on all occasions, to respect the sentiments of the people; and so far as in wisdom they can, to gratify their wishes. But, on no occasion is the legislature precluded from deliberation, with respect to their own acts; or bound to pass laws contrary to its own judgment.

5. There is an express article of this compact, (and without it the right of the people would have been the same) that when the ends of government are perverted, and other means of redress are ineffectual, the people may either dissolve the present government, or suspend, and reform it. It was impracticable to enumerate cases, where the interference of the people will be proper. Of this the people are to judge. But, as such interference amounts to a dissolution, or suspension of the compact, it is not intended by the compact to take place, unless the ends of government be *really* perverted, their liberty *really* endangered, and all other means of redress *really* ineffectual. The people, nevertheless, or any part of them, may, at any time, disclose to the legislature their wants, wishes, and sentiments. That every miscarriage of the legislature, will authorise the interference of the people; was never intended, because most mistakes may be corrected by the successors of the legislature; but any measure that puts the liberties of the people to an immediate hazard, is a proper reason for interference.

6. The legislature being chosen by the people at stated periods, its whole proceedings are published, to the end, that the people may determine whether their trustees have merited a continuence in office.

7. Upon the whole therefore, when a matter, proposed by one branch, is rejected by the other, there is no express or implied provision, that upon an appeal by the proposing branch, the people may oblige the other branch to adopt the proposition. Such a provision would have been repugnant to the institution of two distinct branches, independent of each other, and acting as mutual checks. In a government by representation, where the powers of legislation are delegated, without any express reservation of the people, the legislative possesses the only

power of making laws; and no law can be made by the people, without a suspension, or dissolution of the compact.

The essential difference between Aristides and Publicola is, therefore, only with respect to the weight of instructions. The former considers them merely on the footing of information, remonstrance, or advice; the latter as commands from a principal to his agent, or a master to his servant. Again Publicola not only considers them as positive commands; but thinks, in case of disobedience, the people, consistently with the true meaning of the 4th article of rights, may dissolve the compact. Aristides is of opinion, that, so long as the legislature keeps within the bounds of the constitution, the people ought not to dissolve the compact; and that no disobedience of the legislature can justify a dissolution of the government; unless such refusal shall manifestly spring from the corruption of their trustees, and manifestly endanger liberty, and circumstances will not admit the adoption of other means of redress. All these things must concur: otherwise, the dissolution of the government is a violation of the rights of every individual, not consenting to the measure. I will just put a single case, where an immediate suspension or dissolution would be proper—a certain prospect of a powerful invasion, and the legislature's declining all means of placing the state in a posture of defence.

Aristides conceives likewise, that a practice of frequent interference would totally destroy all energy in the government, and all spirit of obedience in the people; and that, in a little time, we should be in such a state of anarchy and confusion, as would be most favourable to insidious designs on our liberties. For these reasons, he has called the doctrine of his opponents, wicked, slavish, and absurd. The narrow limits of a news-paper will not permit him to go over the ground already trodden. He therefore refers to his former publications.

Publicola's supposition that the case of the United Netherlands, or of Switzerland, is in point, is truly admirable.

Aristides has again got hold of a passage in Mr. Sydney, to which he solicits your attention.

"I believe, that the powers of every county, city, and borough of England are regulated by the general law, to which they have all consented, and by which they are all made members of one political body. This obliges them to proceed with their delegates, in a manner, different from that which is used in the Netherlands, or in Switzerland. Amongst these, every province, city or canton, making a distinct body, independent from any other, and exercising the sovereign power within itself, looks upon the rest as allies, to whom they are bound only by such acts, as they themselves have made, and when any new thing, not comprehended in them, happens to arise, they oblige their delegates to give them an account of it, and retain the power of determining those matters in themselves."

Mr. Sydney's plain meaning in this, and the former recited passage, which are connected in the original, is this. "A single state in the United Netherlands, or in Switzerland, being an entire distinct body, may bind its deputies, at a general meeting of the states. But a county in England cannot bind its representatives in a parliament; because they are at the same time the representatives of the whole kingdom. Nor can these representatives be bound by the whole body of the people; because the whole body of the people cannot be assembled to do any act under the known law or constitution."

Mr. Sydney might have added the following consideration, which from him might possibly have opened Publicola's eyes.—When a single state in the United Netherlands instructs its deputies, the instructions are given by the government of that state, to which these deputies are indeed strictly agents. If Publicola can shew any thing plausible with respect to these states, it must be, that in the domestic legislation of a single state, the people may bind their delegates by instructions. But if he could even shew this, I would then ask him. Do not the people exercise the right, by virtue of a particular law, or by an express article in the form of their government? At any rate, this simple distinction may be made. The deputies of the United States in the Netherlands are bound by the instructions of their respective *governments*, because such is their particular constitution or uniform custom. The legislature of Maryland, is not bound by instructions of the *people*, because the constitution does not authorise them; nor has the thing been ever yet practised.

Mr. Sydney, in the warmth of controversy, has dropt some general expressions, which Publicola has gathered as the most precious pearls. Mr. Sydney was contending against Sir Robert Filmer, a man wicked enough to assert, that things [kings?] have a divine right, that the people must always submit, and that government is, in no case answerable to the people. Mr. Sydney contends, like a *true patriot* that all government springs from the people, and is instituted for the general good. What! (says he in effect) shall the whole people be considered as the property of one man, or set of men, and made for their use? Say rather, that they are the servants of the people. I take what servant I please, &c. &c. &c.

The whole doctrine which I have all along endeavoured to inculcate, is reducible to this single proposition. In every free government, founded on a real compact, neither the governing nor the governed, are to be considered on the footing of either master or slave; they both are possessed of certain rights, which ought to be held inviolable; and the true spirit of the compact must, on all occasions, be considered the law of the land.

Would to Heaven, my beloved countrymen, it had fallen to the lot of a man, more independent in his circumstances, to become the marked object of a base revenge, for inculcating principles essential to the happiness of society. Deserted by the men, from whom I *reasonably expected* support, I sincerely wish, that no future occasions may require similar exertions. The sense of duty must indeed ever impel me to act the part of a zealous and watchful guardian;—but the small services, I have hitherto been able to perform, have been attended with sacrifices greater than, under all circumstances, my duty demanded.

Annapolis   ARISTIDES

William Paca to Alexander Contee Hanson
JUNE 22, 1787

TO ARISTIDES

"WHEN ASSERTION, you say, is substituted for sound argument and pointed authority; when that assertion is mingled with invective, and slander is vented in general terms; when at one moment Publicola maintains almost the doctrine of Aristides, and at the next changes his ground; when he uses words suited to mislead, and then taxes Aristides with indecency and falsehood for not conceiving him aright; the labour of pursuing him appears almost endless."—What shall I reply, or how defend myself against such a catalogue of charges? Shall I content myself with pleading not guilty? or shall I ask Aristides where it is he finds, that to depart from all truth and decorum, is one of the privileges of a judge of the general court?—I have not, Sir, changed my ground; if you knew the subject, and had capacity to handle it, you would not say so; nor have I abused or slandered you, nor sought words to mislead you, nor taxed you with falsehood for not conceiving me aright. I have borne your vain and extravagant effusions with an exemplary patience. But is there no indecency or indelicacy in charging Publicola's defence of the right of instructing as a *seditious and pestilent* doctrine? Is there no calumny, Aristides, no personal reflection, no slander in making observations in a news-paper, addressed to the people of Maryland, and calculated to brand the advocates for the right of instructing as *promoters of sedition and pestilent fellows?* After such freedoms and liberties of speech, what right have you to complain of any animadversions that border upon severity? Do not be mistaken; when a *judge* shall forget his duty, dignity and station, and become a pert, petulant *partisan*, to attack the rights of his fellow-citizens, there shall be one, at least, who will detect and expose his mischievous principles, and repel the assault.

You charge your enemies with devoting you and your *house* to destruction. To construe a contradiction of your political opinions into a personal enmity and opposition, we can readily comprehend as a ridiculous attempt to excite pity and compassion. But what you meant by your *house*, I own I was among the number who for a long time were extremely puzzled to understand. I had heard of mercantile *houses*, and thought at first you had been one of a commercial company, and meant to charge me with devoting your company to destruction. But this it seems was not the case. I had heard too of legislatures, consisting of different branches, being distinguished by *houses*, and recollected the *house* of lords, the *house* of commons, the upper *house*, and lower *house* of assembly. But neither of these could be your *house*. I was then told that the nobility in Europe distinguished their families by *houses*, and I was reminded of the *house* of York, and of the *house* of Lancaster, &c. But I presumed neither of these could be your *house*. In the further prosecution of my inquiries, I recollected to have heard, that during the old government, the upper *house* originated a bill to confer titles of nobility; it passed in that *house*, but on being sent down to the lower *house*, it was there rejected. This bill proposed to confer a variety of titles; there was to be the *Duke of Chesapeake*, the *Duke of Susquehanna*, the *Duke of Patowmack*, &c. The *Earl of Sassafras*, the *Earl of Choptank*, the *Earl of Pocomoke*, &c. *Lord Patuxent, Lord Severn, Lord Patapsco, Lord Gunpowder, Lord Magothy*, &c. Had this bill passed into a law, the noble distinction by *houses*, would have been familiar to our ears; we should have had enough of *houses*. Every day would have told us perhaps of the *house* of Chesapeake, the *house* of Pocomoke, the *house* of Magothy, &c. But as this bill did not pass, and we have no such things as dukes, earls or lords, it is a mighty foolish vanity, Aristides, to assume their noble distinctions, and I appeal to your own judgement, whether such affected pomposity is not much more characteristic of the folly of a *prig*, than of the wisdom of a *judge*.

You have obliged us with a law of Athens, as a justification for your late *extra judicial* opinions and judgments in the news-papers; which law it seems considers every man as a *traitor* who remains *inactive* during *civil commotions* or *treasonable combinations*. And so, Aristides, the adjournment of the house of delegates, to take the sense of their *constituents*, was a *civil commotion* or *traitorous combination* and they who advocated the measure, and the right of instructing, are *domestic enemies*. And hence, I suppose, your animated exertions— in news-papers! But, Sir, is there no *slander* in this quotation and application of the law of Athens?

I would ask, what *active part* the governor and council took in the late *civil commotion* as you are pleased to call it? I know of none; therefore, by your application of the law of Athens, they are *traitors*. And what *active part* did the chief justice, the chancellor, and the judges of the court of appeals take in the affair? I know of none. They too then are *traitors*. Good Lord! What would have become of the government of this country had it not been for the wisdom and patriotism of Aristides! what a pity the general assembly, in consideration of his services, would not accept of his offer, and elect him a deputy to the convention at Philadelphia.

But if your pen did not contradict your heart, if you really considered the late adjournment as a civil commotion, and the right of instructing a *seditious, pestilent* doctrine, how comes it that you never exercised the powers of your office? You were armed with competent authority, and you were bound by oath to execute it. But instead of acting with the resolution of a judge against *domestic enemies*, you pusillanimously shrink from your duty and elevated station, and with wonderful composure and facility sink down into a contemptible *guardian to protest in news papers*; and there whine and blubber that you are "*deserted*, and become a marked object for a *base revenge*."

Having condemned my defence of the right to instruct as a pestilent doctrine, and marked me for a promoter of sedition and your enemy, I ought, perhaps, to thank you for proceeding to charge me, in as delicate a manner as possible, with being a *Cateline* or *Cethegus*. And pray, Aristides, what are you? A patriot no doubt; for you tell the people you are their "zealous and watchful guardian;" and then you address them so often, and publish doctrines so essential, you say, to their happiness! and then you tell them you make such sacrifices for their good! and then you are so affectionate! and you tell them you *love* them! and you call them your *beloved——my beloved countrymen— my beloved countrymen!*—When Judas Iscariot combined to destroy his lord and master, he covered his wicked design with an affected display of the tenderest affection, and in the moment of executing his horrid treachery, he hailed him master, and embraced and kissed him. When you, Aristides, conspire to break down one of the best guards which your fellow citizens possess for their rights and liberties, you assume the same disguise, and wear the same mask, and while you plunge the dagger, you smile in their faces, and hail them *beloved countrymen, my beloved countrymen!*

You never, you say, till after my publication, perused the essays on government of either Sydney or Locke. I really thought so; and this accounts for your understanding neither of them; and I believe you are the only *judge* in the United States who never read Sydney and Locke on government.

But when you stooped at last to consult these authorities, you were utterly astonished to find them both pointedly in your favour; and then you again published to detect misrepresentation, and to turn against Publicola the authors he had cited.

And so Sydney is pointedly in your favour; unfortunate Sydney! Judge Jeffries butchered and murdered his person; you Aristides, butcher and murder his fame, his doctrines and his principles. But how do you turn Sydney against me? Why by again citing his passage respecting the force of instructions from a *particular county*, and then telling the people that all that Sydney says in the passages I cited on the *national right* to instruct, when the people associate as a body, is the mere warmth of *controversy!*

This indeed is a turning of Sydney, and topsy turvey too; but it is a turning of himself against himself, and not against me. And now Aristides, suppose I was to adopt your principle of *turning*, and *turn* Sydney upon *you*. But how you may ask? Why by telling you, that what he says in the passage you cite respecting the force of instructions from a particular county, he meant for a *joke!*—

But it seems the question in England about instructions is a *frivolous* one. And who says so, Aristides? I beg pardon, you cite Mr. Hume. God help us! and is Mr. Hume and such writers the sources from whence a judge of Maryland should draw his *political creed*? How different from Hume is the language of Sydney. He speaks of the right as essential and sacred; to deprive a people of it, he says, is to act upon the principles of *piracy and robbery*, and to violate the laws of God and nature.

To give the right of instructing the *force* of a *command*, you allege, will be productive of the following consequence: either disobedience will produce convulsions, or by the instrumentality of the people, a single man, of great popular talents, or a small combination of such men, may carry measures against the united wisdom of the legislature.

You consider, Sir, only one side of the question. Admit for a moment, that the people are deprived of this right. What then will be the consequence? Both branches may turn, when they please, their backs upon the complaints and grievances of the people; and the people, to obtain redress, must hazard a *revolution* and the *halter*.—Besides, being thus above the reach and control of the people during the periods for which they are respectively chosen, either or both branches might become despotic, or by the instrumentality of the one, or both, a single man, of great popular talents, or a small combination of such men, might destroy the government, establish a tyranny, and make the people slaves.

The right of instructing, you say, leads to licentiousness; the taking it away from the people, I say, leads to despotism and tyranny. And as there is less probability of the peoples destroying themselves by licentiousness, than of rulers, delegates, and senators, becoming despots and tyrants; the right of instructing ought to be sacredly and inviolably preserved. And hence in all governments where the people participate in legislation, this right has ever existed, and been maintained by every patriot as an essential safe-guard of public liberty, and never was questioned but by fools, sycophants, and the partisans of power, till you, Aristides, commenced your opposition.—

But you challenge me to produce instances of governments in which this right of instructing is acknowledged. I refer you to the English government; the British government; the United Netherlands; and, on the authority of Mr. Sydney, I refer you to all the governments he mentions upon this subject, and which at that time admitted a representation of the people by delegates, viz. France, Spain, the states of Languedoc and Brittany, the Diets of Germany, Denmark, Sweden, Poland and Bohemia; and I refer you to the governments of the colonies before the revolution, particularly the government of Maryland; and I refer you to a pointed decision during our *conventions* in the case of the delegates of Anne-Arundel county, who receiving instructions touching the government to be established, and disapproving the same, resigned their seats, and were afterwards re-elected, with different powers. In all these governments, while they existed, the right of instructing was invariably maintained and exercised.

But you say, you have also turned Mr. Locke against me, and as effectually I admit as you have done Sydney. In all your publications you affect to consider the *right of instructing* on the footing of the *right of legislating*. And then you cite Locke to prove that the powers of legislation can never revert to the people but on a dissolution of the government. Wherefore, you conclude, the *right to instruct* cannot exist while the government is in force.

When Mr. Locke says that the powers of legislation can never revert to the people but upon a dissolution of government, it is clear he means those powers which the people possessed *individually*, and exercised *independently* and *exclusively* of each other, in a state of nature, before they established a civil government. But the right of instructing is founded on the *national* and *collected* voice of the people.

Now, Aristides, exert yourself, and prove if you can, that for a people to exercise the right of instructing in their *collective* and *national* capacity, is to resume *individually* the *powers of legislation,* and to exercise them *independently* and exclusively of each other, as in a state of nature, before the establishment of civil government. But this is impossible, and yet Locke is quoted to maintain it. I hope, Sir, you are now satisfied that you do not understand either Sydney or Locke.

The right *occasionally* to *instruct* a legislature, is as compatible with civil government, as the right *periodically* to *elect* a legislature. But to exercise *individually* the powers of legislation, and *exclusively* and *independently*, as in a state of nature, is totally incompatible with every form and principle of a civil government. Well therefore may Locke say, that such powers can never revert but on a dissolution of government.

The simple question you say is this, can the people of Maryland interfere in matters of *ordinary* legislation, and oblige either or both branches to pass a law contrary to their own judgments? But why, Aristides, limit the question to matters of *ordinary* legislation? One would think you admitted the right in matters of *extraordinary* legislation. To your question I answer and say, that if the people find either or both branches *abusing* their powers, or *misapplying* them, even in matters of *ordinary* legislation, they may, if they think the *abuse* or *misapplication* requires it, immediately interfere by remonstrances and instructions; and as the people are the *sole judges* whether there has been an *abuse* or *misapplication* of the powers of legislation, both branches are bound to submit and act according to instructions. And I really should consider it as IMPUDENCE IN THE EXTREME, for either branch or both to set up a claim of *rightful authority* to over-rule the *national voice,* when *clearly* expressed and *decidedly* communicated.

You have been pleased to put a case in which you admit a suspension or dissolution of government would be proper, "a certain prospect of a powerful invasion, and the legislature's declining all means of placing the state in a posture of defence."

I beg your attention to a few observations on the case you put. Who are the judges, Aristides, of the *certainty* of this invasion? And who are the judges whether the legislature has declined the means of placing the state in a posture of defence? You will say, no doubt, *the people;* for on the case put it is admitted the legislature are *delinquents,* and consequently cannot be judges.

But what if it was stated in the case, that the *delegates* were for measures of defence, but the *senate* were of a different opinion, under an impression there was no certainty of an invasion? Are the people still the *judges?* They must, Sir, be the *judges,* or you must maintain that the *senate* have a right to over-rule both the people and their immediate delegates. But if the people are the *judges*, then the judgment of the senate, in the case put, is to be disregarded, and you say the people may suspend or dissolve the government.

Let us now consider for a moment the *blessedness* of your doctrine, and the *pestilence* of mine.

You say the people on the case put may *suspend* or *dissolve* the government. What, Aristides, *suspend* or *dissolve* the government in the moment of a *powerful invasion!* How are troops to be raised, officers appointed, arms purchased, magazines provided, taxes imposed, and money raised and collected? Your doctrine, Sir, no doubt, exhibits a great display of political talents, but it delivers up the people and the country a prey to the invader.

And now for the pestilence of my doctrine. I contend that the peoples right of instructing is and ought to be considered as the constitutional doctrine of the state, having the effect of a command, if the people think proper to speak in that style. And what would be the consequence of it in the case you put? The people instead of *suspending* or *dissolving* the government in the moment of a powerful invasion, would direct and instruct the senate to co-operate with the delegates in measures of defence: the senate would receive the instructions as a constitutional authority, and submit to them; and thus the government would be preserved, proper measures taken for defence, and the people and country saved from ruin and destruction.

But, Aristides exclaims, this is a *pestilent* doctrine; it is a *force* upon the senate; it is a *force* upon their judgments; it is exercising the *powers of legislation.*

And pray, which of our doctrines operates as the *greater force* upon the judgment of the senate? And which is the most assuming of the right of legislation? If to instruct is to over-rule the *judgment* of the senate, and amounts to legislation, surely to *suspend* or *dissolve* the government, *against the judgment* of the senate, is to exert a much *greater force* upon them, and amounts more completely to a resumption of the powers of government.

Having admitted the right of the people to judge in the case of an invasion whether the legislature employ their powers properly or not; and if not, to over-rule the judgment of the senate, and even of both branches, and to suspend or dissolve the government, I would now, Sir, ask you, what it is that forbids the people from exercising the like power *in all cases* where they shall form the like judgment of the conduct of the legislature? And I submit to your serious consideration, whether it is not clearly for the interest and happiness of the state, that the people should possess and exercise the right of remonstrating and instructing, *before* they proceed to the last extremity of suspending and dissolving the government?—

But you want no other ground to destroy the right of instructing than our compact, constitution, and government. "This compact, you say, defines the rights of the people, and ascertains with precision the powers delegated, &c. Wherefore during the *existence of the compact,* there can be rightfully exercised no powers whatever except those therein mentioned and defined." And you have said, the right of instructing is not therein mentioned, and so does not exist.

I deny, Sir, the position, that during the existence of our compact no powers or rights can be exercised, but those that are therein mentioned and defined. I maintain all powers and rights may be exercised, which the people possessed before the compact, and which are not therein mentioned, parted with, and *transferred.* I maintain that the right to instruct a *deputy,* or *agent* or *trustee,* was a natural right *paramount* the *compact,* and not being therein mentioned or *transferred,* it still exists, and may be rightfully exercised.

When America resisted the tyranny of Great Britain, the then colonies had charters, compacts, constitutions and governments. Did congress rest the rights of America upon these charters or compacts? Or did they deduce them from a higher source, *the laws of God and nature?* Did any *patriot* or *judge* broach the absurd doctrine, or make the absurd position, that the people could exercise no other rights or powers, except those mentioned and defined in their respective charters, compacts and constitutions? Read, Sir, the proceedings of congress, be assured it will be no imputation upon you to trust *more* to the authority of books and the writings of others, and less to your own powers and faculties.

But you admit the *right of instructing* so far as to give *advice and information*; this, no doubt is a great *kindness* to the people; but where shall we find even this right *mentioned or defined* in our compact? No matter that; you are a *judge,* and you so decide.

Again. By our constitution and government delegates are to be chosen annually to congress; and the legislature claims and exercises the right of instructing and binding them by such instructions. But according to your position, the legislature has no such right; for there is not one word about it in the compact; it is neither mentioned nor defined.—

You see, Aristides, if the *compact* is to destroy the right of instructing, it lies upon you to shew that the right is *parted from* and *transferred* by the compact; if it is not *mentioned* in the *compact,* it cannot be *parted with* or *transferred,* but remains with the people; for I have already observed, that in a state of nature, antecedent to government, it was a natural right to instruct a delegate, deputy, agent or trustee. But independently of this ground, the very relationship between principal and delegate, implies and maintains the right.

You complain that you are *deserted*. I think I understand you; you stood, you mean to say, by the *senate*; and the *senate* have not stood by *you*. You were certainly thought *a laborious partisan* for them; as such you at least deserved their thanks. But when you aspired to be a *deputy* to the convention, your ambition took too lofty a flight, and they could not gratify you. A person may be well qualified for a *partisan* in a news paper, but not for a *deputy* to the convention. A deputy ought *at least* to be *acquainted* with the rights and liberties of his fellow-citizens, and to respect and regard them. But do not despair, Aristides; the *senate* may remember you in due season, and reward you for your *services*. At present perhaps they have taken a *personal disgust* to you; for you know in human affairs it sometimes so happens, that we love the treason but *hate* the *traitor*.

Annapolis   PUBLICOLA

Alexander Contee Hanson to William Paca
JULY 12, 1787

ARISTIDES TO PUBLICOLA

IF YOU POSSESSED the vast superiority, you affect, your treatment of Aristides would be different. The experience of almost half a century might have taught you, that, in controversies like ours, the world ever considers clamour and reviling as signals of defeat. Although you manfully persist in calling him the partisan of power, and insinuate, that he looked for some kind of compensation from the senate, you have assigned no reason in support of the suggestion. Unless they shall succeed in their aristocratic views, it will be difficult for them to reward him, so long, as he shall remain obnoxious to the other more numerous, and more powerful branch. But one eminent proof of your "exemplary patience" is an attempt to lay him under the displeasure of both branches. The meaning of that passage in my last address, which you so ingeniously misconstrue, needs no explanation to those, who are acquainted with the proceedings alluded to. On account of his recent "*exertions*," and for no other reason, as he believes, was his character traduced, in a place, where he had no opportunity of defending it. This was done too, at a most critical time; and the men, who thought as he did, on the great political questions, which called forth those *exertions*, sat by with the most frigid indifference. Perhaps the term "given up," or sacrificed, might have been more proper, as in some measure, denoting the inferiority of Aristides. Be that as it may, the *desertion,* or giving up, or sacrifice, affected him far more, than the open enmity of his prosecutors. And yet neither of them affected him so far, as to produce "whining or blubbering."

You have not scrupled to assert, that he offered himself as a delegate to the convention. I shall not inquire what are *your* "privileges." I deny, that either directly, or indirectly, I ever made the offer. Your eagerness to depreciate my character may be very commendable, but it has induced you to mention an affair, which, from a regard to your own reputation, and the honour of the state, you ought, if possible, to bury in oblivion. What circumstance is there relative to that affair, which can dishonour Aristides? As he does not mean to write a pretty general satire, he will content himself with remarking, that the appointment was subsequent to his opposition against paper, and that every method was, by some men, practised to prevent his election; whilst on that, as on every other occasion, he disdained to use the vile acts of intrigue.

My non-appointment to that arduous ticklish employment, I consider as a circumstance favourable to me in a variety of lights. One consolation is that I shall save the effusion of that precious cash, which could be as illy spared from my "house," as from many other noble houses. Do you take it as a settled point, that every failure at an election must render a man unhappy? I ought perhaps to return you thanks, for consoling me, in pretty nearly the same manner, as the affectionate FREEMAN, in the sadness of his soul, administered comfort to his beloved friend, the associate of his youth and manhood, his faithful counsellor, and the reviser of all his productions, intended for the press, save only one. "Regard them not, thou beloved of my heart! thou mirror of patriots, thou perfect pattern of every political moral, and christian virtue! What though, after manfully *standing by* Annapolis, its citizens have turned their backs upon thee! thou art now leaving this ungrateful city. Peradventure *in the dispensations of Providence,* thou mayst have it in thy power to return them *evil for evil.*"

Another mark of your exemplary patience is your entertaining comment on the word "house," "that Jemmy Twitcher should 'peach me, I own, surprised me." You here shine in a new light; for, amongst your manifold attributes, no man ever yet thought of enumerating humor and wit. Had I the pomposity of the mighty Ventosus, of the great Pomposo, or even of yourself, your comment might have been spared; because foreign from the dispute; because a plain man might well use "house" for "family," and because half a column is taken up in proving nothing but a determination, at all events, to load your

adversary with abuse. It would have been infinitely better to save yourself the fatigue of your learned researches; more especially, as the
laborious exercise of your fancy has not, in the slightest degree, soft-
ened your rancour. When a man jokes, there ought to be some appearance of good humor.

I had before heard of the old foolish proprietary scheme for
introducing into Maryland an order of nobility. Happily the good sense
of the people saw the matter in its true light. I am, however inclined
to believe, that, if the titles you mention, could be conferred, we might
probably hear something about the most illustrious, high, noble, and
puissant DUKE of WYE. But you are out, with respect to DUKES, EARLS,
and LORDS. You forget that such could not have been created. If they
could, the plan would, in all human probability, have succeeded to the
condign praise of the projector, the emolument of the Lord PARAMOUNT,
and the gratification of his trusty adherents. There were to have been,
alas! only such paltry things as POTENTATES, POTENTEES and POTENTESSES.
You thought there was some how or other, a good joke, and you had a
mind to tell it, "having a fine opportunity to bring it in." But, like
many other tellers of good jokes, you unluckily forget the cream of the
story.

A third mark of exemplary patience is your application of the
Athenian law. At first no civil officer had a right to meddle with politics.
It was next monstrous in a judge to interfere; because his whole time
should be devoted either to the administration of justice, or the study of
the law. Now forsooth the enormity of one officer's interference is
demonstrated by the passiveness and silence of the rest. With wonderful address my citation of the Athenian law is converted into a charge
of high treason against the governor and council, the chancellor, the
chief justice and the judges of appeals. With all these gentlemen nevertheless, I hope to remain on good terms. They will perceive that I
quoted this law merely on account of that salutary principle upon
which it was made, and which ought ever to prevail in all republican
governments. I never thought them under an obligation, to imitate my
conduct. I never once mentioned or alluded to them. My idea is, that
any of them may speak, write, or be silent, as inclination or judgment
may determine. They might not think the situation of our affairs to be
critical. I *did*. It appeared to me, that, although there was little danger
of the peoples interference in favour of an emission, it was of the last
importance to their future welfare to set them right, with respect to the
doctrines contained in their delegates address. In the discharge of my
official duty, I have always construed the constitution and laws upon
the plain principles of common sense. *I have ever reprobated arbitrary
or occasional constructions.* I knew of no law, under which that

address, the appeal, and the adjournment could be fairly construed into a crime punishable by the courts of justice. Besides, I considered a majority of the delegates as men acting under a full persuasion, that they were doing what was right. God knows, that in addressing the people, I wished not to expose their representatives, provided I could otherwise perform the part, to which I found myself strongly impeded.

My *exertions* were not indeed so *animated,* as the harangues at Chester mill, &c. and as certain debates in the house of delegates. My aim was to convey instruction; and he, that seeks it, will do well to prefer the perusal of a publication, written with care, and open to the examination of all the world, to the frothy, noisy declamation at public meetings. Of the former he may at leisure examine the arguments, divested of all ornament, and wanting those dangerous aids, derived from the personal influence of the orator, the force of look and gesture, the charms of utterance, and all "the pomp, pride, and circumstance" of glorious speechification. To men of sense and candour, Aristides will perhaps appear entitled to some credit, even if his doctrine be errone- ous, for his *"laborious exertions,"* and for pursuing the dictates of his conscience, at the hazard of interest, and with the certain prospect of provoking the indignation of interested, powerful, vindictive men. How is it, you dare to speak so contemptuously of news-papers, of all other publications the most proper for conveying general information? How often by their means have insidious views been exposed and defeated! How often have they kindled, far and wide, the flame of patriotism! Their importance is so well known, that I should expect objections to news-papers from a *partisan of power,* much sooner than from a friend to the people, and an assertor of liberty, and equal rights. It is true they do not always afford either entertainment or instruction, but they can seldom do harm. Is there any man, who has resorted to them oftener than Publicola? But Aristides has not only descended into news-papers. After charging with high treason the house of delegates, the executive and the judicial, "he pusillanimously shrinks from the duty and dignity of his elevated station," and suffers all those daring offenders to go at large. Alas! Publicola, how art thou shrunken and fallen!

> Mourn, mourn ye people! join them patriots all!
> In concert *"whine* and *blubber"* at his fall.
> How often, in that stadt-house, has he said,
> Curse on all laws, except what ye have made.
> *My people want—my people* did I say?
> My *masters order,* and ye *shall* obey.
> How oft, in list'ning raptures, have ye hung,
> And caught those glorious accents from his tongue!

"*You towering steeple*" echoed back the sound,
Whilst the glad throng their plaudits buzz'd around,
Blot from the calendar the fatal day!
He fell by curs'd "aristocratic sway."
Tho' sycophants and "partisans of power"
Deride your tears, and hail the lucky hour,
Come, all ye patriots! bear the plaintive call,
Whine for your leader, blubber one and all!

Accept, Publicola, these few elegiac lines, in return for your friendly consolatory remarks. But every thing you have said or written against Aristides, is nothing more than an opposition to his doctrines. If you have even a little deviated, Aristides began, and therefore has no right to complain of the poignancy of your satire. This kind of morality is as novel as your politics and logic. I did not, after all, mean to call any person "a pestilent fellow." I trust, that I have more sense and good manners. I did not charge you with high treason, or insurrection. I did not compare you to Catiline or Cethegus, and (if it will give you any satisfaction) I declare, that I do not think, such a comparison would be just.

Having said more than perhaps was necessary, in reply to the abusive part of your address, I proceed to speak fully to the very little you have said by way of argument.

In a genuine republic, there is no such political idea as that of master and servant, applied to the governing and governed. The idea of the people being masters is one of the most incongruous, and absurd, that ever entered into a human brain. Every person is subject to the constitution. This is the sovereign and the protector. This is the bond of union. And if in a regular system of government, there can be such a department as the *people having a constitutional legislative power, as a collective body, the constitution is its creator.

* The common and proper acceptation of the word "people" is all the inhabitants of a country, existing in the same society, and under the same laws. It comprehends the governing as well as the governed. By Mr. Locke, and from him by our declaration of rights, the word is used to signify either the governed as distinguished from the governing, or a majority of the individuals, bound by the compact. In each of these senses it is used, at different times. If by people be understood a collective body, as such, having certain powers and rights, as a part of the government, my idea is, that there can be no such thing, unless created by the compact. Should we ask some of those who are continuously acclaiming about the people, the people, what they mean by the people, it is possible the question might put them to a stand. Are the governor and council a part of this people, which may control the legislature? No. They are the servants of the legislature, as well as of the people. Are the judges, the other magistrates, and the rest of the civil list? They are the bloodsuckers of the people. The senate and the delegates cannot be a part of this people, from the nature of things. Is then the body of merchants? Surely not. They

That the people as a collective body, possess rights *"paramount"* the compact or institution of government, I will allow you the full credit of discovering. Notwithstanding you may have read Locke and Sydney before Aristides could read at all, if your pen and heart be in union, you never understood the whole of these, or other writers on government. You could not otherwise utter such jargon about *"paramount"* rights, not transferred by the compact, and the natural right of controling *"agents, deputies and trustees."* Admitting now, that, in a state of nature, an individual might have an agent, deputy, or trustee; how, in the name of every thing profound, was this agent deputy, or trustee, to be controled? In a state of nature, (if ever such there was) no man had any authority over another, except that which was temporary, and derived from superior cunning, or strength. Admitting again, that this agent, deputy or trustee, might be controled; who ever heard of the people, or a collective body, in the state of nature, having the right of controling their agents, deputies, or trustees? Suppose even this absurdity, that, in a state of nature, there was this people or collective body of individuals, who had the right of constituting, and controling, their agents, deputies or trustees. Let them still continue to control all those agents, deputies or trustees, which they had in the state of nature. Neither a house of delegates, nor a senate were among them. Besides if delegates and senators were amongst these agents, deputies or trustees, there is this further consideration. When the people entered into a compact of government, and thereby parted with the whole legislative power, although this natural right, which you talk of, be not mentioned in the compact, yet, as it is incompatible with the exercise of the legislative power, conferred on a body, or bodies of men, common sense must decide, that it is given up, as clearly, as if it had been mentioned.

You most erroneously imagine the constitutional legislature to be nothing more than agents, deputies or trustees. Suppose our compact had instituted a different form of government. It was debated in convention, whether there should not be three distinct branches of the legislature. Had the proposition been adopted, would you have called

---

are the enemies of the people, as much as the lawyers. They have quite distinct and opposite views and interests. Are the country gentlemen, and respectable landholders? These are your aristocratic gentry, the friends of the senate. Were the inquiry pursued, without disclosing the intent, we should probably find, at last, that what some zealous patriots mean by the people is in reality, (if they have any precise meaning at all) those who possess the least of knowledge, worth or property the most likely to be inflamed by declamatory harangues, to be driven forwards, and drawn back at the will of a few. By means of this engine, would these few manage the senate and the house of delegates. Blessed be Providence! Not a great many of our countrymen can be reckoned amongst this people. The attempts to convert them into this political engine have been most miserably defeated.

them all agents, deputies or trustees, subject to the orders of their principal? All good writers, that speak on the subject, agree, so far as I have read, that the compact confers rights as well as duties, on the governing, whilst you would make them mere tools of the governed. I demand whether the king of England be this agent, deputy or trustee, to be directed and controled by the people, his *masters*. Is even the house of peers under the constitutional control of these masters? Understand me now Publicola. The king of England would do wrong to fight the opinions of his people. Our legislature, I trust, will never presume to despise the wants, sentiments and wishes of the people. All that I have ever contended for, is, that this legislature, whilst it lasts, is not to be precluded from the freedom of deliberation. The general sense of a nation is supposed to be always right, and without doubt, it must ever, to a great degree, influence a wise and honest legislature that *knows it*.

If then the people, or a collective body of men, having rights as such, cannot exist without a compact of government, either express or implied; it is plain they can have no rights *"paramount"* the compact. After all, the dispute is precisely the same; although I flatter myself, its merits are now better understood. I say, that not even a majority of the individuals, composing the society, can rightfully control the constitutional legislature. You say, it can. *"I beg your pardon."* Your position, I believe, is, that a majority of voters can do it. Here is a fresh absurdity. For when you confine your *"paramount"* right to voters, may not paupers, and some others, well demand, why you do so, seeing that the right of suffrage is regulated by the compact only? If you correct yourself and admit paupers, I would then ask, how is it you admit to control the legislature those men, who have nothing to do, in electing the legislature?

Of tracing the absurd consequences of your doctrine there is no end. I have before said, that the right of the people to interfere, when the ends of government are perverted, &c. exist independent of the express provision in the compact. Perhaps, to anticipate cavil, it may be proper to explain myself, so as to reconcile the position, with the ideas just disclosed. I there use the word "people," in the same sense, as it is used by Locke, and, from him by the declaration of rights. I use it to signify a majority of the individuals bound by the compact—a number of individuals, entered into a compact of government, creating various political powers, connected with, or dependent on each other, so as to form a complete system, for the protection of their natural rights, not transferred, and of the rights thereby created. Should this compact be violated, in such a manner, as that the end of it is defeated, and it affords within itself no redress for the injury; the individuals, or several parties to the compact, (and those living under the government, and enjoying the rights of citizens, must be ever considered as parties) are then, independent of any force, which may render them otherwise, on the same footing, as before the compact, except certain rights of property, &c. They are again a number of independent persons, who must again form an entire new compact, or resume their old system, after correcting its errors, and abuses. If you must be gratified with the idea, that the constitutional legislature consists of agents, deputies, or trustees, I would then tell you, that the parties to the compact, *in which each has a right that ought not to be violated*, have agreed that those agents, deputies, or trustees, shall act according to their own judgments, so long as they shall act at all. I would ask you, whether even a number of merchants may not, by articles of agreement, enter into partnership, and place their affairs in the hands of agents, being a part of the company who are in all cases to act according to their own judgment, so long as the partnership continues.

Do you seriously assert, Publicola, or is it only one of your jokes, that Mr. Locke, in the passage I cited, means nothing more, than that whilst government lasts, the people cannot *"individually,"* exercise those powers, which in a state of nature they possessed, *"independently"* and *"exclusively"* of each other? I must again call your attention to that passage, first giving you the sentence which preceeds it.—

"The power that every *individual* gave the *society*, when he entered into it, can never revert to the individuals again, as long as the society lasts; but will always remain in the community; because, without this, there can be no community, or commonwealth, which is contrary to the original agreement."

In this sentence, he speaks directly as you say; but that sentence I had not quoted. He then goes on as I had before quoted.

"So also, when the *society* hath placed the legislative in any assembly of men, to continue in them, and their successors, with direction and authority for providing such successors, *the legislative can never revert to the people, whilst that government lasts*; because having provided a legislative with power to continue for ever, *they have given up their political power to the legislative, and cannot resume it*. But, if they have set limits to the duration of their legislative, and made the supreme power in any person, or assembly, only temporary; or else, when by the miscarriages of those in authority, it is forfeited; upon the forfeiture, or, at the determination of the time set, *it reverts to the society*; and the people have a right to act as supreme, and continue the legislative in themselves, or erect a new form, or under the old form, place it in new hands, as they shall think good."

If this be not a most pointed authority for the whole of my doctrine, and particularly *against* the right of the people to bind those to whom is delegated the power of legislation, then am I labouring under an unaccountable delusion. As you are so very *ingenious at construction,* I wonder indeed, that you have not twisted this passage into an authority *for* your doctrine. Locke has indeed called the *governing* deputies and trustees; but, in no passage of Locke, is there a single syllable about dictating to these deputies and trustees. In laying down his principles, he evidently had the government of England in his eye; writing, as he intimates himself, "to establish the throne of the great restorer, king William," and yet he says not a single word, in support of the right of the people to bind this deputy, king William, nor even the house of lords, nor even their immediate representatives, the house of commons.

To get over (as I imagine) something in the above quotation, that bears rather hard, you have made a distinction between binding by instructions, and exercising a legislative power. Now, Publicola, exert all your talents of wit, humor, railing or ratiocination. Consult your friend, before you publish. Prove if you can, that for the people to prescribe to both branches that to which these branches are obliged to give the sanction of law, be not, in effect, an exercise of legislative authority.

You intimate, that, having admitted the propriety of instructions, on the footing of opinion, remonstrance, or advice, I ought to have admitted them as binding and conclusive; one kind being no more mentioned in the compact, than the other. Wonderful indeed! Publicola can *advise* Aristides. To give an opinion or advice, is no exercise of authority. But I thank Heaven! Publicola cannot require obedience to his *commands.* It might even be said, that the constitution actually provides for the first kind of instructions, in securing the liberty of speech, the freedom of the press, and the right of petitioning. You say too, that our legislature dictates to our delegates in congress; and yet the constitution does not confer that authority expressly. There is little analogy between the cases. If there be any, it is in my favour. Delegates in congress may, in some respects, be considered as the deputies of their respective legislatures. In other respects, they are more. Where congress has authority under the articles of confederation to do any act, the ratification of the several states is not necessary, and therefore, if a delegate votes contrary to instructions, his state may recall and disgrace him; but still his vote remains good. Where congress is about an act, requiring ratification, delegates must be bound by instructions; because, in that case, they have no authority without the instructions.

My main position ever was, that the question between us depends on the construction of the compact. As reasoning from analogy always has weight, I called on you for instances in other governments by representation, either with, or without any provision in their constitution, or laws, where the people have prescribed to, and precluded the deliberations of, the legislature; or where the national voice, as you call it, has laid on the legislature its positive commands; or where the *legislature* has recognised the authority of the people to lay these commands. I called on you to produce any approved book, asserting, that, where an express compact delegates the power of legislation to a body, or bodies of men, without reserving any part of it to the people, this legislature shall notwithstanding, in all cases be bound by the directions of the people. In answer to this, you say, you refer me to the English government, the British government, the United Netherlands; and, on Sydney's authority, to many other governments. For the sake of common sense, give me one particular example, or one particular quotation from an author, such as I demand, or at once honestly allow, that you cannot.

You and I cannot agree upon the meaning of either Sydney or Locke. The case of the several states of the United Netherlands, instructing their deputies, is most pointedly distinguished, by Sydney, from the case of the people in an English county, instructing its representatives. You get over that, in a manner, becoming yourself. Aristides had imputed some *general* vague expressions in Sydney to the warmth of controversy with the wretched Filmer. In return, you tell him, that this very *particular* intelligible passage is all a joke. ("Gentle dulness ever loves a joke.") And, when I quote no less authority than Hume, to shew the state of the controversy in England, respecting instructions, you break forth into abuse both of Hume and myself. This kind of reasoning has often browbeaten an adversary at a bar, and influenced those, who even pretended not to understand the debate. I have you, Publicola, before a more respectable tribunal, which will determine according to the true merits of the case without examining which is the greater man, Publicola or Aristides. But alas poor David! Thou wast no more a friend to paper money than to the doctrine of binding instructions. With thy acknowledged skill in politics, and thy deep historical researches, thy name would not otherwise have been so grossly insulted by a man, so very little *thy* superior.

You refer me, however, on your own authority, to a case, which happened during our conventions,—a case of instructions from a particular county. It was a case too of instructions for forming a compact, not for making laws, under a compact already formed. Suppose now, those instructions had been disobeyed. You say too, that, in all the governments of America, the right was formerly exercised. Admitting that, either in America, or in England, the representatives of particular counties have obeyed the directions, handed to them as the instructions of their constituents, what would that prove as to the *right of controling*, if it should, on the other side, be shewn, that other representatives have disobeyed instructions, and, notwithstanding their votes have been held good? I might very justly contend, that the bare consideration of such votes being universally held good, settles the question in my favour,—that instructions are to be considered, on the footing of opinion, remonstrance, or advice. I do not believe, that a majority of voters in a county have ever joined in one letter of instructions; although it be a common thing for representatives to say, they are instructed, and, although popular men have often attempted to avail themselves of instructions. Most men would choose to follow instructions, for a variety of reasons; but surely no man would have the impudence to claim a right of controling another, because that other had generally, or even on all occasions, followed his advice.

But, to confine myself to the point,—admitting, that the practice of instructions prevailed throughout the American colonies; that they were never disobeyed; and that every man had held them to be binding; all this would be nothing at all to your purpose. You do not pretend, that the practice was anything more than the practice of particular counties, directing their respective immediate representatives. Our controversy is respecting *"national"* instructions, to bind not only the immediate representatives of the people, but every other branch of the legislature if there were an hundred. And these same *national* instructions, given by the people at large to their legislature, I verily believe, were never before contended for.

When first I quoted Sydney, you told me, he was speaking only of instructions from particular counties, concerning the force of which, you said, there were various opinions. You said too, that the passage impliedly admitted the right of *national* instructions. Well then! "I met you on that ground." I shewed, that Sydney considered these same national instructions given by the people, entirely out of the question. I told you too, that the instructions of the several states in the Netherlands to their deputies, were instructions given by government, not by the people at large, and that all cases like that of the Netherlands of instructions by governments or states were foreign from the question. To this you gave no answer, except, as aforesaid, that what Sydney said was all a joke. I suppose it was a joke too in Publicola to refer me to the practice of particular instructions, binding immediate representatives, to support this same *"new fangled doctrine"* of national instructions, binding the whole legislature. You may rest assured, that such conduct will never establish your claim to the amazing superiority, you have all along affected over Aristides. Suppose him to retort, and ask, pray, Publicola, what are you? Suppose too he should give an answer to his own question. Why then he would do a thing, which he sincerely despised in another. From your conduct, your speeches, and your writings, let the world form an estimate of your principles and character. I will not gratify the malignant by pouring forth a torrent of invective. Of all species of composition, personal *abuse*, or even personal *satire*, demands the least of parts, or laudable knowledge, because every thing of that kind is but too well relished by many, who affect to condemn it. Aristides holds it as much beneath his character, as contrary to his principles and inclination. It requires scarcely any effort for him to preserve his temper, when he is conscious of his superiority in the argument, and when he is satisfied, that the indulgence of a petulant overbearing disposition does not, with those about whose good opinion he is chiefly solicitous, enhance a man's reputation for wit, understanding, courage, or patriotism.

You demand, under what articles of their charters did the Americans resist the tyranny of Great-Britain. Is it necessary again to declare the same thing in different words? Know then that the right of the people to throw off a government, which aims to enslave them, is founded on this plain principle. When the real or supposed compact is violated on one side, the other side is absolved from its obligation.

That the people's exercising a legislative authority, so far as to dictate to the legislature, would inevitably lead to licentiousness, cannot be denied. That having once begun this practice of dictating, the lowest classes of the citizens would be too apt, at the slightest call, to leave their employments, and assemble tumultuously, for the purpose of hearing the different propositions and harangues, and of then exercising this transcendent right, is greatly to be apprehended. As they are not competent to decide on complicated questions of policy, affecting a variety of interests, and as these would be more likely to be brought before them, the most ruinous plans might frequently be adopted. But I need not, at this stage, enlarge on the consequences of introducing a practice, which, would either preclude all deliberation in the legislature, or compel one branch to adopt the opinion of the other, for which it was evidently intended as a check. If you, and every body else, would allow, that the practice ought never to be introduced, the question about abstract right would not be so material.

Was it ever known, that, in any republic, the introduction of licentiousness was not soon followed by usurpation? You maintain that the independence of the legislature must lead to tyranny and despotism. I beseech you, Publicola, as a citizen, interested in preserving our free and happy constitution, to reflect on these things. Is it no security that elections are frequent and free; that the liberty of speaking and writing is secured; that each citizen has a right to petition and remonstrate; that there is no power capable of corrupting the legislature, (if there were, the right of instructing would be a poor safeguard to the people) that the members of the legislature are subject to the laws they enact, and at a near period, return into the general mass of citizens; and finally, that in cases of extremity, even the constitution expressly authorises a suspension, or a dissolution of the government?

The case, which I put, where an immediate interference would be necessary, implied the corruption of the legislature, and the incompetency of all other means of redress. Of what avail would it be for the people to instruct a body of men, who evidently design to betray them? In such a case, the people would be irretrievably ruined, if they did not act as *we* did, 13 years ago. Remember the suspension of the old government, and the vigorous proceedings of committees and conventions. You were too precipitate in supposing my own case might be turned against me. To do you justice, I dare say, in a case like that, you, as one of the people, would be for suspending or dissolving. Were an invasion intended by a rich powerful enemy, I should be afraid, that a few corrupt demagogues might be employed with success, in procuring instructions.

And now, Publicola, exert all your powers to parry the following questions: Might not the right of binding by instructions the legislature have been expressly surrendered by the constitution? Again. If the framers of that constitution intended, that the people might, *in all cases*, exercise a legislative authority, so far as to control, and prescribe to, both branches of the legislature, where was the necessity of providing so carefully for the peoples interference *in extraordinary cases*? Again. If they conceived that intention, wherefore did they not plainly express a matter of such vast importance, and, at once, preclude all cavil and doubt?

It will be no derogation from your real consequence, to treat Aristides as an equal. It was not generous in you, Publicola, to use against him his confession respecting Sydney and Locke. His readers will perceive, that he understands at least what he quoted. These authors, however, have not enlarged his ideas. He had read later authors improving on both. He may add, that he has profited, by exerting the powers of his own mind; and happy would it be for mankind in general, *if other men would dare to think more for themselves.* Had Aristides suffered Publicola to think for him; had he changed as Publicola changed, and, for him, become a *"laborious partisan;"* then possibly might not Publicola have deemed him the most unlettered judge on the continent. But surely, Publicola, however vast the superiority of your genius, your achievements, and your services, you do not imagine, our acquaintance will give you credit for more extensive reading and knowledge. If to say this be *boasting,* Aristides most humbly intreats the indulgence of his *readers.* Not only this, but many other egotisms have been exerted by your illiberal deviations. As they are uttered in defence of my character, I trust that no candid man will think them improper.

Annapolis   ARISTIDES

Alexander Contee Hanson to William Paca
AUGUST 2, 1787

ARISTIDES TO PUBLICOLA

So FAR AS I can discover, the "new-fangled doctrine" of *national instructions* binding the whole legislature has never yet been broached in England. In the hundreds and thousands of books, continually issuing from the press, there may be something of the kind; but I have never had the fortune to stumble on it. Indeed, were this doctrine established in England, in how short a time might we not hear of a *national* bankruptcy, followed by a revolution in their government? Borne down as the people are by the enormous taxes, laid for the purpose of discharging only the interest of their national debt, there can be little doubt that, with activity and perseverance, a majority of the electors might be induced to subscribe an instruction to the parliament, for abolishing a great part of those taxes, *"imposing burthens on the whole for the emolument of a few."*

But although this doctrine of national instructions be unknown to the English, much has been said and written, amongst them, about instructions given by the electors in a single county, or in a single borough, to its own representatives. Mr. Hume has incurred your displeasure, it seems, for saying that the dispute about that kind of instructions is frivolous. Mr. Hume, however, was well skilled in the history and politics of that country; and was perfectly acquainted with the state of parties. He states the admissions of the disputants respecting instructions. One side acknowledges, that a representative ought not to disregard the opinions of his electors. The other side admits, that he is not absolutely bound by their instructions. Now if Mr. Hume be not guilty of a gross misrepresentation, is there any person that can say, the general question concerning the operation of instructions is not frivolous?

The question between Publicola and Aristides is, simply and precisely, whether or not the direction of a majority of the people or of the voters in Maryland, be so far the foundation of a law, as to bind both branches of the legislature to frame a bill agreeably to that direction. In maintaining the negative Aristides has called upon all those, who maintain the affirmative, to produce from history the case of any government in the world, (whether founded on express compact or not) in which the direction of the people at large had laid the foundation of a law, to which the regular established legislature was bound to give all the sanctions of its authority. He further called upon them to produce even the opinion of any approved writer, that such a direction, in a free government, should preclude the deliberations of the legislature, and oblige it to pass the law. In answer to this, as it seems, you gave the following reference: "I refer you to the English government, the British government, the United Netherlands; and, on the authority of Mr. Sydney, I refer you to all the governments he mentions on this subject, and which, at the time, admitted to representation of the people by delegates, viz. France, Spain, the states of Languedoc and Brittanny, the diets of Germany, Denmark, Sweden, Poland and Bohemia; and I refer you to the governments of the colonies before the revolution, particularly the government of Maryland." You preface this reference by saying, I had challenged you to produce instances of governments, in which the right of instructions was acknowledged. You there seem disposed conveniently to confound national and particular instructions; to consider me as having denied, that the practice of giving any kind of instruction ever prevailed; and to claim the victory, in virtue of this reference. Now Aristides never denied, that the practice of giving particular instructions prevailed in England, and in the English colonies. But he maintained, that instructions given by a particular county or borough, could operate, only as an opinion, a remonstrance, or advice. And this position he has fully established by Sydney and Hume; to say nothing of judge Blackstone, Sir Edward Coke, and several others, whom in the course of the controversy he has quoted. I now call upon you to produce the opinion of any writer, good, bad, or indifferent, that if a representative in England, should vote contrary to the instructions of his county or borough, his vote ought not to be received; or, that if a bill should be passed, contrary to the instructions of a majority of counties and boroughs, by the house of commons, and receive the assent of the peers, and of the king, it ought not to be considered as a law.

Mr. Sydney informs you, that the deputies of the several states in the United Netherlands are subject to the instructions of their respective governments; and I have before told you, that the case of the United Netherlands is nothing to your purpose of establishing the doctrine of *"national instructions"* given by the people at large. Let us examine whether there is any thing relative to the other countries, mentioned in your reference, that will better answer your purpose.

France, ever since the dissolution of the Roman empire, has been under a king. It formerly consisted of twelve provinces, each of which had a parliament, composed of peers and landholders, whose consent was necessary to the passing of laws and the levying of money. It is now divided into many more provinces, whose parliaments still claim a kind of negative to the kings edicts, which always have been the law of the land. Will you be pleased to explain how the circumstances of France can make for your purpose? Languedoc and Brittany are provinces of France. Is either of them governed by laws dictated by the people at large? Has either of them a legislative body which is bound to obey the instructions of the people at large?

The *cortez,* or courts of Spain are, in point of form, somewhat similar to a British parliament. They consist of the nobility, the clergy, and the representatives of commons. But whatever their former privileges have been, these cortez now meet, only to confirm and record the decrees of the court. It is not impossible, that the representatives of commons were formerly somewhat on a footing with the English house of commons.

In Denmark, although it has always had a king, the legislative power was once in the nobility, the clergy, and the representatives of citizens and farmers. Ever since the year 1661, the king has been absolute, from the solemn act of the several orders, passed at that time. History does not inform us, that any one of those orders, on that momentous occasion, pursued the directions of the people. With respect to particular instructions from particular districts, it is probable enough, that such might have been formerly given, by way of communicating the opinion of the particular citizens and farmers.

In Sweden, Poland and Bohemia, the people have a share in the legislature, by representation. Whether or not the people in particular districts make a practice of instructing their respective representatives, or how far their representatives would hold themselves bound, I cannot positively say. But it is incumbent upon you to show (if your reference is to answer any purpose) not only that representatives are there bound by the instructions of their electors; but that the whole legislature, or at least the whole representative body in the legislature, receive and invariably hold themselves bound to obey directions, given by a majority of the people. It would throw much light upon the subject, if you could shew likewise, in what manner the sense of the people, or the *"national sense,"* in those countries, is collected. I take it for granted, that the people, in those countries, were never more tenacious of their liberties and rights, than the people of England, whose rights

Mr. Sydney asserts to be unimpaired. Now, admitting, that in all those countries, and even in England, the representatives of the people are considered as passive instruments without any right of deliberating in those cases, where their constituents choose to determine for themselves, you have not shewn, nor can it be shewn, that the people in those countries ever thought themselves entitled to dictate to the other branches of the legislature.

The diet of Germany consists of the emperor, of a vast number of princes and great lords, who are absolute in their own estates, and of the deputies of free cities. This diet is the supreme power which takes care of the interests of an immense confederacy. The princes and great lords speak for themselves. The deputies of cities pursue the instructions of the respective *governments* which they represent. For each of these cities has an internal government of its own. The diet then of Germany is nothing to your purpose; because in this diet there is no representation of the people at large.

But you refer me to all these governments, on the authority of Mr. Sydney. *Unfortunate Sydney! how hast thou been misrepresented and abused. But I trust that thou wilt look down with complacency on him, who vindicates thy fame.* If Publicola will be pleased to examine attentively, he will find that, when Sydney speaks of deputies obliged to pursue the orders of those, who send them, he means the deputies of the states of the United Netherlands, or of the cantons in Switzerland, or of the free towns in Germany. It is true, he says the deputies of Castile, in the cortez held at Madrid, in the time of Charles the fifth, did excuse themselves from giving supplies, as Charles desired; because they had received no orders from the towns, which sent them. Sydney says likewise, that no grants of importance were ever made, without consulting their principals. He says too, that so long as the general assemblies of estates in France continued, the deputies acted in the same manner; and, when these general assemblies were laid aside, the same custom was used, in the assemblies of lesser estates in Languedoc and Brittanny. Now, Publicola, consider how far this authority operates in your favour. It amounts to no more than that certain deputies did not choose to grant the money of their constituents, before they were certain, it would be agreable to them. Is there any thing in Sydney, to prove the custom in Spain and France, of the peoples dictating laws even to their own representatives? Why, Sir, these very representatives seldom did more than consider the propositions, that came from the court. It would puzzle you, with all your reading, to discover one single instance, where a majority of the people at large, in either France or Spain determined, that this, or that law, should be passed, and so gave order to the whole representative body, that this body might propose it to the assembly of nobles, &c. and to the court. But, could you even do that, it would be insufficient, unless you could shew likewise, that the people dictated to all the branches.

That the question between us is determinable only upon a fair construction of our compact, is a position, I shall make a point of always repeating. I have however examined the question on every ground, and in every point of view. To a slight thinker, after all, the question may appear not very material. I shall ever contend, as strenuously as Publicola, that all rightful government originates from the people; that in every free government, there is a sacred compact, either express or implied; and that society and government were instituted solely for the good of the whole. I admit too, that whenever the legislature shall be possessed of the peoples sentiments and wishes they must in most cases, and indeed, in all cases, without some weighty reason to the contrary, do as the people would have them. Publicola seems to admit, that the people ought not to dictate, except on occasions of importance. Where then is the mighty difference between the doctrines of Publicola and Aristides? Why is not their contest about instructions as frivolous, as the contest in England? The difference consists in this. According to Publicola, if a majority of the people, or of the voters, shall at any time be prevailed on to subscribe instructions the business is as good as done. The legislature must pass a bill, agreeably to that direction. But Aristides maintains, that the legislature are at liberty to examine, whether these instructions, although signed by a majority really contain the general sense, and whether that general sense be right. There may be a variety of circumstances to render improper that measure, which appears salutary to the people, from the narrow view each individual has of the subject. It may be requisite too, in many cases, for the legislature immediately to adopt measures, contrary to instructions. According to Publicola, I should suppose, the utmost which the legislature could do, in such cases, after receiving *"national instructions,"* would be to adjourn, and address the people, *to prevail on them to rescind those instructions.*

If Aristides be right, there will be little encouragement for a party at any time, to make a pretext of obtaining the peoples sense, in order to force upon the legislature, or upon a dissenting branch, a measure, which they have rejected, upon the maturest deliberation. If the thing had not actually occurred, it would hardly be believed, that any man of character could have the presumption to call another inimical to liberty, and ignorant of the peoples rights, merely for contending, that each branch of the legislature may exercise its own judgment, in passing, or rejecting bills.

On a dispassionate, and disinterested view, it is impossible to conceive, that the peoples having a right to dictate measures to the legislature, and to preclude its deliberation thereon, can operate as a security to liberty, or advance the true interests of the people. That the frequent exercise of such a right must tend to render of no avail the salutary institution of two distinct branches, and indeed to confer all power on a few men, can hardly be doubted. *Your* position is, that, if the right exists not, both branches "may turn their backs upon the complaints and grievances of the people; and, to obtain redress, the people must hazard a revolution and the halter." I have before, more than once solicited your attention to the securities we enjoy against such deplorable corruption in our trustees. Should they *really* prove false to their trust, would not their influence think you be exerted, to prevent instructions, or to defeat them, after they were given? *Where are the individuals who would dare to stand against the resentment and power of a corrupt senate and house of delegates united?* If this unaccountable degeneracy, should prevail in each branch, and circumstances should render it unsafe to wait for the next period of election, would it not be better, at once, to resort to that grand remedy, prescribed by the 4th article of the declaration? But wherefore should you Publicola, by way of preventing a disorder, which you dread, use constantly a medicine, which is too apt of itself to produce worse diseases? There is little reason to believe, that the legislature or either branch will disregard those sufferings, of which they and their connexions cannot fail to participate. But admitting that instructions are binding; and admitting too, that they ought not to be given, except on important occasions; how apt will popular men be, whenever disappointed in a favourite measure, to tell the people it was of infinite importance, and that, by rejecting it, the legislature had turned their backs upon the people. Take now a passage from *your old* and *my new* acquaintance, Mr. Sydney—

"They may make prejudicial wars, ignominious treaties, and unjust laws. Yet when the session is ended, they must bear the burthen, as much as others, and, when they die, the teeth of their children will be set on edge with the sour grapes they have eaten. But it is hard to delude, or corrupt so many. Men do not, in matters of the highest importance, yield to slight temptations. No man serves the devil for nothing—small wages will not content those who expose themselves to perpetual infamy, and the hatred of a nation for betraying their country."

Let us now quit for a while the theory of "national instructions," and consider the method of reducing it to practice. On a recent occasion, the mode adopted was nearly the same, as has heretofore been attempted, to bind individual representatives. In each county, were papers carried about among the people; and, if it had so happened, that a majority of voters in each of ten counties, had signed for an emission, these local instructions would have been held binding not only upon the house of delegates, but upon the senate likewise. Now the senate, although its members are not endowed with extraordinary privileges, as individuals, nor invested with their dignities for life, were intended, by the constitution, to be as independent in legislation, as the orders of nobility in the countries mentioned in your reference. The idea that senators are representatives of the people of Maryland, is no more just, than is the idea, that the king, and the house of lords, are representatives of the people of England. The notion too of senators being only deputies or trustees of the people, and therefore subject to their direction, *whilst they act as senators*, is just as well founded, as that of the king and house of lords being deputies and trustees, and therefore controlable by the people. You remember all which Locke says about deputies and trustees; and yet Locke does not place them on the same footing, as you would place *our* deputies and trustees.

You must, at least, allow, the method of conveying the national sense is no where prescribed. Who then has authority to declare *that*, about which the constitution and the laws are silent? The right of binding by *"national instructions,"* you have told me is *"paramount"* to the constitution. The manner then of exercising this right perhaps ought to be fixed by the national voice. How is it, we find the manner adopted, without previously consulting the people. There is indeed an old law maxim, *omnis ratihabitio retrotrahitur et mananto æquiparatur.* That is, according to this maxim, any man of competent zeal and assurance may assume an office belonging to no other. He may prepare a draught of instructions; and, if a majority shall sign them, it will be the same thing as, if the people had previously agreed on that mode. I will not perplex the case, by supposing a number of different draughts, carried about by different people. Suppose one of the self-created offi-cers hands to the senate a paper, purporting to be instructions of a majority of voters in Anne-Arundel. The senate not being representa-tives of Anne-Arundel, may very probably be inclined to reject it. But then the senate is informed, that there are nine other papers, containing instructions from nine other counties; and that these, taken altogether, convey the national sense of Maryland. The senate thereupon deter-mines to receive them all. However, these papers not being on the footing of sheriffs returns, the senate is not, on any principle, precluded from examining into their authenticity, the number of voters in each county, whether the names appearing belong to men residing, and having a right of suffrage in the respective counties, and whether these names were set down by the owners, or with their consents. Suppose, that, after a minute, laborious, expensive investigation, the senate finds one or more of the self-created officers guilty of a thousand frauds and forgeries. What then? Why then they may hold themselves not bound by those papers. Suppose a variety of forms, all tending nearly to the same point. The legislature must be perplexed in framing the law.

I have selected a few circumstances, to expose the lately adopted method of conveying the national sense, which was to lay the foundation of a law, and compel the senate to adopt that measure, which, without any imputation of corrupt views, they had before unanimously rejected. Let us now return to the theory. Suppose the instructions of a majority of the people, prohibiting the passage of a particular bill depending in the assembly. The bill, notwithstanding, is passed in the usual form, and has all the sanctions prescribed by the constitution. Will you maintain, that this act of assembly is unconstitutional and therefore no law; and that the executive and judicial ought to regard it as a mere *nullity*? Would you, in a court of justice, make the point, that it is no law? If you should, would you expect the court to make the inquiry, whether or not it was passed, contrary to the instructions of the people? In pursuance of your principle, I imagine you would. And, if your doctrine be right, the court ought, undoubtedly, to institute the inquiry. I would then demand *"by what authority"* they do this? Do they derive it from the constitution, or an act of assembly, or an adopted British statute, or the provision of the common law? The more we consider this "blessed doctrine" of instructions, signed by the people, controling and prescribing to each branch of the legislature, which notwithstanding, agreeably to our sacred compact, is to be at full liberty to exercise its own judgment; the more we shall be convinced, that, not being mentioned in this compact, nor in any preceding or subsequent law, the doctrine is altogether inadmissible upon any other ground.

There have been great occasions, on which, amongst a free people, the national voice has been *heard*. It has then constituted a law of the most exalted kind. The occasions I mean are, when the people have found it necessary, for the preservation of their rights, to interfere; and either make a total, or a partial, change in their government, or, under the old form, to place it in new hands. I need not remind you of the English revolution in 1688, or of the late astonishing revolution in America. Did any man, on occasions like these, ever think of going about with a paper, requesting and urging to subscribe, one after another, men who either knew nothing about the subject, or were totally indifferent what became of the paper after they were freed from his importunity? Did any man ever suppose that such a paper was to obtain a redress of all grievances? On the great occasions, just mentioned, and more particularly the last, the people acted from their own knowledge and feelings. They assembled together in every part of the country; and one opinion only, respecting the main question, prevailed. In cases like these, the national sense is collected without setting down names, and the national voice is always decisive. And, on occasions only of evident necessity like these, ought any man to solicit the national voice. I think, it may safely be affirmed, that never, before the late appeals, was it any where attempted, to procure the authority of the people at large, as a legal constitutional power, to oblige the regular legislature to adopt a measure of mere domestic policy, concerning which a variety of opinions had indeed prevailed, but which, till very lately, had been reprobated by all the best characters in the state. If history records any other instance, I doubt not, that, in the most decided manner, it censures the attempt. Never was it known that a determined attempt in the people at large, to exercise an authority, did not produce a convulsion, or a suspension, or a dissolution, of the government. But I will not again tread over that ground.

When an adversary appears to me disposed to misconceive every thing I can say, I shall always take care to repeat and enforce my principal positions and arguments. Should the voice of the people, at any time, decidedly declare for an ordinary measure of policy, and no after circumstances should change the complexion of affairs, it will be prudent for the legislature, upon the principle of avoiding a greater evil, to submit. Should it plainly appear, that the national voice proceeds from delusion, and that obedience would be fatal to our interests, the legislature would be in such circumstances, as render it most difficult to determine what ought to be done.

But should, at any time, the activity and perseverance of a party or set of men prevail so far, as by mere dint of persuasion, to obtain the signatures of a large majority of their fellow-citizens to instructions framed by themselves, I should hold those papers so far from laying the foundation of an indispensable act, that the legislature ought to make a determined point of withstanding an innovation, which might speedily overthrow the salutary institutions of the constitution. When there is not the least shadow of a provision in that constitution for conveying the sense of the people, so as to leave the legislature nothing more than the mere forms of reading a first and second time, passing, engrossing, &c. &c. when I say there is no provision made any where for this most important purpose, I am almost ashamed to have laboured so long, and against such an adversary, in disproving a doctrine, which I am sure must have appeared preposterous to almost every intelligent man, so soon as it was fairly stated. Your efforts, to rouse the public indignation against the man, whom you represent as endeavouring to break down the best guard to their liberty, can tend only to your own dis-honour. It is impossible they should produce the intended effect, on any mind, that will attend to what is said on both sides, and to the whole conduct of each of the men. Would to Heaven! That every man of candour and intelligence, after taking the trouble of perusing our whole controversy, would openly declare, whether Publicola, *by this dispute*, hath manifested a regard for liberty and equal rights, superior to that of Aristides. Were perpetual exile to be the doom of him against whom the *"national voice"* should declare, be assured that the man, whom you idly affect to despise, would feel no uneasiness, *before* the decision, on his own account.

There is a plain and material distinction between laudable and impertinent egotism. When a man voluntarily and without provocation addresses his fellow-citizens with discourses about himself and his affairs —it is truly unmanly and disgusting. But when his reputation is wan-tonly attacked, they ought, with patience, to hear him so long, as he confines himself to the charge, and overleaps not the bounds of mod-esty. However as I have some reason to be satisfied, that the public on no occasion *wishes* to hear a man speak of himself, I shall conclude, without doing that, which, at first, I intended. My comments on the proceedings relative to the editor of a late publication shall hereafter appear, provided I shall be convinced that they are necessary, or that the public wishes to see them.

Annapolis   ARISTIDES

William Paca to Alexander Contee Hanson
AUGUST 6, 1787

TO ARISTIDES

YOU HAVE at length *honoured* me with a *personal* address. What-ever my "manifold attributes" may be, I find they are sufficient to make you *feel*, when I think proper to give your vanity a public correction. If I have shone in a *new light*, you were determined, it seems, not to be behind hand. I think there is at least as much humour in my *comment*, as there is in your *poetry*. That "Jemmy Twitcher should 'peach me, I own surprises me."—Your humble servant captain Mac-heath! I do not wonder that you are so ready to assume the character of Macheath; there seems between you to be a correspondence in prin-ciple; he was a highwayman, and plundered the purses of his fellow-citizens; you plunder too, but strike at higher game; you plunder your *beloved countrymen* of their liberties. Your *gibes* and *sneers* upon my *friend,* might have been spared; he had no concern whatever in the publications under the signature of Publicola; but a malignant spirit, such as yours, Aristides, must be gratified. As to *Freeman,* spare him not; do him however the justice to acknowledge, that the extract you have given is not his, but one of your *pathetic* exhibitions. And yet there was no necessity that you should give a fresh proof of your talents at the *pathos.* Your *beloved countrymen* cannot forget your affecting memorials to the general assembly, and *moving tales* about the scantiness of your salary. Whatever sensibility *Freeman* may exhibit for a friend, he disdains to *whine* and *spaniel* at the feet of any public body upon earth for tea and sugar!*

In a former publication you made the position, that no rights or powers could be exercised during the existence of our compact, but what were there mentioned, defined and ascertained; and you then asserted, that the right of instructing was not *there* mentioned, defined or ascertained, and then concluded, no such right existed. To this I replied, that the position was not a just one; and contended, that all rights and powers which a people possessed in a state of nature before compact, and which were not transferred by such compact, may be exercised, although not mentioned, defined or ascertained, by such compact; that the right to appoint and instruct a deputy, agent or trustee, was a natural right, which the people possessed in a state of nature, before compact, and therefore, if not transferred by compact, might be exercised, although not mentioned therein, defined or ascertained.

But this reasoning of mine, you are pleased to tell me, is all *jargon* and *absurdity.* It is *jargon,* you say, to talk of rights paramount and not transferred by compact; and it is equal *jargon,* you say, to talk of a *natural right* to *appoint* and *control deputies, agents* and *trustees.* I mean, Sir, to prove, that, positive and dogmatical as you are, you do not understand the subject you are upon.

By men versed in legal technical phrases, the word *"paramount"* is well understood; by others it may not. By rights paramount, we mean, rights which the people hold by a title or tenure other and higher than the compact, constitution or government, of a country.

You deny there are such rights, and say, to talk of such is *jargon.* I maintain the contrary position. What then are these rights? I will tell you. The right to private judgment in matters of conscience and religion; the right to life; the right to liberty; and the right to the pursuit of happiness. These rights are held by a title and tenure other and higher than our constitution and government; they are held by the

---

* *Aristides in the estimate of expences accompanying the memorials.*

grant of the Supreme Being. Our constitution does nothing more than provide guards and securities for their better defence and protection. To these rights, I add, the right to judge whether the legislature exercises the powers of legislation properly or improperly; the right to complain of grievances, to petition, to remonstrate and instruct, for a removal of them; and the right to dissolve the government, if such petitions, remonstrances or instructions, are disregarded, and the powers of government still abused—

All these rights, Sir, derive no part of their existence from any compact, constitution or government. Nor are they parted with or transferred by any compact that we have made. For what power, I would ask, can take away my life, or my liberty, &c? In whose hands have I lodged such a power? If, indeed, I commit certain crimes or offences, I forfeit both life and liberty to the state; and so in a state of nature, if I commit the like crimes, I forfeit both life and liberty to the party injured. But as in a state of nature the party injured does not take my life upon any compact or transfer, but upon the ground of forfeiture for crimes, so the state, standing in the place of the injured individual, can deduce no right to my life from any transfer of it by compact, but takes it upon the like ground of forfeiture.

But, most learned judge! you assert, that to talk of a natural right to appoint and control a deputy, agent or trustee, in a state of nature, is also *jargon.* And pray where is the *jargon?* Did the Supreme Being ordain that mankind, while in a state of nature, should always act *personally*, and never by *deputy, agent or trustee?* Where do you find that He has declared that such was his will and command? Or was mankind at that time of day not only *morally* but *naturally* disabled from making such an appointment? Was there no intercourse in a state of nature, no dealings or contracts, no exchange of kind offices no mutual dependence from mutual wants and necessities? Why then suppose that the Supreme Being should with-hold or decline to grant them, while in that state, the right, if they think proper to make a deputy, agent or trustee, and to control him occasionally, by instructions.

But this is impossible! says Aristides; for in the name of all that is profound, how was such a deputy, agent or trustee, to be *controled?* Why most profound Sir, just in the same manner as delegates or senators in civil society, viz. by instructions; if that is not sufficient, then *by force.* But this cannot be! says Aristides, for in a state of nature every man is upon an equal footing, and no other force can be applied than what arises from superior cunning and strength. And, most profound Sir! when force becomes necessary to be applied to delegates and senators, and a dissolution of the powers of government ensues, I wonder what other force can be applied than what arises from superior cunning and strength.

But admitting, says Aristides, that the people might individually, in a state of nature, make a *deputy, agent or trustee,* yet the absurdity still remains to be maintained, that the people in collective bodies could do it. Where, Sir, is this absurdity? Are you to be taught that there were not only individuals in a state of nature, but *societies* of individuals? Was there no such society as man and wife? No such society as parent and child? No such society as master and servant, by contract and stipulation? Might not families *then* spread to the like extent as now, and form numerous distinct societies, and yet all upon equal footing, without any superior invested with legislative powers? And might not these societies or collective bodies have dealings and transactions that required the intervention of a deputy, agent or trustee? If so, did the Supreme Being forbid such appointments by any moral or natural impediment? If not, where, Aristides, is the *jargon* you charge upon Publicola?

Well! but if *collective bodies* could make such appointments in a state of nature, yet there were no *delegates or senators* in a state of nature. And what then? Therefore the people, in collective bodies, have no natural right to make delegates or senators, or in collective bodies to control them. Excellent reasoning indeed! I suppose in a state of nature, the people, both *individually* and *collectively,* had a natural right to *drink*. Will it follow, that because in a state of nature there was no *claret,* therefore in civil society they have no *natural* right *individually* or *collectively* to drink *claret?*—I think not.

You doubt, you say, whether there was such a state as a state of nature—the partisans of power, and advocates for despotism, not only doubt, but deny it. They contend, that rightful government is not founded upon compact; that the original government of mankind was an *absolute monarchy,* established by *divine authority.* They further contend, that it is ridiculous to say that God placed mankind in a state of freedom and equality; that there was a monarchy from the beginning of the world; that men are not born free, but born in subjection to that monarchy; that there being no such state as the state of nature, there are no such things as rights to life, liberty or happiness, or rights paramount the authority and sovereignty of the first monarch, and his dependents and heirs.—And that mankind hold their lives, their liberties and properties, at the will and pleasure of the monarch.—Such were the doctrines and principles of the partisans of power, and advocates for despotism, and Mr. Filmer was the chief and principal.

But these absurd and slavish principles were opposed and exploded by Mr. Sydney, Locke and other patriotic writers. They contended there was such a state as a state of nature, a state of freedom and equality; that mankind were placed originally in this state; that in this state there was no superior, but every man stood upon an equal footing. That this being the original state of mankind, they never could be rightfully removed out of that state but by their own consent. And therefore, that all rightful government is founded upon compact. But Aristides it seems, doubts whether there was ever such a state as a state of nature.—

Hear Sir, Mr. Locke.

"I affirm all men are naturally in that state, that is, a state of freedom and equality; and remain so till by their own consent they make themselves members of some political society." Page 153.

Again. "It is often ask'd, as a mighty objection, where are, or ever were there any men in such a state of nature? To which it may suffice as an answer at present, that since all princes and rulers of independent states, all through the world, are in a state of nature, its plain the world never was, nor never will be, without numbers of men in that state." Page 152.

Again. "To *understand* political power aright, and derive it from its original, we must consider what state all men are in, and that is a state of perfect freedom, and also of equality." Page 144.

But the learned Aristides differs from Mr. Locke. This celebrated writer is received as an oracle by the enlightened part of mankind, upon all questions touching principles of liberty and of government. When, Sir, shall we see the blessed day when your laborious memorials, laborious pamphlets, and laborious addresses to your *beloved countrymen*, shall be cited and admitted as equal authority?

You ask, whether I seriously assert, or *whether it is one of my jokes*, that Mr. Locke, in the passage you cited, means nothing more than while government exists the people cannot exercise the powers of legislation, *exclusively* and *independently* of each other? I do Sir, assert it most seriously, and your miserable evasion of my construction is a clear evidence that you cannot meet it upon fair argument.

Let us once more have this passage before us.

"So also when the society has placed the legislature in any assembly of men, to continue in them and their successors, with direction and authority for providing such successors, the legislative can never return to the people, whilst that government lasts; because having provided a legislative with power to continue for ever, they have given up their political power to the legislative, and cannot resume it. But, if they have set limits to the duration of their legislative, and made this supreme power in any person or assembly only temporary; or else, when by the miscarriages of those in authority, it is forfeited, upon the forfeiture, or, at the determination of the time set, it reverts to the society; and the people have a right to act as supreme and continue the legislative in themselves, or erect a new form, or under the old form place it in new hands, as they think it good."—

Does this passage disprove my assertion? Is it not the meaning of Mr. Locke, that the powers which the people give up on the establishment of a legislature, cannot revert back to them whilst that legislature or government exists? And how were these powers exercised before they were transferred? I know of no other way, but *individually* and *exclusively*. And how are they to be exercised when they revert to the people, under the contingencies which Mr. Locke mentions? I know of no other way than they originally exercised them, that is *individually* and *exclusively*—If you know of any other way, pray Sir why not mention it? It is no doubt very material that you should; for if my construction be right, nothing can be more ridiculous than your citing this passage as an authority against the people's right of instructing.

You still persist, and demand to know, whether this passage is not a pointed authority against the people's right of instructing; I again reply no. It is no more an authority against the people's right of *occasionally* instructing, than against the people's right of *periodically* electing the senate and delegates. For I repeat it, the power which Mr. Locke speaks of as incompatible with government while it lasts, is the power of legislating individually and exclusively, in the manner as exercised before the establishment of the government. Now, Sir, for the people to instruct is not to legislate *individually* and *exclusively*; for the *majority* only can *bind* and *conclude* by instructions. And this right of instructing is perfectly consistent with the idea of an established form of government; whereas the right to legislate *individually* and *exclusively*, is incompatible with any established form, and therefore cannot, as Mr. Locke observes, revert to the people, or be exercised, whilst the government exists.

I have laboured, you say, to distinguish the right of instructing from the right of legislating; I hope you mean legislating *individually* and *exclusively*, for I have hitherto distinguished it from no other kind of legislating.

But "now Publicola, exert all your talents of wit, humour, railing or ratiocination. Consult your friend before you publish. Prove if you can, that for the people to prescribe to both branches that, to which these branches are obliged to give the sanction of law, be not in effect an exercise of legislative authority." Born, Aristides, for your use, I live but to oblige you. I answer, Sir, without hesitation—and even without consulting my friend—and say Yes.

Having with such candour and plainness answered your question,

I hope, with equal candour and plainness, you will answer me a question.

Suppose the senate and house of delegates should pass an act of assembly imposing a tax for five years, for the purpose of raising one hundred thousand pounds, to erect a monument in memory of Aristides, for the great and signal services done his country, by publications, inculcating principles, essential to the welfare and happiness of his *beloved countrymen*. Suppose remonstrances and instructions should come from every county, stating this act to be oppressive and grievous, and instructing both branches to repeal it.

I demand to know, whether under such circumstances, the *judgment* and *voice* of the people is not conclusive upon both the senate and house of delegates; that is, whether they are not bound by such judgment and instructions, and have no rightful authority to over-rule them?

If you admit the senate and house of delegates bound, then the people may prescribe, and your question becomes impertinent. If you deny that they are bound, then you must deny that the people are the *judges* of what is, or what is not, *legislative oppression*.

You still persist in maintaining the position, that delegates and representatives may *rightfully* over-rule the voice and instructions of the people, and you again demand authorities, if any, which assert the binding force of the people's voice, when communicated to their delegates.

Hear Sir, if you please, what Mr. Pitt, afterwards the *earl of Chatham*, says upon this point.

"The misfortune is, that gentlemen who are in office seldom converse with any but such as are in office, and such men, let them think what they will, always applaud the conduct of their superiors; consequently, gentlemen who are in the administration, or in any office under it, can rarely know what is the *voice* of the people. The *voice* of this house was formerly, I shall grant, *and always ought to be, the voice of the people*."

Mr. *Pitt* then maintains that the delegates and representatives of the people ought always to speak the *voice* of the people; consequently, instructions, communicating the sense or voice of the people, must therefore be binding and conclusive. But the learned Aristides differs from Mr. Pitt.

Hear, Sir, if you please, the celebrated Mr. *Charles Fox*, upon this point.

"The whole body of the British legislature, as well as every separate branch of it, is calculated to protect the freedom, and guarantee the various and minutest franchises of the subject. The parliament is only a *substitution* for the community at large, in which her delegates are stationed and ordained to act as one aggregate body, to *hear* her *united dictates*, and without consulting *their own*, to adopt them as principles of action. She ought to *judge* for them, and not they for her. They only constitute that organ to whom she devolves the power of giving form and effect to whatever plans or measures the settled routine of public affairs, or any sudden emergency, renders necessary."

And now, Sir, hear if you please, the illustrious *Sydney*—not on the force of instructions from a particular county—which you catch at as a drowning man would at a straw—but upon the right of the people, as a body, to limit and direct their delegates and public servants.

"I take what servant I please, and when I have taken him, I must, according to this doctrine, suffer him to do what he pleases. But from whence should this necessity arise? Why may I not take one to be my groom, another to be my cook, and keep them both to the offices for which I took them? And if I am free in my private capacity to regulate my particular affairs according to my own discretion, and to allot to each servant his proper work, *why have not I, with my associates, the freemen of England,* the like liberty of directing and limiting the powers of the servants we employ in our public affairs."—But the learned Aristides differs from Sydney, and considers such limiting, instructing and directing, of the legislature, as incompatible with an established government—

A motion being made, says my *Lord Coke*, in parliament, for a subsidy to be granted of a new kind, the commons answered, "they would have conference with those of their several counties and places who had put trust in them, before they treated in any such matter."

He also says, "the king declared to parliament, that he, with others about him, stood bound for furnishing him and his allies in £.30,000, which he ought to pay, and therefore wanted aid of his commons to pay the same; but the commons made answer, that they knew and tendered the kings estate, and were ready to aid him; only in this new device they *durst* not agree, without further conference with their counties, and so praying respite until another time, they promise to travel to their counties to consult them in this grand affair."

The deputies from the *Swiss cantons* to the general diet, receive instructions from their constituents, and hold themselves bound to conform to them. Simler. Helv. Dess. p. 276, 310.

The *procuradores*, or members for Castile, in the *corte* held at Madrid in the beginning of Charles the Vth, excused themselves from granting the supplies he demanded, because they had received no *orders* from their *constituents*, and afterwards, receiving express orders not to do it, they gave Charles a flat denial. Bu Pol. D. 204.

The same was the custom in *France*, when the people had a share in the government. The same custom is still used in the lesser assemblies of the states in *Languedoc* and *Britanny*. The same is observed by the deputies of the cities of Germany to the *diets.*—State tracts, time of king William, III. 112.—

I trust the above authorities will give you complete satisfaction; if not, let me beg you to produce some *approved* authorities on your side of the question; for as to *your* reasoning, I have really had enough of it; but if I am doom'd to have more, I pray you to put it *in verse*, and then I shall be sure to find wit and humour at least for my entertainment—

One or two observations more Aristides, and then I shall have done with the subject of instructing.

It is a fundamental principle of liberty, that a people cannot be bound by laws without their consent. Suppose the senate and house of delegates should propose to lay an exorbitant tax upon the people. Suppose the people apprised of it should remonstrate and instruct both branches against the imposing of it. And suppose both branches overrule the voice of the people, and pass an act imposing the tax. I ask, whether this act can be said, upon any principle of construction whatever, to have been passed *with* the consent of the people, when passed directly *against* their positive instructions and declared sense?

Again. If the senate and house of delegates may rightfully overrule the voice and instructions of the people, and pass laws in direct opposition to their declared sense and opinion, I ask, what participation it is that the people have in the legislature of Maryland? I take it, the people's participation, if any at all, must either be *personally* or *representatively.* But is it not nonsense in the extreme to say, that the people participate *representatively*, if the doctrine be admitted that the *representative* can rightfully over-rule the *declared sense* and *instruction* of his constituent, and adopt his own opinion in direct opposition?

Reflect, I beseech you, Aristides, upon the above observations, and cease to spread doctrines so fatal to public liberty, and subversive of that part of our excellent constitution, which asserts and declares, "that the right of the people to participate in the legislature is the best security of liberty, and the foundation of all free government." There is no preserving, Sir, first principles—no maintaining the people's right of participation in the legislature—without adopting the doctrine, that the voice of the *representative* ought always to be the voice of the *constituent.* Away then with the idle question, can the people prescribe a law; and, for justice sake, do not insult Mr. Locke again by your miserable construction of his writings.

But you are dreadfully alarmed about the people's possessing this right of instructing. You think it too great a power for them; they may abuse it and be licentious. And yet you admit the people to be the judges whether the legislature exercise the powers of legislation properly or improperly, and that they may even dissolve the government, if they think the powers are abused. I should be glad to know, if the people have judgment enough to decide upon the conduct of the legislature, whether they have not judgment enough to instruct? And if they have prudence and discretion enough to be intrusted with the power of even dissolving the government, why should it be doubted, whether they would have prudence and discretion enough to exercise the right of instructing?—

You are pleased to enumerate the guards and securities which the constitution provides against the despotism and tyranny of our rulers, and you ask me, whether they are not sufficient checks, without the right of instructing. I answer no.—nor certainly sufficient, even with the right. Hear what the excellent Gordon says upon this subject.

"There is not upon earth a nation, which having *unaccountable* magistrates, has not felt them to be *crying* and *consuming* mischiefs. In truth, *where they are most limited*, it has been often as much as a whole people could do to restrain them to their trust, and to keep them from violence; and such frequently has been their propensity to be lawless, that nothing but a violent death could cure them of their violence. *This evil has its root in human nature*; men will never think they have enough whilst they can take more; nor be content with a part when they can seize the whole."

The history of mankind for two or three thousand years back, says an admired writer, is a sermon upon this text.

How is it, you ask, that I dare to speak so contemptuously of news paper information? No, Aristides, I have not dared to do any such thing. But I have dared to say, that when a *judge* turns a *news-paper scribbler* upon every political crack—embroils himself with his fellow citizens—abuses and villains unblemished characters—brands and stigmatizes them as promoters of *sedition* and *pestilent fellows*—such a judge, I have dared to say, dishonours his station, dishonours the bench, and dishonours his country.

But, you pursued, it seems, the dictates of your conscience! and therefore opposed the right of instructing, and *published* to give light and information to your *beloved countrymen*. The man who undertakes *to inform*, ought first *to be informed*. There is not only such a character as a *quack* in physic, but such a character as a *quack* in politics; both are dangerous and fatal to the welfare and happiness of society; and both are *public curses*.

Annapolis   PUBLICOLA

Considerations on the Proposed Removal
of the Seat of Government

I DOUBT NOT, my countrymen, that before the next general election, you will be strongly solicited for your instructions, and I apprehend, from the industry, perseverance and influence, of Baltimore-town, that most of the solicitations will be in its favour! I could invoke Heaven to witness, that in writing this address I have the sincerest wishes to promote your happiness. And all the return I ask from you, is to weigh well the arguments I have used, to carry them with you to all public meetings in your respective counties, and to call upon every man who shall solicit your countenance to the proposed measure, to give them a full, clear, and satisfactory answer.

As the election of a senate is at hand, attempts may likewise be made to instruct the electors. You surely must remark, how improper it would be to instruct men who are to choose upon oath. It is the evident intention of the constitution, that these men shall always be at perfect liberty to exercise their own judgments. If not, wherein is the use of that refined mode of election? It were much better for the people at once to elect the senate, than to choose electors who are bound to obey their instructions. It would indeed be a prostitution of language to call them electors, if instead of naming their own choice, they are only to utter the opinion of others.

Permit me now, my countrymen, to remark, that although I do not question your right of dictating to your delegates, you ought to exercise that right in a very sparing manner. Perhaps instructions have never yet been fairly obtained. I will inform you what alone I conceive to be fair instructions, and such as your representatives may be bound to obey. If at a public meeting, of which general notice has been given, any matter shall be freely discussed, and instructions respecting it be produced, and read to the people there assembled, approved, and signed by a majority of the voters in the county, and by their directions presented to their delegates, then ought their delegates either to pursue those instructions, or to resign their seats.

But when busy artful men, who are not even residents of the county, shall go about soliciting the people, one after another, to sub-

EDITOR'S NOTE: *Considerations on the Proposed Removal of the Seat of Government, Addressed to the Citizens of Maryland, by Aristides.* Annapolis, March 17, 1786, pp. 57–60.

scribe their instructions; and when the people have never heard a discussion of the subject; and when even a majority has not signed them; instructions like these cannot, and ought not, on any principle whatever, to be binding. It is notorious, that instructions like these may be obtained for almost any purpose whatever. Sometimes indeed, your representatives take a fancy that they are instructed, when they have not even a writing to shew; when they have not conversed on the subject with a tenth part of their constituents; and when perhaps the subject has not in their county been generally talked of. The truth is, these men have not a proper sense of their own dignity, and they suffer themselves to be dictated to by a few bustling noisy men, without whose assistance they are apprehensive they cannot maintain their seats.

It is rarely that the people of a county can have a fair comprehensive view of a subject to be discussed in the general assembly. Indeed it is seldom at a popular meeting that both sides of a question are permitted to be stated and examined. Besides, the representatives of each county are, at the same time, representatives of the state, and bound to consult the good of the whole. For all these weighty and most substantial reasons, I would advise you to give your instructions in those cases only where your rights and liberties may be endangered. In a case like the present, when every engine will be put in motion to carry a most pernicious measure, and when too there is a danger that your representatives may be swayed by personal motives; it is in cases like this, that you may, without the least scruple, interfere.

But I do not urge you, my countrymen, even on this occasion, to bind your delegates by instructions. I have ever observed, that the men fondest of procuring them, are those who are fearful of being borne down by superior reason. You will be told, that the friends of Annapolis, at the last session, would not consent to refer to the people the proposition for a removal. It is true that a motion was made for leave to bring in a bill for removing the seat of government. This motion being both seconded and opposed, a day was assigned for the debate. On that day, after a fair and dispassionate discussion, and when every member was *at perfect liberty* to vote his opinion, the motion was rejected by 35 against 18. A second motion was then made, for leave to bring in the same bill, to be published under the direction of the house for your consideration. This motion too was rejected almost without a debate. It was the publication of this bill, by order of the house of delegates, that the Farmer thinks would have been "a reasonable expedient for collecting your sense." It would have been indulging the friends of Baltimore-town in a manner, of which, in this state, there never was, and never ought to be, an example; and a small minority had not the least colour of right to expect it. You must indeed have despised the conduct of your representatives, had they published for your consideration, a bill which, after deliberation, they would not suffer to be brought into their house.

It has been generally believed, that a majority of the gentlemen composing the present senate, was opposed to the measure. Of course, one great object may be (if I may use the expression) to pack a senate; and for that purpose it will be expedient, in the first instance, to pack their electors. You will remember, however, that the senate to be chosen in September next, is to last five years, and in that time an improper senate might subvert the constitution. The convention were so fully impressed with an idea of the necessity of having the best characters for that elevated station, that they invented the most admirable mode of election which has ever been known in the universe, and for any single purpose to defeat their salutary provision, would be a disgrace to the people of Maryland. I wish not to be understood, that any person who shall vote for a removal of the government would be unworthy of a seat in the senate. I have no such contracted narrow way of thinking. My position is, that such men only ought to be elected, who possess the most cultivated minds, the most independent spirits, the greatest love of country, the most inflexible integrity, and the greatest dignity of character. As few men, indeed, possess all these requisites of a perfect senator, the electors should discard no man of whose worth we have had ample experience. I would dismiss no man merely because he is an advocate for the removal, and I would not elect even a plain, honest, ignorant man, merely because he is a staunch friend to Annapolis. Let the electors examine the merits of our present senators, without any regard to their sentiments on any one particular question. Let the opinion of the electors on the present question be what it may, they cannot suppose every thing depends on carrying the measure. I conceive, that if an elector wishes to fix the government at Baltimore, he ought to redouble his care in electing a good senate, because the qualifications of a senator, who will on all occasions perform his duty in that town, must be rare indeed.

I beseech you, my beloved countrymen, to be exceedingly circumspect in your choice of electors, and attempt not to lay them under any injunction whatever, except that of examining the conduct of each member of the present senate, and of making very particular inquiries concerning all those who shall be proposed as objects of their choice. As to the general proceedings of the senate, from the commencement of the government, the whole state bears ample testimony of their worth; and I know not the man in the present body whose conduct, on the whole, has not merited your approbation. However, it is the duty of your electors to make the strictest scrutiny, and let them not think of dismissing any gentleman, until they shall be certain of finding a more worthy successor.

Remarks on the Proposed Plan of an Emission of Paper

HOW LONG a constitution, under which we enjoy equal rights, may endure, it is not for short-sighted mortals to predict. In the annals of the world there are few instances, where a direct attack has been made by any part of the citizens of a free state, against the liberty of the rest. It has even been the practice of those, who meditated its destruction, to avert suspicion from themselves, by warning the people of danger from others. Thus it is that a people are sometimes precipitated into that state of anarchy and confusion, which is most favourable to insidious designs.

Although the frequent prostitution of professions renders it almost disgraceful to use them, I must assure you, that from the moment I began seriously to reflect, your happiness has been dear to my heart. At the hazard of my peace and fortune, without the least hope of reward, and with the certain prospect of provoking the malice of weak and wicked minds, I have for many years devoted my attention to the public concerns. On this head however I should have maintained a becoming silence, had not certain ungenerous remarks been thrown out in a place where it was impossible for me, in a proper manner, to expose them. Besides these there is a recent publication, in which my real name has been used with an unwarrantable freedom; but this I consider as the effusion of habitual insolence, not meriting a more particular notice. A sufficient answer may be collected from the following remarks.

When a disagreement takes place between the two branches of the legislature, on a question involving with it other questions of still greater moment, every freeman in the community is concerned in its decision. The freedom of the press has been indirectly attacked by men who should guard it with the fondest care. It has been repeatedly asserted, that the officers of government have exerted their influence,

EDITOR'S NOTE: Remarks on the Proposed Plan of an Emission of Paper and on the Means of Effecting It; Addressed to the Citizens of Maryland, by Aristides. Annapolis, February 26, 1787, pp. 3–16.

acquired through public money, in opposing the wishes of the people, and that therefore they have merited punishment from the representatives of the people. An assertion repeatedly made is generally the result of reflection. The purpose of this is to wound the feelings of some, restrain others by their fears, and bind the rest by their interests. The spirit of a genuine republican must revolt at the idea. What? Shall he, who in some respects, is constituted the guardian of your rights, be himself debarred the common right of speaking his opinions? Does his situation separate his interests from those of the people, or render him less capable than the most illiterate demagogue of deciding on questions of policy?

Thus far is premised to remove unreasonable prejudice. The author has been charged with adhering to the senate, courting their favour, and reposing a faith in their decisions. The truth is, on the maturest deliberation, he thinks them justifiable in rejecting the bill for an emission of paper; and it is partly his intention to adduce some arguments in their vindication.

When a man coolly and deliberately acts against his interest, there is a presumption, that he conceives himself in the right. It cannot escape your penetration, that if a servant of the people were capable of sacrificing on the altar of ambition his opinion, his conscience and his duty, he would, with every appearance of the most fervent zeal, espouse the cause of those who might most effectually requite his endeavours.

The senate having rejected the proposed plan of an emission upon loan, the house of delegates declines all overtures of a conference, and determines to close the session without making any provision for the necessary supplies. In an address to the people they state the disagreement, and urge many arguments in support of their own system. They tell them an appeal is made by both branches of the legislature, that the opinion of the people only can decide, and that both branches will be equally bound by instructions. The senate makes no direct address; but as they conceive their fellow-citizens entitled to know the principles of their conduct, the messages respecting the money bill are published by their direction. In one of these is a declaration, that they make no appeal; and they suggest the inconveniencies which they apprehend may flow from the precedent. The house of delegates adjourns to the 20th of March, and the senate to the 20th of April.

This brief narrative suggests a variety of points, a thorough discussion whereof is absolutely necessary, before you can prudently take any step on this peculiar great occasion.

In the first place it is proper to decide, whether an appeal is made by both branches, and your instructions requested by each. Whatever might *possibly* be implied from the senate's first message, their subsequent express declaration, published at the same time, must render void that implication. This construction is conformable to a known maxim of law and common sense—*Expressum facit cessare tacitum*; that is, according to a liberal translation, *positive words set aside that which without them would be implied.* I conceive, that nothing can be fairly construed into an appeal to the people, except an address soliciting their instructions in the most plain unequivocal terms.

But it is insisted by a crowd of writers, that although the senate make no direct application, if the people shall think proper to instruct, the senate is constitutionally bound to obey.

This second point must be determined on a view of the constitution and the declaration of rights. To me this point also is abundantly clear, from the single consideration, that the constitution creates two distinct branches only; and that neither that nor the declaration any where intimates, that the people at large are immediately a part of the legislature. Had the respectable framers intended, that whenever a bill proposed by one is rejected by the other, the people may afterwards direct it to be passed into a law, they would have said so in plain positive terms; but then they would have rendered of no avail the institution of the two branches. The senate would have been calculated for little more than to produce delays, and to afford occasions for inflaming the passions, and disturbing the public quiet. There would not have been two distinct regular branches to decide, but two distinct branches to propose. A bill proposed by either would be a law, not being dissented to by the other, or, in case of a dissent, the people would constitute a third or a single branch occasionally. No business would be settled in the appointed legislature, unless the two branches agreed. Had the framers entertained such ideas, they would unquestionably have prescribed the manner of collecting the peoples decision.

I believe there never existed a government, in which, notwithstanding every freeman had a suffrage in framing laws, the question was decided by a majority of single voices. In the purest democracies, the people have voted by classes, tribes or companies, into which they were distributed, agreeably to some rational principle. I pretend to no great historical researches. I conceive that many ages have elapsed since any civilized nation, state, or even single independent city, has placed the power of legislation in the people at large; and I think, that no virtuous citizen, who is acquainted with the history of ancient democracies, would wish this power amongst us to reside *constantly* in the people. In abstract theory, such a legislation appears consonant to their natural rights; but the shocking inconveniencies attendant on the mode, have long since occasioned mankind to renounce it. It was calculated only for small cities in their beginnings; and he that wishes for it in a state of equal extent and population to ours, must either be a political madman, or, under the convenient cloak of public good, he veils the most dark and traitorous intent.

Let us examine the true import of the fourth article of the declaration of rights; for on that article, if on any, is founded the doctrine that both branches of the legislature are bound to obey the instructions of the people, and that by so doing, they act agreeably to the constitution. The article speaks so plain a language it will be difficult for any exposition to render it more intelligible:

"That all persons invested with the legislative or executive powers of government are the trustees of the public, and as such accountable for their conduct; wherefore, whenever the ends of government are perverted, and public liberty manifestly endangered, and all other means of redress are ineffectual, the people may, and of right ought, to reform the old or establish a new government; the doctrine of non-resistance against arbitrary power and oppression, is absurd, slavish, and destructive of the good and happiness of mankind."

If the period has actually arrived, when it is necessary for the people to interpose, they should act in a way very different from that of commanding the senate's assent to a bill, which, on the maturest deliberation, they have unanimously rejected. Such an interference of the people might only prevent, for a season, that, which without many subsequent interferences, would be likely to take place; and the danger threatened from the corruption of their trustees would probably continually increase. The truth is, that from the obvious meaning of the fourth article, and upon every sound principle of government, the interference of the people is a resumption of all delegated powers; the whole frame is *ipso facto* dissolved; and it becomes their business either to reform its errors and abuses, and to declare it again in force, or to adopt an entire new system. If experience hath evinced two distinct legislative branches to be inconvenient, they will probably abolish that which is not of their immediate appointment. But to say, that the senate shall still subsist, and enjoy their powers and privileges uninterrupted, and that notwithstanding they shall be obliged to give their assent, which, after a full interchange of sentiment with the delegates, they have unanimously declined, seems uttering manifest contradictions to be saying, that a thing is so, and is not so, in the same sentence.

This fourth article was unnecessary, as indeed are many others. It affords a striking lesson to legislators never to use sentences or words without necessity or meaning. It was never surely foreseen, that an article asserting only a natural right, could by any possibility be construed into a positive institution. I have on many occasions lamented, that the convention in composing a declaration did not content themselves with recognising generally the law, and laying down certain maxims of government for the conduct of future legislatures. Instead of that they have thrown together natural rights, principles of government, and particular provisions of the common law. Had this and the first article been omitted, there would have been no sentence or word in the whole declaration or the form of government, countenancing the doctrine in question; and yet the rights of the people would have been precisely as they are. With respect to the fifth article, which speaks of the people's right to participate in the legislature, that article is manifestly opposed to the doctrine; because it explains the right into a right of immediate representation, and frequent elections.

When the happiness of the people, the true end of all society and government, cannot be preserved on account of some original fault in the constitution, or when the trustees betray their sacred charge, and the people are roused by a sense of injuries no longer to be borne, the indelible rights of nature authorise them to enforce that redress to which all constitutional means are incompetent. This is the principle of the English revolution in 1688. This is the principle of the revolution in America, which every good man still flatters himself will be deemed the most important era in the history of the world. It would be slavish to imagine, that without the first and fourth articles, or even with one directly repugnant, the people might not annul a compact intended for their good, when experience evinces the framers of that compact to have been mistaken; or that a mode of government which suited its framers, might not be changed by their posterity.

But whether a right be inherent in the people, and whether this be a proper occasion for using it, are two distinct questions. Has ten years experience demonstrated the senate to be either a dangerous or useless body? Has the rejection of the paper system perverted the ends of its appointment, or exposed your liberties to danger? The warmest advocates for the measure surely will not maintain the affirmative of these questions to be a self-evident position. Let them remember, that the attempt to introduce *this very scheme* miscarried two years successively; and yet the people murmured not. In the third year the house of delegates were induced to adopt it. The senate unanimously dissented. The people still made no complaints. Indeed, had the conduct of the senate excited their displeasure, it might have been easily manifested in the late election. In this election the gentlemen most distinguished for opposition to paper were honoured with almost every suffrage. It will be strange indeed, if you can now be persuaded, that the new senate has perverted the ends of government by declining an expedient rejected by the old, and by two successive houses of delegates.

The mode of appointing your senate is esteemed by wise men the most admirable institution in all the United States; and I make no doubt, that in Europe it has done honour to American genius. The senate of Maryland has been continually acquiring the esteem and confidence of the people, whilst other senates have fallen in repute. The difference arises from the different modes of election. It is not a man's popularity in a single county or district, it is his general good character, and his real dignity and importance, that confer on him this honour. The suffrage of the electors is a tribute paid to worth. The arts of intrigue, and even the magic powers of eloquence, should these be essayed, will probably be found unavailing.

In spite of these circumstances attempts are made to excite your suspicions of the senate. You are told, that in this select body prevails a baneful aristocratic spirit. Enemy as I am to arbitrary sway *of every kind*, I was at first startled at the suggestion. But as this was a weighty charge, I thought some proof should be required superior to the bare assertion of any man. An aristocracy is properly when *the sovereign power of a state resides in a permanent body of men distinct from the people*. At present the senate is not that permanent body; because it is appointed once in five years, and the supreme power resides not in it to so great an extent as in the house of delegates. Neither of them alone can pass a law. If an aristocracy be the government of a few, *uncontroled and unchecked by any other power*, an aristocratic spirit must mean a disposition to bring about such a government. In what instance has even a single senator evinced an inclination to confine the powers of legislation to the senate, or to change that branch into a permanent hereditary body. I now ask, whether the address of your delegates be not an attempt to have their own proposition passed into law, without the consent of the senate. I beseech you to reflect soberly, whether this conduct of the delegates does not tend indirectly to confer on them alone the power of making laws.

I am thoroughly, and upon the best grounds, persuaded, that no man in the senate conceives himself at liberty to disregard the wants, wishes, or sentiments of the people. He is perfectly apprized, that the institution was not intended to cloathe individuals with honour merely for their own gratification; but, like every other part of the constitution, to consult the general good. There may be a variety of instances where this general good is promoted by gratifying the inclination of the people. But is there a man so lost to common sense as not to foresee, that if the people shall take upon themselves to decide nice questions of policy by a majority of voices, they may frequently be wrought upon to choose things which will injure them the most. I repeat that their will, provided they persist long enough to pursue effectual measures, must stand for a law. But on what ground can a man who breathes the true spirit of patriotism, persuade them to exercise their will on the present occasion? Can he seriously believe them better qualified than the senate to decide on the expediency of an emission? It is not sufficient to say, they best know their own wants; because that is only a begging of the question, which is, whether an emission would supply those wants. Behold the glaring monstrous absurdity. The people do not immediately choose the senate. They appoint their most intelligent men to choose for them; and their electors make the most diligent inquiry into every corner of the state. Well, the senate, after all, is ignorant of the true interests of the state; and the general body of the people, from which they were selected, is to supply their wants, and enlighten their understandings.

If any man says the senate are interested, or otherwise corrupt, let us have an opportunity to decide on his testimony; for confident assertions, and noisy declamation, will, I trust at last, stand for nought.

It may be said the comparison is not proper between the people and the senate; that the people are called to decide between their immediate representatives and the senate, on a question, the right decision of which is essential to your happiness; and that, until this decision, all operations of the legislature will be suspended. In the same way might any other rejected bill be brought before the people. It is indeed natural for every projector to esteem his own *system* of the last importance. In a contest between the two branches, to be determined in the proposed manner, is it at all probable, that the question will come fairly before the people? The number of delegates exceeds that of the senate in a ratio of five for one. This circumstance could not fail to operate, if even the arts of popularity were laid aside, the inhabitants of each county assembled, the merits fairly discussed, and instructions signed only at that, or a subsequent meeting of the same kind. The delegates being far more intimately connected with their constituents, it must be a plain question indeed, which the people will decide in favour of the senate. Would to Heaven my countrymen could see the business in a true light. Their representatives appeal to them for instructions—So far I should have no objection, if their representatives were themselves undetermined. But these instructions are to govern the senate, and at the same time to be dictated by the delegates. In this kind of service the *people are not volunteers, and they feel not enough to stimulate them to a voluntary exertion. Can the interposition of the people thus obtained, be termed an interference, dictated by a sense of wrongs, a defence of natural rights, and a promotion of the true ends of government? Can a man wish the free unbiassed

* My readers will understand that whenever I speak of the people, I mean a majority of the great body of our citizens.

sentiments of the people to prevail, when he exerts every nerve to obtain their decision before each side of the question can be fairly examined? A draught of instructions is circulated before the close of the session. Its preamble asserts the appeal of the senate and the people are pressed to subscribe before they can possibly examine the allegation, or hear the senate's reasons.

Is this such a mode as naturally suggested itself to men anxious in the pursuit of truth? Were these instructions in other respects constitutional, they would be void on one certain ground. Had the senate, being at a loss how to decide, really appealed to the people, instructions would be strictly proper; but the personal influence of any member of either branch, would even in that case have been extremely improper.

Were I an advocate for the principle, I should be puzzled respecting the true manner of communicating the sense of the people. Are instructions to be signed only at public meetings? Is there to be one meeting only? Is that meeting to take place at each county court-house, or in each hundred? Is one general form to be pursued? Or may each man choose his own form? By whom are the several papers to be collected in each county or district? With whom shall they all be lodged? What shall be deemed a sufficient authentication? On a suggestion of forgery, how shall the fact be ascertained, or the crime punished? A thousand such questions may be asked, and the ingenuity of many gentlemen might be sufficient to prescribe suitable provisions But as to these questions no answer is found in the constitution, the conclusion is obvious, that its framers had no idea of the thing, consistent with the regular administration of the government by *them* devised. I repeat, that whenever the great body of the people shall declare their will (in whatever way it be done) this declaration, agreeably to the fourth article of the declaration, and the unalienable rights of nature, ought to be law; but then the whole frame of the government is either dissolved or suspended. I mean not, that any act of violence committed by only a part, and obstructing the exercise of a constitutional authority, would amount to this dissolution or suspension. I mean such an interference as is mentioned in that article. I contend that, according to the plain import of the words, the authors had not in comtemplation an interference, without a total dissolution or a suspension, until it could be reformed, and again declared in force.

Had the constitution made express provision, and prescribed the manner in which instructions should be given, so as to bind both branches of the legislature, the people ought nevertheless to be extremely sparing in the exercise. Were the corrupt motives of the senate apparent; if by their conduct your liberties were manifestly endangered; if proving false to their trust, they sacrificed the public good to their own private views—it would be proper to teach them their duty, and at the same time to address them in the terms of a severe reprimand. And further, as the people are to exercise the right, the people only should determine on the occasion. I repeat again and again, that with or without a constitutional provision, the people ought unquestionably to interfere on occasions like these. The difference between me and my adversaries is whether an interference will not abolish or suspend the constitutional legislature; and whether this be a proper season for an interference. The doctrines imputed to me by scribblers, I detest as much as I do all insolence, domineering, sedition, malice and calumny.

I should imagine any prudent, cautious, disinterested citizen, who has a valuable stake in the community, whose welfare is intimately connected with the public prosperity, who wishes no change in a government under which none hold superior rights, who would hazard all, and could gain nothing by a new revolution—I should imagine that such a man, let his opinion respecting an emission be what it may, will be induced by no solicitation to subscribe. The point was simply, whether bills of credit should be emitted on loan. The house of delegates was divided. A member whose reputation is not limited to these states, who, sometime ago, possessed your almost unbounded confidence, and to whom nothing had since been imputed, this gentleman, with about two fifths of the house, was stedfastly opposed to the plan. The senate were unanimous. But what again is the senate? It is a select body of men of enlarged minds, and unblemished characters, having no interest whatever distinct from yours, bearing with you a full proportion of burthens, and out of the senate-house at their own homes, to all intents and purposes, composing a part of the people. If these fifteen men can harbour a design of erecting an arbitrary power on the ruins of the constitution, of enjoying their dignities for life, and bequeathing them to their issue, they have conceived ideas of which I did not think the brain of man susceptible. Suppose the last convention had conferred the whole legislative authority on the senate, appointed fifteen men senators for life, and rendered the office hereditary. Is it possible such an odious establishment could have subsisted even unto this day. No senator under the present form can meditate an extension of his authority, and no rational being, on a moment's reflection, can retain his suspicions, unless jealousy of your trustees be like the jealousy of love, excited without cause, and subsisting on idle fancies. If a senator were really capable of such designs, he would become a much fitter object of derision, than of any well grounded apprehension. Happy will it be for you, my countrymen, if that constitution which perhaps owes its existence, and has done honour to men, who no longer view it with a parent's eye, shall withstand this powerful attack. Oh! listen to a man who defies the tongue of envy and detraction to fix one improper motive for this address, who has long been a faithful guardian to that constitution, and feels for it more than a father's love. Be assured, if it must receive a deadly wound, the fatal blow will be dealt by yourselves, or your immediate representatives. Far from me be the wish of narrowing the powers of the popular branch of the legislature. The defect of human policy, arising from human nature, is such, that in instituting the frame of a government, it is impossible to guard against dangers on one side, without being exposed on another. Were every thing submitted to my discretion, I declare solemnly I would not abridge the established power of your delegates. My only wish and aim is to protect that sacred palladium of your rights, which you have sworn to defend, against all open and secret combinations. Permit not either branch, *by any method*, to exercise the office of both. The very use and intent of one is to check any unadvised hasty proceedings, or intemperate sallies of the other more numerous assembly. Think not, that a predilection for the former has blinded my understanding. I further declare, that if it were left to me to abolish one or the other, I would by all means preserve the house of delegates. There is nothing more hateful to my soul than the idea of a proud, worthless, tyrannical order of nobility, like the senate of Venice. But, although this government may hereafter possibly degenerate into an arbitrary one, there is no reason to dread, that it will become an aristocracy erected by the senate.

If it be the meaning of the fourth article, that the people shall act as an umpire, wherefore is it, that in every instance of a dissent the bill is not laid before them? To this may be said, they are called upon only with respect to bills of the last importance. The constitution however creates no distinction. The constitution contains no provision in any case.

An idea has been started, that both branches are to be considered as agents of the people, and the constitution a letter of instructions; that as it was impossible for the principal to foresee the necessity of an emission at this time, he may now give additional instructions. There is a disposition in mankind to be imposed on by similitudes. They captivate the imagination, and are much better received than solid argument. Behold another similitude.—

There are fifty persons, the far greater part having no knowledge or experience in trade, who agree to join stock, and commence merchants. In a little time they find it extremely inconvenient for so large a company to transact their own affairs. They enter into articles to be binding until at two several meetings of the company a majority shall vote for dissolving the partnership. By the principal clause in the indenture, the business for a limited time is committed to the management of only two, without any proviso, that if these two should differ respecting a proposition made by either, the matter shall be referred to the company. One of them, a fine, bold, enterprizing spirit, scorning the ordinary profits of a slow progressive trade, and delighting only in capital strokes, proposes to embark a considerable part of the stock in a venture to China. His object is to import rice for supplying the want of Indian corn, the apprehension of a short crop having suggested the thought. The other merchant, a cautious, calculating man, considers it as a mere chimera. The first thereupon calls a meeting of the company, produces his calculations, displays his brilliant prospects, and actually brings over a majority. His associate continues fixed. His judgment is not convinced, and he adheres to his opinion. Should the law authorise the majority, notwithstanding their agreement, to displace their agents, and should they take the management into their own hands, they are again in the situation which induced them to choose managers. Again they perceive the necessity of appointing; and it is not improbable, that they will trust the whole concern to him who has impressed an high opinion of his talents.

The meaning of this allegory is to guard you against sophistry.

Let us trace the consequences of the doctrine, that, notwithstanding the express provisions of the constitution, the people, without violating or suspending, may control a delegated power. If it be good with regard to the legislature, it must likewise be good with respect to the executive and judiciary.

A citizen levies constructive war against the state. He is thereon indicted in the general court, arraigned, takes his trial, and is found guilty by the unanimous suffrage of twelve men, the petit jury. This man is a favourite of the people. His friends make strenuous exertions, and a great majority of the people are induced to sign a declaration of their will, and an order, that he be discharged. There is no doubt the prisoner will escape punishment, provided the people shall enforce their mandate. But will any man pretend, that it authorises the judge legally and constitutionally to pronounce the discharge? And yet the court may be considered the agent of the people, deriving authority like every other department of government, immediately or ultimately from the people.

Suppose now the address to succeed, and in ten counties a greater number to have signed the instructions for an emission, than have either signed against it, or declined signing at all.* The senate taking the constitution for their guide, and finding it no where expressed, that in any case they shall be bound to pass laws against their own opinion, still viewing the system as injurious to our affairs, esteeming it their inviolable duty to preserve the constitution unimpaired, and thinking too, that the free unbiassed opinion has not been obtained, will most probably continue firm in rejecting the bill. The house of delegates will then most probably decline for a season all further intercourse. The people then, or a part of them in behalf of the rest, mistaking the firmness of virtue for an obstinate contempt of their rights, will perhaps repair to the capital, and *in thunder* pronounce their will. If then the senate, still holding themselves bound by superior obligations, and manifesting a zeal for their country's *permanent* happiness, shall disdain to assent to that which their judgments disapprove, and thereby establish a precedent, leaving to their successors little more than a name, and shall either instantly adjourn, or relinquish their seats, this posture of affairs will, in all human probability, be construed a dissolution of government. Immediately may ensue scenes, the bare contemplation of which must touch the stoutest heart, not interested to produce them. But passing over these scenes of discord, riot, violence, and perhaps bloodshed, let us calmly consider what best can possibly happen. On a resignation of the senate, provided such a measure would not be construed void on the principle of duresse, there can be no senate under the present form until the year 1791. In such a case the house of delegates may do one of two things. They may proceed, on the pretext of necessity, to exercise alone the powers of legislation, or they may address their constituents to elect a convention. The latter being more safe and decent, will probably be adopted. Alas, my beloved countrymen, we shall be fortunate indeed, if the convention will recognise the present constitution, reforming only a few errors and abuses, and rendering it from this convulsion more stable than before, or if a new constitution from its ashes shall arise superior to the present! The members of a convention will be composed principally of the present delegates, irritated and inflamed as they are against the senate.

You will be told, that this is an attempt, by alarming your fears, to intimidate you from doing that which is right. To him who attentively, and with a proper frame of mind, considers the conduct and address of

---

* *It surely will not be maintained, that any writing can be justly styled the declaration of a county's sense, unless more than half of the voters, or of the free-men, shall have signed it. If it can, where shall the line be drawn? Or what prevents a paper signed by a dozen, when there is no counter paper, from being styled instructions?*

your delegates, the messages of the senate and the aforegoing remarks, the condition of our affairs will appear critical and alarming. If I know my own heart, although I were thoroughly convinced, that bills of credit would produce the promised effects, I would stedfastly set my face against this mode of effecting the plan. Nothing short of a conviction, that on the scheme depended your safety and happiness, would reconcile me to the idea. At the same time were I certain that the people, left to themselves, would feel the want of an emission, and without it could not be content, I would renounce my opinion, and reprobate the man who could hold out against the free voice of the people, his masters.

When I consider, that independent of impelling the people, like a blind machine, to break down the fixed barriers of the constitution, the scheme for an emission is pregnant with a thousand ills, I regret the poor extent of my powers. I wish for immediate inspiration. When indeed alone, and in my study, I contemplate on all these things, my whole frame becomes agitated and convulsed. I feel as it were the resistless impulse of an invisible agent.

Index

Adams, John, 3, 5
Addison, Joseph, 59
"America," 3–4
Anne Arundel County, 133, 156; and constituent instruction, 54; on paper money, 53–54
Appeals: and legislative independence, 17–19, 48–49, 76–77; practice of, 11, 12–14, 16, 21, 65–66, 67, 69, 81, 173, 179
Arendt, Hannah, 5, 20
"Aristides," See Hanson, Alexander Contee
Association of Freemen, 3
Athens: Athenian law, 119, 130, 131, 139; Athenians, 58

Bailyn, Bernard, 8
Baltimore, 3, 48, 89, 90, 169, 170
Bank of England, 14
Barnard, Sir John, 58, 92, 93
Bicameralism, 5, 6, 13–14, 89, 96, 154–55, 174; and appeals, 17–19, 48–49, 76–77 ,82, 120
Blackstone, Sir William, 59, 92, 94, 151
Bohemia, 113, 133, 152
Bolingbroke, Henry St. John, Viscount, 98
Brittany, 113, 133, 152, 153, 167

Camden, Earl of (Charles Pratt), 67–68
Carroll, Charles, of Carrollton, 17, 27, 80, 81
Carroll, Charles, Sr., 13
Charles I, 117
Charles V, 153, 166
Chase, Samuel, 3, 9, 27; and bicameralism, 18; on constituent instruction, 55, 56, 57, 60; on representation, 16–17, 55, 56–57, 59
Chatham, Earl of (William Pitt), 165

Coke, Sir Edward, 94, 151, 166
Commonwealthmen, 3
Compact, conceptualization of, 21, 25–26, 28, 95, 175. See also Hanson, Alexander Countee; Paca, William
Confiscation, 12–14
"Constituent," 19, 20, 25; on Bolingbroke, 98; on British constitution, 97–99, 101; on depreciation of currency, 69–73; on instructions, 76–77, 78, 106; on Locke, 101–4, 107; on money bills, 100; on representation, 79, 99, 101, 104; on Rutherford, 104–5
Constituent instructions, 2, 4, 11, 12–13; and constitutionalism, 18; and representation, 16–17. See also Chase, Samuel; Hanson, Alexander Contee; Paca, William
"Country Party," 4
Crowl, Philip A., 15

De Lolme, John Louis, 94
Democracy, deferential, 4–5, 20, 21
Demosthenes, 58
Denmark, 113, 133, 152

England: constitution and government of, 79, 94, 97–99, 101, 113, 143, 146; and instructions, 57–58, 89, 94, 123, 128, 133, 150, 151

Federalist, The, 1
Filmer, Sir Robert, 112, 120, 128, 162
Fox, Charles, 165–66
France, 113, 133, 152, 153, 167
Franklin, Benjamin, 94

Gale, George, 17, 27
George III, 3
Germany, 113, 133, 153, 167

185

Goddard, William, 9, 90, 122
Gordon, Thomas, 168
Greece, 49
Grotius, Hugo, 104, 105
Grove, Sylvanus, 14

Hamilton, Alexander, 1
Hampden, John, 63, 90, 92, 109, 114
Hanbury, Osgood, 14
Hanson, Alexander Contee ("Aristides"):
  on compacts, 24–26, 89, 124–27,
  128–29, 141–44, 146, 154, 175;
  on constituent instruction, 21–22,
  23, 27, 88, 94, 120, 123, 124, 127,
  128, 145, 147, 151, 154, 158,
  169–70, 178–79, 180; on Hume,
  146, 150, 151; on Locke, 89, 91,
  121, 124, 144–45, 156; on the people,
  143; on representation, 90, 95–96;
  on senatorial electors, 171, 176–77;
  on Sidney, 92, 121, 122, 146, 147,
  153; on state of nature, 142
Henry, John, 17, 27
House of Delegates: appeal of, 2, 35,
  46, 47; Committee of Aggrievances,
  9; confiscation, 12–14; debtor relief,
  45–46; emission proposal of, 40–42;
  as immediate representatives, 11, 17–
  18, 35, 49, 54, 56, 76, 84, 97;
  loyalty oaths, 9–11; paper money,
  15–18, 38–40, 44
Howe, Gen. William, 10
Hume, David, 100, 123, 132, 146, 150,
  151

Ireland, 97

Jay, John, 1
Jeffreys, Judge George, 108, 114, 120,
  132
Jenifer, Daniel of St. Thomas, 5–6, 7
Johnson, Thomas, 3, 19, 27

Kent County, 91, 112, 122

Languedoc (France), 113, 133, 152,
  153, 167
Lee, Thomas Sim, 27
Lewes, 91, 112, 122
Locke, John, 6, 63–64, 66–67, 90, 91,

102, 103, 106–7, 109, 114, 125,
  144–45, 163–64
Loyalty oaths, 8–11

Madison, James, 1
Maidstone, 91, 112, 122
Main, Jackson Turner, 4
Mann's Tavern, 80, 85
Maryland: constitution of, 4, 7, 10,
  101, 102, 103, 106–7; Declaration
  of Rights, 4, 5, 7, 10, 16, 61, 78, 102,
  114, 124, 175–76
Mixed government, 1–2
Molesworth, Robert, Viscount, 63, 90,
  92, 109, 114

Netherlands. See United Netherlands
New York State, 43
Norman Conquest, 98

Paca, William ("Publicola"), 1, 16,
  27; on the compact, 23–24, 114,
  135–36, 160; on constituent instruction, 22–23, 64, 107, 113, 114–17,
  132–34, 136–37, 164; on Locke, 24,
  116, 132, 133, 162–63; on national
  instructions, 111, 116, 133; on
  people as constitutional judges, 62–63,
  64, 110, 114–16, 134, 161; on
  representation, 17, 61, 167; on Sidney,
  110–11, 112, 113, 114, 132, 162–63,
  164; on state of nature, 161–63
Palmer, R. R., 1, 26
Paper money, 15–27, 69–75, 81
Parsons, Theophilus, 6
Pennsylvania, 43, 48, 57
Philadelphia, 27, 48, 131
Pitt, William. See Chatham, Earl of
"Plebean," 13
Poland, 113, 133, 152
Pole, J. R., 6
"Publicola." See Paca, William

"Rationalis," 11
Ridgely, Richard, 17
Rome, 49; Roman empire, 80
Russell, James, 14
Russell, William, Lord, 63, 90, 92,
  108, 109, 114
Rutherford, Thomas, 104–6

Senate, 1, 2, 7; and appeals, 17–19,
  48–49; on confiscation, 12–14; on
  debtors and creditors, 50, 51–52;
  independence of, 156; on judicial
  salaries, 51; on loyalty oaths, 9–11;
  on paper money, 15, 17–21
Sidney, Algernon, 58, 63, 90, 91–92,
  94, 108, 109, 110, 111, 112, 114,
  122, 127–28, 166
Somerset County, 9
Sovereignty: constitutional, 25, 26, 89,
  95, 104–6, 125–27, 141–44, 174;
  popular, 2, 4, 7, 20, 62, 64, 85
Spain, 113, 133, 152, 153
Stone, Thomas, 3, 17, 27; on appeals,
  82; on instructions, 19–20, 22, 82–85
Sussex County, 91, 112, 122
Sweden, 113, 133, 152
Swift, Jonathan, 97
Switzerland, 127, 153, 166

Tate, Thad W., 20–21
Tilghman, Matthew, 3
Trenchard, John, 63, 90, 92, 109, 114

Unicameralism, 5, 6
United Netherlands, 113, 127, 128, 133,
  146, 147, 151, 153

Virginia, 48

Whigs: doctrine, 6; Club, 9
Willes, Sir John, 93
Wood, Gordon S., 1–2, 6
Worcester County, 9
Wright, Robert, 16
Wyndham, Sir William, 58, 92, 93

Yonge, Sir William, 93

THE JOHNS HOPKINS UNIVERSITY PRESS

This book was composed in Linotype Electra text and Weiss display type by The Maryland Linotype Composition Co., Inc., from a design by Susan Bishop, and printed on 60-lb. Warren 1854 regular paper. It was printed and bound by The Maple Press Company.